Empires of Belief

Empires of Belief

*Why We Need More Scepticism and
Doubt in the Twenty-First Century*

STUART SIM

EDINBURGH UNIVERSITY PRESS

© Stuart Sim, 2006

Edinburgh University Press Ltd
22 George Square, Edinburgh

Typeset in Palatino
by Servis Filmsetting Ltd, Manchester, and
printed and bound in Great Britain by
The Cromwell Press, Trowbridge, Wilts

A CIP record for this book is available from the British Library

ISBN-10 0 7486 2326 4 (hardback)
ISBN-13 978 0 7486 2326 6

The right of Stuart Sim
to be identified as author of this work
has been asserted in accordance with
the Copyright, Designs and Patents Act 1988.

Contents

Acknowledgements

My thanks go to my editor at EUP, Jackie Jones, for excellent advice and encouragement throughout this project; to Fiona Sewell for copy-editing; and to Dr. Helene Brandon for a quarter-century of being an invaluable sounding-board for ideas.

Introduction: Empires of Belief, Campaigns for Scepticism

It is this book's contention that unquestioning belief is pervading global culture, and that the most effective way of countering it is by an engaged scepticism, an open-minded and continually questioning and probing sense of doubt. Unless we can develop this, our democratic lifestyle is under severe threat from the narrow-minded purveyors of dogma. In the current world order we are confronted by an array of what can be called 'empires' of belief. These empires – dominant organisations or groups led by the powerful that exercise dominion over ordinary people – are investing an immense amount of time and effort in trying to dictate how we should think, consume, and behave. Like all empires run by the powerful they have expansionist ambitions and we are all their targets, not just the true believers who have already bought the message in question and can be relied on to do what they are told by their leaders without demur, only too eager to uphold the cause. The dramatic resurgence of religious fundamentalism on an international scale indicates that there is a significant constituency of people receptive to unquestioning belief of the kind that empires traditionally foster, as does the rise of various other kinds of fundamentalism – market, nationalistic, political, ecological, to name some of the most prominent.[1] It is not the least of the ironies connected with such empires that everyone outside one's own empire is to be treated as a non-believer, as if there was not enough, rather than a surfeit of, belief in the world.

Political, economic, and scientific theories can command the same unquestioning support from the general public as do their religious counterparts. Sometimes this support is imposed on us, but more often than not the public has indeed, to repeat the phrase, bought the message – and of its own accord, because of the emotional security it can bring to individuals (illusory, but none the less potent). Systems of belief depend on such complicity. Neither organised religion, chauvinistic politicians, nor the multinationals like opposition; in fact, they do their very best to quash it and force conformity and obedience on the rest of us wherever possible. As one recent commentator has remarked, 'globalisation has declared war on other cultures', and there are few empires of belief which do not aspire to such a condition.[2]

This book confronts those empires in all their breadth – they can even include the institutions of science and technology, as Chapter 4 will go on to outline in greater detail – and the effect they are having on our lives. It insists that their expansionist aspirations must be resisted if we are to maintain anything like a democratic, pluralist, lifestyle that enshrines freedom of expression as a natural right for all individuals without exception. And by freedom of expression I mean explicitly to be able to criticise those running the empires and all their beliefs: to criticise them until their activities are brought into public disrepute. Generating fear among people about terrorism is a tactic which political empires, for example, use to maintain their power over their sceptically minded citizens – a way of undermining freethinking criticism. We find ourselves embroiled in a complex argument about this in the UK at the moment over the issue of identity cards, one of the primary justifications for which has been to help combat terrorism; although there is little proof that they will have much effectiveness in this regard.

There is a pressing need for a concerted campaign on behalf of a sceptical attitude, and this book is designed to stir up as much debate as it can towards that end. I am at least as interested in why individuals buy into systems of belief that support empire-building as in the systems themselves: I want to argue the case for buying out. In scepticism, I would argue, lies the way to a more egalitarian future, in which conformity and obedience need no longer be seen as our destiny. We are under no obligation passively to submit to the power of empires of belief: that would be a betrayal of all that is positive about modern, post-Enlightenment society, such as freedom from superstition and authoritarianism in both public and private life. Post-Enlightenment society has also seen a rise in the more radical ideas of postmodern theory. Postmodernists envisage a world in which authority is kept under constant surveillance by the general public, and is never allowed to become authoritarian: sentiments many of us would be only too happy to endorse. Postmodernism is essentially anti-empire-building, and this commitment can sometimes cause its more ardent supporters to lose sight of the positive side of the Enlightenment, seeing it as giving birth to an empire of belief in its own right. It would be more in the spirit of postmodern anti-authoritarianism, however, to reinterpret the Enlightenment's legacy than to reject it – and that is what I will be arguing for. I will be aiming for a *rapprochement* between an anti-authoritarian, 'oppositional' postmodernism and the best of Enlightenment scepticism from here onwards: I think we share the same enemies.

The West is generally regarded now as a secular society, and since the Enlightenment period religion has been steadily marginalised in terms of its impact on politics and social policy. Even if this does vary somewhat from country to country (Catholicism has been more persistent in its socio-political influence in its traditional European heartlands, such as Italy, Spain, and Ireland[3]), the overall trend towards secularism has nevertheless been very clear. The Enlightenment saw a great flowering of scepticism, particularly towards traditional authority (even more oppressive then than now, in the grip of the *ancien régime* with its penchant for absolute monarchy), and this has passed into our general cultural outlook. Yet religion, that most traditional, that most obedience-demanding, of authorities, is a resurgent force on the global scene, with fundamentalist notions coming to the fore in all of the world's major religions in recent decades.[4] The activities of Al-Qaeda immediately come to mind, but that organisation is merely the tip of the iceberg: equivalents can be found in other religions, just as imbued with the absolute rightness of their cause and the desire to extend this over the rest of humanity – whether the rest of humanity wants it or not.

Those in possession of 'the truth' are rarely concerned with such niceties as the right of opposition. In America, evangelical Protestantism has become deeply involved in the political process, at both national and state level, and has succeeded in overturning progressive social legislation on issues such as abortion and homosexuality. In Israel, Jewish fundamentalists campaign for the expansion of the state and the expulsion of the Palestinian people from within its borders in order to return Israel to its (supposed) biblical contours – hardly a tactic designed to help the already beleaguered peace process. In the UK, the Anglican church is in ferment over gay priests, with reactionaries demanding their removal, particularly when they are put forward for high office such as bishoprics. The dogmatists are now setting the agenda for twenty-first-century religion, and becoming increasingly aggressive in their approach: they want a new age of faith, however achieved, however received.

Dogmatic attitudes can be found in many other areas of our lives as well, such as politics and economics, and the sceptical outlook that we have inherited from the Enlightenment is under considerable threat. Unquestioning belief is deeply embedded in our culture, and is striving to become even more so. It is all the more urgent to restate the case for scepticism under the circumstances, a scepticism acting on behalf of all of humanity. The claim here will be that we are in need of less belief and more doubt; less fundamentalism and dogmatism, and more scepticism – *far* more scepticism. That case will be made by placing the current clash between belief and scepticism in a wider cultural and historical context. Elements of scepticism can be identified in all cultures, and certainly pre-date the Enlightenment, so this need not be seen as a Eurocentric or Western-centric project that is being undertaken (we can find some Islamic scholars querying the basis of the Koran's authority as early as the tenth century, for example). The aim instead is to encourage the growth of a sceptical anti-authoritarianism within all cultures, since the capacity for authoritarian dogmatism is equally present in all cultures. None of us can feel superior, all of us are at risk. It is worth remembering that religious fundamentalism is, in the first instance, a product of Christian culture: others may have developed their own form since, but it was the West that formulated the concept and allowed it to become a force in political life.[5] Most of the other fundamentalisms that we mentioned above are Western in origin too, with market fundamentalism – the scourge of many a Third World economy when imposed by the World Bank and the International Monetary Fund – being a prime case in point.

Arguments for scepticism and doubt in public life are beginning to crop up in the daily press and the broadcast media in the West on a regular basis, and a fear is increasingly being voiced there, amongst the more liberal commentators, that the legacy of the Enlightenment is in very real danger of being eroded unless some action is taken, and taken very soon. A full-scale defence of the sceptical outlook is therefore timely. The empires of belief constitute a threat which must be countered as rapidly as possible: they will not simply wither away – there is too much of an investment in them by interested parties for that to happen. True believers are nothing if not indefatigable, and unless they are met with the same degree of commitment and persistence from the sceptical side, then they will continue to make the inroads into our individual and collective freedoms that they are currently making. Scepticism simply has to become a much more prominent part of our daily lives.

I should point out at this early stage that Enlightenment scepticism will be differentiated from the more anarchic version favoured by many postmodernist thinkers ('super-scepticism', as I have referred to it elsewhere[6]), although both will be seen to have a part to play in the campaign that is going to be advocated. Scepticism does not naturally lend itself to politics, since its bias is essentially negative, concerned mainly with casting other positions in an unflattering light by revealing their internal inconsistencies and contradictions. That will always remain its core activity. But if politics as an arena of opposed viewpoints is to continue to exist in a meaningful form, then sceptics will need to become more actively involved on that scene, becoming a visible presence that others must take into account when bidding for power.

The project of an engaged scepticism suggests that we should sketch out the history of scepticism, particularly in the Western and Islamic traditions (although from elsewhere as well, where appropriate), in order to understand what a politics based on scepticism might be like and how reasonable doubt – as opposed to suspicion – can play a positive part in the ordinary citizen's life, and how satire, too, can be used to prevent the build-up of dogmatism in politics and elsewhere. The alternative, a culture run by unquestioning believers, is not a pleasant prospect to contemplate. Let's now consider how it can be kept at bay; how we can maintain a bias towards open-mindedness rather than the closed-mindedness of a zealotry which, sad to say, is all around us.

Defining Scepticism

Scepticism is a term that can be used in a variety of ways, some looser than others. We'll need to narrow down its meaning for this study, to render it more precise. In the first place, it is a technical term in philosophy, and that will be the source of its use here. Some of that philosophical sense is present in all appearances of the word, no matter how loose they may prove to be. Our task will be to show how that philosophical interest can be turned into a basis for political action. Scepticism in philosophy is the position which questions the possibility of there being any absolute ground for theories of truth or knowledge, or for belief. All such theories depend on the existence of some basic principle, or central criterion, taken to be beyond doubt; that is, self-evidently true and therefore ideal as the basis for a system, which can then build outward from that point to construct a larger body of knowledge. Sceptics draw attention to the contradictions in such an assumption: that it is more an act of faith than reason. If something is assumed to be self-evidently true, then it has not been proved to be self-evidently true – and philosophy as a discipline depends very heavily on the notion of proof. Without rational proof, arguments are to be considered suspect.

Introduction

The problem non-sceptics face has been summed up very neatly by the Hellenistic philosopher Sextus Empiricus (active around AD 200) as follows:

> in order for the dispute that has arisen about standards to be decided, we must possess an agreed standard through which we can judge it; and in order for us to possess an agreed standard, the dispute about standards must already have been decided. Thus the argument falls into the reciprocal mode [circular reasoning] and the discovery of a standard is blocked – for we do not allow them to assume a standard by hypothesis, and if they want to judge the standard by a standard we throw them into an infinite regress. Again, since a proof needs a standard which has been proved and a standard needs a proof which has been judged, they are thrown into the reciprocal mode.[7]

Philosophical sceptics are fond of trapping their opponents into an infinite regress in this manner, and it can become an irritating game if pushed to extremes – as super-sceptics, for example, are wont to do (for there to be an origin there must be the origin of an origin, etc.). A key point is being established none the less; that much authority – and not just in the field of philosophy – rests on unsubstantiated assumptions. Sceptics will always want to draw attention to this state of affairs, and to question the continued existence of such authority as well. In a sense, all modern sceptics are to be considered the heirs of Sextus Empiricus.

Scepticism can take various forms, some more pertinent to our argument than others. In his classic study, *The History of Scepticism from Erasmus to Spinoza*, Richard H. Popkin notes how scepticism in classical Greek thought was eventually formulated in the Hellenistic period into two main types, Academic and Pyrrhonian, describing these as follows: '(1) that no knowledge was possible [Academic], or (2) that there was insufficient and inadequate evidence to determine if any knowledge was possible, and hence one ought to suspend judgment on all questions concerning knowledge [Pyrrhonian]'.[8] Whereas Academic scepticism became a form of dogmatism in its own right (there were no shades of opinion on the topic; Academics were certain, paradoxically enough, that knowledge simply was not possible), Pyrrhonian was more of a 'mental attitude' for opposing such claims to certainty, seeing itself as 'a cure for the disease called Dogmatism or rashness'.[9] Pyrrhonians, such as Sextus Empiricus, further wanted to achieve 'a state of *ataraxia*, quietude, or unperturbedness, in which the sceptic was no longer concerned or worried about matters beyond appearances'.[10] I incline more towards the Pyrrhonian position with its sense of being a free-floating critique of received ideas rather than yet another dogmatism seeking converts to the cause. While not wishing to suspend judgements altogether – particularly on dogmatism, in whatever form it may take – I want to retain the open-endedness of Pyrrhonian scepticism with its refusal to take on any aura of authority, its desire to remain a thorn in the flesh of dogmatists everywhere. One contemporary philosopher, Christopher Hookaway, has made a case for what he calls 'soft scepticism', a similarly open-ended form which avoids the blanket generalisations of Academic-style scepticism.[11] Although not subscribing to it himself, he nevertheless concedes its virtues for philosophical enquiry, and we'll return to these later.

Scepticism is essentially an argument against authority, contesting the assumptions on which this is based and the power that flows from these. That is certainly how we want it to operate in the new century, causing institutional and governmental authority in particular to be extremely circumspect in its ways and constantly aware of the possibility of challenge from within its own domain. Unless it is kept under constant scrutiny, such authority has a distinct tendency to become authoritarian and to strive to maintain its power base at all costs: scepticism will form the basis of that scrutiny, the perpetual source of dissent. We shall go on to consider the history of philosophical scepticism, including the pivotal role of Sextus Empiricus, in more detail in Chapter 1.

There are, however, many who define themselves, or are defined by cultural commentators, as sceptics who cannot really count as such for our purposes. The press in the UK often talks about Eurosceptics, those who oppose the European Union (EU) – or at least Britain's membership in it, which ideally they would like to terminate at the earliest opportunity. As we shall go on to discuss in

Chapter 5, this is not scepticism as we understand it, since it is generally underpinned by quite a reactionary brand of politics that is, if anything, *over*-respectful of authority. Euroscepticism is a defence of British national sovereignty, rather than a genuinely open-minded critique of social or political authority as wielded by large-scale bureaucracies. Its motives are somewhat less noble: Eurosceptics want to retain traditional authority rather than cede it to a more remote one based outside the UK (the dreaded Brussels, as Eurosceptics conceive of it). It is an argument about who should be in control, rather than a scepticism about the notion of political control itself. It is that latter notion that we shall want to hold onto.

Creationists are sceptical of the claims of evolutionary science, but hardly qualify as open-minded either, espousing what has been called 'faith-based' science in stead; that is, a science that constructs a narrative based on the biblical account of creation, contracting the Earth's life-span quite drastically in the process of reinterpreting the physical evidence. Bishop Ussher (1581–1656) famously claimed in 1654 that the Earth was created in 4004 BC, whereas recent creationist scholarship is willing to extend this to somewhere around 8000 BC. Others in the faith-based science camp can offer more sophisticated accounts than that ('Old Earth Creationists' as they have been called to differentiate them from the more fundamental 'Young Earth Creationists'), yet still feel the need to incorporate a supernatural element into creation. Old Earth Creationists argue the case for 'intelligent design', where we are all deemed to be the product of a divine plan – Christian, of course. While ostensibly more scientific, intelligent design still demands that we take Genesis as the starting point of our physics and biology, and the claims of other religions are simply disregarded. Given that so much of the Big Bang is still shrouded in mystery, the biblical account is capable of exerting a certain appeal, but in real terms it adds nothing to scientific explanation. It may provide answers, but those come with considerable ideological baggage. What initially looks like scepticism is soon revealed to be the most unyielding and literal-minded form of unquestioning belief – the very opposite of the Pyrrhonian spirit we wish to promote.

The theory of global warming has its sceptics too, who claim that the data on which global warming proponents rest their case is capable of being interpreted in different ways. Rather than humankind being responsible for global warming, as most scientists in the field contend, these sceptics argue that it is all part of the Earth's natural cycle and that arguments to the contrary amount to a conspiracy by the scientific community to gain funding for their research projects: a 'scam', in the words of one particularly forthright critic.[12] Such critics are closer to our idea of a sceptic, but again, they are not necessarily as open-minded in their general outlook as we would like. This is especially so since their scepticism is often in the service of big business (the international oil companies, for example), for whom action on global warming could mean a significant curb on their operations and consequent drop in their profit margins. Such 'special interest' scepticism has to be treated with a considerable degree of caution.

Holocaust sceptics deny this shameful event even took place and contest the reliability of all confirmatory evidence, which is often presented as part of a large-scale Jewish conspiracy to make the West feel guilty for its history of persecution of Judaism and thereby gain political leverage. Their objective is not to raise questions about the nature of historical truth and how it is constructed and disseminated, a very interesting topic in its own right, but rather to resuscitate the reputation of the Nazi party. Most Holocaust sceptics turn out to be Nazi sympathisers – the British historian David Irving being a notable example of the species, with his attempts to clear Hitler of responsibility for the death camps in the Second World War. One account simply replaces another, which cannot qualify as a philosophically informed scepticism: again, special interests are to be seen in play, distorting the character of the debate.

All such cases as the above need to be investigated, however, to reach a more precise understanding of what scepticism really should be in order to be effective against dogmatism, and we shall come back to them at various points later in the volume.

The 'Little Narrative' of Scepticism

Becoming a sceptic is, of its nature, a very personal decision, and I offer no grand vision to resolve all the world's political problems by adopting it as a tactic. Instead, it will be a matter of putting forward reasons for developing a sceptical outlook, and promoting that as widely as possible as a desirable view to hold in our public life for the benefit of all. Those who choose to take that route will argue the case against unexamined beliefs and uncritical believers alike, pointing out where their systems rest on nothing stronger than circular reasoning and infinite regress, and should therefore at the very least be reconsidered. We should think of scepticism more as an approach than a theory as such (although as we shall see in Chapter 1, it has had a long and distinguished history within philosophy, attracting some of the most acute minds in the field). Scepticism will be presented as a 'little narrative': a loose conglomeration of interests resisting the might of the many empires of belief that have come to dominate our social and political landscapes.[13] A pressure group, if you like; but none the worse for aiming no higher than that, and one moreover that is open to all motivated by a genuine spirit of enquiry.

The little narrative of scepticism aspires to be a genuinely open-minded, public-spirited critique of authoritarian paradigms which are more interested in protecting their own power bases than in upholding genuine intellectual rigour about their beliefs and principles. To be a little narrative is to have specific objectives, generally directed against the abuses being committed by the world's powerful and dogmatic individuals, institutions, and corporate organisations, but to resist becoming a source of dogma in one's turn. That last point is crucial; the primary motivation must be to remain a pressure group. This is not to say that sceptics do not, or cannot, have beliefs and principles they hold dear; rather that they will feel themselves under an obligation to keep examining these with the same open mind they do those of others. If one's own ideas and principles cannot stand up to such scrutiny, then they ought to be changed. It is something of a balancing act that is required of us, but one worth persevering with, as there is no lack of empires to be confronted. I will strive to be the representative sceptic in these pages, drawing attention to where dogmatism is getting the upper hand over open-mindedness and suggesting how we can set about redressing the balance; deploying a Pyrrhonist-influenced soft scepticism, with some other additions as we go, to give the project a political edge.

Reasons to be Sceptical

There is no shortage of reasons to be sceptical. I'll enumerate some of them before developing them in the chapters to follow.

Religion is an almost endless source of examples to the sceptic. As noted above, it is currently flexing its muscles worldwide, and trying to see just how far it can go in dictating the socio-political agenda of today's culture. No sceptic wants to live in a theocracy, or even a semblance of one (as some claim even America is fast becoming these days), where religion constitutes the basis of all social existence. Any move at all in the direction of what has been dubbed 'theocratic fascism' has to be seen as unacceptable, a betrayal of our humanist heritage.[14] Sceptics would prefer it if religion played no part in politics at all. That was the thrust of the more radical Enlightenment thought, such as Baron d'Holbach's (1723–89), to exile religion from the political process and drive it into the private domain, where it would be tolerated but not encouraged (a formula I am more than happy to subscribe to myself). Instead, we now have faith-based politics entrenching itself in both the Western and Islamic worlds (and to some extent elsewhere as well), bringing faith-based science in its wake. As we shall go on to discuss in Chapter 5, however, it is possible to imagine a context where religion and scepticism engage in political debate – if not one that religion would be entirely happy with, since it assumes both the necessity and the permanent presence of an anti-religious bloc in politics. What is worrying at present is that so many political systems are so open to manipulation from fundamentalist religious groups that have no real interest in democratic debate or wider participation in political life. Their goal instead is to remove all trace of opposition to their own ideas – this is what sceptics are up against.

Politics would certainly benefit from an injection of scepticism. Indeed, I intend to argue that scepticism should be right at the heart of the political process; that this is the only way to ensure we can keep democratic traditions of pluralism alive. Building on Chantal Mouffe and William E. Connolly's concept of 'agonism', I will examine the prospects for a new kind of adversarial politics that, while rejecting consensus and compromise, still guarantees a basis for principled opposition. While it may not provide all the answers as to how to banish authoritarianism from our lives, agonistic politics does have some very interesting suggestions to make on how a change of emphasis could reinvigorate our somewhat moribund, compromise-ridden political system, which induces apathy in so much of the populace in the West (turnout in general elections is steadily declining in most countries). There are arguments to be made for compromise and consensus, but these activities can so easily become a means of protecting authority from challenge, of defusing dissent. That is where sceptics have to step in and make their presence felt.

Science, too, provides reasons to develop a strong sense of mistrust of those in positions of power, especially when it is translated into the kind of advanced technology we are familiar with today. 'Techno-science', as Jean-François Lyotard has dubbed it, has the capacity to dominate our lives to an unhealthy degree. Artificial intelligence (AI), artificial life (AL), GM (genetically modified) crops, stem-cell research, and cloning, for example, all raise complex ethical issues which cannot be left to scientists and politicians alone, and demand at the very least that a sceptical eye is turned on them to monitor their progress. Faith-based science can be an even more sinister opponent, since its founding premises lie outside the field of science proper, thus rendering them oblivious to counter-evidence reached through empirical scientific enquiry. Creationists are not disposed to debate; they feel they have no need to when the Bible has the answer to all possible queries. The fact that such ideas are creeping back onto the syllabus of schools in the West has to be a matter of considerable concern to the sceptic, since they encourage unquestioning belief within the heart of the scientific enterprise – which at its best is one of the great monuments to the sceptical temperament.

The Empires Strike Back

The case for developing scepticism into more of a force in our public life is plain. Sceptics are confronted by determined opposition from the many adherents to the empires of belief we shall be examining, however, and those will not give up their power base lightly. Such adherents have extensive resources at their command, both financial and psychological, and they will use these to curb the spread of a sceptical outlook that is clearly inimical to their interests. I am speaking here not just of those in control of the empires, the officials at the top, but the ranks of believers whose commitment ensures that empires become monolithic in character. The power-holders of these empires traditionally display a pathological hatred of opposition as an expression of their zeal, and our twenty-first-century adherents are no exception. It is up to sceptics collectively to make life as difficult as they can for these exponents of empire; to worry away at their authority, to question their ideas, to call attention to their totalitarian leanings, and to refuse to give up when they strike back with all their considerable power and support. We'll start that process by considering how scepticism came to be the position we know it as today; then place it in confrontation with unquestioning belief across its many empires, in particular those of science and technology, politics and religion. How scepticism actively can be fostered by the university sector and the media will close the case being made for an engaged scepticism to take us forward in the new century.

One historian of scepticism has commented that, 'once upon a time scepticism was a serious challenge and no-one thought to insulate it from affecting, or being affected by, the judgments of ordinary life'.[15] I want to return us to that position, where scepticism can be seen to have a moral value for all of us.

1
Scepticism: A Brief Philosophical History

Scepticism has been a major part of Western philosophical history, from classical times through to the present, and we can now consider what it has contributed to this tradition. While an essentially negative mode of thought (C. H. Whiteley memorably has described it as 'an uncomfortable position . . . tolerable only if it can be employed to make self-important people still more uncomfortable'[1]), scepticism has played a critical role in countering philosophy's often-problematical system-building pretensions. And philosophical history is littered with examples of grandiose systems of thought that attempt to override all that has gone before: think of Hegel (1770–1831) and Marx (1818–83) above all, with their universally operative dialectics of history. In Marx's case, this philosophical system-building went on to have a profound impact on global politics for the greater part of the twentieth century, with the Soviet empire and China living by the 'laws' of dialectical materialism and doing their best to make the rest of humanity conform to them too. Against this tendency, scepticism from Sextus Empiricus onwards represents a call to preserve a sense of proportion in our thought. It is a call for suspension of judgement – particularly of hasty judgements. When we reach modern times, the work of David Hume (1711–76) continues to constitute a relevant warning against the system-building impulse, with all the imperialistic aspirations such a process involves (in the realms of both philosophy and religion). The value of such 'negative' projects as this for philosophy as a discipline will be emphasised in this chapter.

Consideration also needs to be given to the role of scepticism in non-Western philosophical traditions. To that end, attention will be paid to scepticism in Islamic philosophy – which in its early days can be seen as a bridge between classical and pre-modern Western thought. This will be a way of suggesting that the Islamic world can deploy its own history in the struggle against fundamentalism: a struggle which Islam surely cannot avoid undergoing in the longer term if it is to be anything other than a reactionary creed. Even a former aide of the Ayatollah Khomeini has felt moved to complain of 'the absolutist and authoritarian system which has resulted in a fascist version of Islam in Iran, where everything has to be unified, singular, one: a total state'.[2] (The declaration by the Iranian president Mahmoud Ahmadinejad (elected 2005) that his country, 'did not have a revolution in order to have a democracy', is a stark reminder of what reformers are up against in that system.[3]) Anything from within Islam that can help to dissipate the drive towards theocratic fascism should be advertised as widely as possible. A professor of philosophy at Cairo University has also openly called for resistance to the Islamic clergy (*ulama*), whom he regards as collectively responsible for preventing the modernisation of attitudes that Islamic societies desperately need if they are to prosper and develop.[4]

Relating such ideas back into Islamic history can only be a good idea. Scepticism should not be regarded as a Eurocentric or Western-centric phenomenon: it can, and should, be promoted from within other cultural traditions. Given the prominence of Islam in the current world order, and its increasingly fractious relationship with the West (much exacerbated since 9/11 and the Iraq war and subsequent occupation), that becomes a highly desirable objective. Scepticism has to be supported, and turned to account, wherever it can be found. From the perspective adopted here, the emergence of scepticism is always a good sign.

Classical Scepticism

Western philosophical scepticism begins with the Greeks, and as we saw in the introduction soon settles down in the Hellenistic world into two main forms, the Academic and the Pyrrhonian. As I noted before, the latter is the one for which I feel the most sympathy, the one most inclined towards undermining 'the disease called Dogmatism' – the enemy of true sceptics everywhere. Its virtue lies in its very lack of claims; in its desire to be a technique for analysing the claims of others, and identifying their shortcomings, rather than a new source of authority in its own right (a condition that Academic scepticism tended to gravitate towards). While classical Pyrrhonians wished to reach a condition of quietude, I am more concerned to use scepticism to create *disquiet*, not just amongst dogmatists, but within the sceptical community itself. Our own position should be under constant review, and should never become too comfortable. Nevertheless, I think we can reasonably appropriate elements of Pyrrhonism into the current project. As the noted scholar on the classical Pyrrhonian tradition, Jonathan Barnes, has argued, its 'forms and structures remain today among the central issues in the theory of knowledge; . . . they still provide the subject of epistemology with some of its most cunning puzzles and most obdurate problems'.[5]

Pyrrhonism is to be considered, therefore, more than just a historical curiosity. It provides an extremely useful point of reference for rethinking the project of scepticism in the twenty-first century. This is particularly so since, as Julia Annas and Jonathan Barnes point out, Pyrrhonism's emphasis was very firmly on belief: 'The ancient sceptics did not attack knowledge: they attacked belief' (whereas in modern scepticism it is often the opposite).[6] As it is precisely belief that we are concerned to call into question too, it is appropriate for us to link up as much as we can with the classical sceptical tradition.

Pyrrhonism can be traced back to Pyrrho of Elis (c. 360–275 BC), and his disciple Timon (c. 315–225 BC), but was only subsequently developed as a proper theory of scepticism by Aenesidemus (c. 100–40 BC). Sextus Empiricus owes his key position in the history of scepticism to

being the author of the only surviving texts from the Pyrrhonian tradition, *Outlines of Scepticism* and *Against the Mathematicians*, rather than
to any originality of interpretation of his own (one theory is that he
owes a considerable debt to an obscure figure from the previous
century called Agrippa[7]). The theories of his forebears are channelled
through these works by Sextus, which provide us with an extensive
body of arguments – arranged into ten 'modes', such as 'disagree-
ment', 'infinite regress', and 'reciprocity' (circular reasoning[8]) – as to
why we should desist from making judgements on matters of knowledge. In every case these modes prevent clear-cut decisions being
made about disputed issues. For Sextus,

> Scepticism is an ability to set out oppositions among things which
> appear and are thought of in any way at all, an ability by which, because
> of the equipollence in the opposed objects and accounts, we come first to
> a suspension of judgement and afterwards to tranquillity. . . . The chief
> constitutive principle of scepticism is the claim that to every account an
> equal account is opposed; for it is from this, we think, that we come to
> hold no belief.[9]

('Equipollence' means for Sextus, 'equality with regard to being convincing or unconvincing'.[10]) Scepticism is presented in the *Outlines*,
as we noted in the Introduction, as a 'mental attitude' (much as postmodernism has been defined by some commentators in our own
day), 'a purge that eliminates everything including itself'.[11] Sextus
himself emphasises the social utility of the sceptical project, arguing
that '[s]ceptics are philanthropic and wish to cure by argument, as far
as they can, the conceit and rashness of the Dogmatists', clearly signalling his belief that the world would be a much better place were
scepticism to become the dominant outlook.[12] After the Hellenistic
period, however, the Pyrrhonian tradition largely disappears for
several centuries, with philosophy in the West increasingly being
drawn into the web of Christian theology and made to serve its more
specialised interests (enquiries into the nature of God and his properties, proofs for the existence of God, concerns of that nature).

In Richard H. Popkin's summation, the Pyrrhonist sceptic 'lives
undogmatically, following his natural inclinations, the appearances

he is aware of, and the laws and customs of his society, without ever committing himself to any judgment about them'.[13] I find this an attractive character portrait, particularly when coupled with the Pyrrhonist's focus on belief; but I would like to build a few more elements into it, such as a more robust attitude towards dogmatism and a desire to see it challenged whenever it raises its head, as it almost always will, in institutional authority. Pyrrhonism can sound a bit passive and interior to the discipline of philosophy: I would like it to be more active and outward looking, an encouragement to making links and establishing common cause with the like-minded rather than a retreat into the personal. That way we can begin to see how we can develop a scepticism for our own times, politically engaged and directed against abuses of power rather than trying to be clever for its own sake (as so much of negatively inclined philosophy can be, especially when it is denying the grounds for knowledge). As far as I am concerned, that is the acceptable face of relativism.

Not everyone finds the Pyrrhonian ideal desirable. One recent robust attack has come from R. J. Hankinson, who wonders whether following its prescriptions really will lead to a more contented existence for all as Sextus claims: 'perhaps some people need a good hearty dose of naive Dogmatism (as religion apparently comforts the bereaved)'.[14] Hankinson argues that Pyrrhonian-style scepticism will only have a therapeutic value for those of a particular temperament and that it will have nothing to say to others. But that is to concentrate on its psychological impact rather than its philosophical and ideological implications. I have no wish to mock the beliefs of the bereaved, for whom religion may well provide a source of solace at a very trying time (and most of us have seen it do just that with relatives or friends at one time or other), but religion is about more than helping the emotionally distraught. It goes well beyond that laudable enough aim to build-up empires that inevitably seem to gravitate towards repression of other viewpoints. Neither is dogmatism just a personal matter; invariably it becomes a group dynamic, and in that form it turns into something much more sinister whose will is hard to counter. But as I said above, it is my intention to build on the Pyrrhonian base so that it achieves a political dimension; hopefully, that will deflect the criticisms of such as Hankinson to scepticism's shortcomings.

Scepticism in Modern Philosophy

Scepticism undergoes a revival in sixteenth-century Europe, with Michel de Montaigne (1533–92) being instrumental in fostering renewed interest in the Pyrrhonian tradition (particularly in his essay 'An Apology for Raymond Sebond' (1780)[15]). It is Pyrrhonism, as Popkin notes, that 'became central in the intellectual battles of the late sixteenth century'.[16] Popkin speaks of a *crise pyrrhoniene* in the period, with scepticism being brought to bear on theology in the wake of the Reformation and the fierce doctrinal conflicts that flared up between Protestants and Catholics. Authority is a key issue in this context, with both sides claiming to be the sole authority for the Christian faith, and freely accusing each other of scepticism with regard to the fundamentals of belief. This was a damning indictment in that culture: in the ringing words of Martin Luther (1483–1546), '[t]he Holy Ghost is not a Sceptic', so no true Christian could be either.[17] Pyrrhonism is even mocked in the work of Rabelais (?1494–1553), through the figure of the philosopher Wordspinner in *Gargantua and Pantagruel* (1532, 1534). Wordspinner's intellectual evasiveness leaves both Panurge and Gargantua bemused and exasperated; the latter declaring of his convoluted arguments that, '[i]t will be easier to seize lions by the mane . . . than to catch philosophers of this kind by the words they speak'.[18]

It is Descartes (1596–1650), however, who is generally considered to be the figure who brings scepticism most fully into the modern philosophical world, in his quest to find a secure basis for a theory of knowledge. He subjected all his beliefs to scrutiny, seeking to locate that elusive starting point from which he could then build outwards with assurance. This proved to be the famous proposition, *cogito ergo sum*, 'I think therefore I am.' The one thing that Descartes could never doubt was that he was thinking, even if the truth of the content of his thoughts posed more problems for him. Once he started investigating these thoughts, however, they soon provided more reinforcement for his new system.

Descartes is generally regarded now as only a quasi-sceptic, since although he describes himself in the *Third Meditation* as 'a being that doubts' he proves only too ready to embrace proofs for the existence of God.[19] Indeed, he regarded himself as the enemy of the new Pyrrhonism in French thought, considering this to be a particularly dangerous trend which needed to be countered if Christian belief was to prevail. Descartes' brand of scepticism was designed to overcome scepticism: 'strategic', in one commentator's assessment.[20] On the subject of God Descartes' philosophical radicalism slips. Once that proof is in place, based on principles such as that he has an idea in his mind of a perfect being against which his own imperfection can be measured, Descartes moves rapidly to build-up a series of propositions in which he can believe with complete confidence. In sceptical terms of reference, the existence of God is never really placed in question, which makes Descartes' project of formulating a theory and system of knowledge considerably easier. As Bernard Williams has observed,

> The road that Descartes constructed back from the extreme point of the Doubt, and from the world merely of first-personal mental existence which he hoped to have established in the *cogito*, essentially goes over a religious bridge. Taking his concern to be the foundations of scientific knowledge, these are provided by God; taking it to be the foundations of the possibility of knowledge, these too, and in a more intimate sense, are to be found in God.[21]

The belief undermines the scepticism, in other words, whereas for the true sceptic it would be the other way around: faith would be out of bounds as a basis for proof, yet another unsubstantiated assumption looking around in vain for a criterion to justify it.

Ultimately, Descartes is not really a philosopher who leaves one feeling too 'uncomfortable', although he does succeed in establishing scepticism as a key element in modern philosophical discourse. As one commentator has put it, the irony of Descartes' researches is that '[h]is "refutation" of scepticism left it in better shape than before'.[22] Negatively oriented though it may be, scepticism is nevertheless now firmly a part of the philosophical mainstream.

David Hume: The Sceptic's Sceptic

When it comes to thoroughgoing scepticism few can rival David Hume, who might justifiably be described as 'the sceptic's sceptic'. Until postmodern times anyway, Hume can outsceptic almost any of his competitors. Neither faith nor religious belief will get in the way of the conclusions in this instance, with Hume making it quite clear in various works how low his opinion is of organised religion and the religious impulse. Hume is particularly critical of monotheism, arguing in the *Natural History of Religion* that polytheism is the preferable option of the two, being generally more tolerant than monotheism: 'The tolerating spirit of idolaters, both in ancient and modern times, is very obvious to any one, who is the least conversant in the writings of historians or travellers'.[23] Religion in general, however, is considered to have a bad influence on public morals, its adherents so often being motivated 'by intemperate zeal, by rapturous extasies, or by the belief of mysterious and absurd opinions'.[24]

Descartes may have resolved his difficulties over finding a starting point for philosophical enquiry, but Hume never did, and bravely faced up to the consequences. It is in his researches into the nature of causality that Hume's importance for the history of scepticism mainly lies. He called into question the connection between cause and effect, arguing that this was contingent only. There was no 'necessary connection' between causes and effects; we merely assumed there was on the basis of previous experience, and had no justification other than 'custom', as Hume put it, for projecting such experience into the future:[25] repetition could not be depended upon. The uniformity we assumed to be all around us in nature was just that, an assumption, and could be breached at any point. Just because the sun had risen every day did not mean it would do so again tomorrow – and even if it subsequently did, that offered no greater probability for the day after that.

Hume offers us a genuinely disturbing view of the world, although there are positive aspects to note as well: we are left with an open future and a powerful argument against determinism or predestination (those great standbys of monotheistic religions, and powerful ways of preventing us from questioning the order of things). We simply do not *know* what will happen next, although we can of course make an educated guess based on past experience, which will generally be confirmed (but you cannot bet on it). This is a state of affairs that some will find alarming, others exciting, depending on how much security you crave in your everyday life. An open future, as we shall go on to see in Chapter 3, is one of the cornerstones of poststructuralist and postmodernist thought, and those thinkers certainly consider it to be a liberating notion, worth disseminating and celebrating.

Hume went on to call into doubt the notion of personal identity, claiming that each of us was the recipient of a stream of sense impressions that had no connecting link holding them together. Many other philosophers, Hume contended, believed that 'we are every moment intimately conscious of what we call our *self*', and that this was central to our understanding of the world: 'nor is there anything of which we can be certain if we doubt of this'.[26] Hume disagreed strongly, arguing that '[u]nluckily all these positive assertions are contrary to that very experience which is pleaded for them'.[27] Personal identity was for him a state of permanent change, with no central essence to it that defined us as individuals. At any one point the self was simply the series of sense impressions that were flowing through it, and these would endlessly change over time:

> For my part, when I enter most intimately into what I call *myself*, I always stumble on some particular perception or other, of heat or cold, light or shade, love or hatred, pain or pleasure. I never can catch *myself* at any time without a perception, and never can observe anything but the perception. . . . I may venture to affirm of the rest of mankind, that they are nothing but a bundle or collection of different perceptions, which succeed each other with an inconceivable rapidity, and are in a perpetual flux and movement. Our eyes cannot turn in their sockets without

varying our perceptions. Our thought is still more variable than our sight; and all our other senses and faculties contribute to this change; nor is there any single power of the soul, which remains unalterably the same, perhaps for one moment. The mind is a kind of theatre, where several perceptions successively make their appearance; pass, repass, glide away, and mingle in an infinite variety of postures and situations.[28]

Even memory, although it did give us a sense of past events, could not stamp unity on this process. There was no fixed personal identity that we carried with us through our lives, no central 'self' that endured no matter what happened to us; therefore, we must also assume, no certainty as to our knowledge either. With the mind as 'a kind of theatre', there could be no basis for unquestioning belief. Indeed, belief of any kind at all would be hard to sustain, with ideas constantly passing, repassing, gliding away, and mingling indiscriminately. We were deluding ourselves to think that we had anything solid to hang onto with which to construct a stable world-view. Again, this was a conclusion which some would find alarming, some exciting, depending on their psychological make-up.

Hume certainly did prove to possess the talent to make the self-important feel distinctly uncomfortable, and his scepticism continues to resonate in similar fashion through to our own day. So does, more positively, his insistence that sceptics have to do their best to engage with the everyday world: 'To whatever length any one may push his speculative principles of scepticism, he must act, I own, and live, and converse like other men.'[29]

Before turning to more recent engagements with scepticism, we'll dip into some other philosophical traditions, and then briefly consider some gestures towards super-scepticism (our topic in Chapter 3) in Western philosophy.

Scepticism in Islamic Philosophy

Islamic philosophy developed largely out of a dialogue with classical Greek philosophy, with the work of Aristotle (384–322 BC), Plato (c.427–347 BC), and the neoplatonist Alexandrian philosopher

Plotinus (AD 204/5–70) being key sources. In fact, it was largely through the Islamic tradition, and the work of Averroes (Ibn Rushd; 1126–98) in particular, that the work of such philosophers was kept alive after the break-up of the Roman Empire.[30] The Orthodox Byzantine empire, ruled from Constantinople, had turned its back on Greek philosophy – the Emperor Justinian closing the famous School of Athens in AD 529 – because of its pagan heritage. When a reaction to Aristotelianism set in after the first few centuries of Islamic culture it brought in its wake a measure of scepticism, with philosophy as a discipline itself coming to be called into question by some thinkers. One such prominent anti-Aristotelian was the eleventh-century philosopher Al-Ghazali (or Algazali; 1058–1111), who was noted for exhibiting sceptical leanings at several points in his career, although he ended up as a mystic, turning to Sufism. He is described by the commentators Arthur Hyman and James J. Walsh as someone who 'had a skeptical streak within his nature, sampled a number of theological and philosophic positions, and left an auto-biographical record of his spiritual quests'.[31] The work in which his scepticism is most evident, as well as his anti-philosophical bent, is *The Incoherence of the Philosophers* (written between 1091 and 1095).

From our point of view it is unfortunate that Al-Ghazali's scepti-cism ultimately was overcome by his religious belief. Whereas for Pyrrhonians dogmatism was the 'disease' to be feared, for Al-Ghazali that was scepticism. He speaks of God having 'cured me of this malady' in his autobiographical work *Deliverance from Error* (c.1100), after a prolonged period in which he felt himself to be 'a sceptic in fact though not in theory nor in outward expression'.[32] Al-Ghazali then goes on to denounce philosophy in the same work, dismissing the claims of the various schools on the grounds that 'unbelief affects them all', and that their influence on Muslims is 'baneful and mis-chievous'.[33] It is a claim that many in the Muslim world would uphold still today. But at least we can see the seed of scepticism present there within the Islamic tradition, and it is fascinating to observe the dialectic between scepticism and theology unfolding in this context – as it was later to do in Descartes, another philosopher for whom God was in some sense the 'cure' for his intellectual 'malady'. When that scepticism is directed against philosophy it fits into the tradition of Western scepticism, and there are similarities to be noted between Al-Ghazali and Hume on the subject of causality. Both philosophers deny any necessary connection between cause and effect, although with Al-Ghazali there is a theological aspect in God being the only source of causes in the universe. There can even be 'causeless' effects in Al-Ghazali's scheme; as Hyman and Walsh note, it is a consequence of Al-Ghazali's conception of divine omnipotence that, 'God is able to produce any effect without any intermediate cause at all.'[34] Al-Ghazali is also thought to have influenced the fourteenth-century French philosopher Nicholas (sometimes spelled Nicolaus) of Autrecourt, who has been dubbed 'the medieval Hume', so he genuinely has a role to play in the Western as well as the Islamic tradition.

In *The Incoherence of the Philosophers* Al-Ghazali systematically works his way through twenty philosophical doctrines to prove that they are inconsistent with the Koran. In each case he offers a detailed refutation, and although his position is theologically based – Koranic doctrines are taken as given and felt to require no proof – he argues his case, in the words of some recent commentators, 'with great philosophical acuity'.[35] The doctrines in question can be traced back to Greek philosophy, and in Al-Ghazali's reading they have come to infect Islamic philosophy with heretical notions. He speaks disparagingly of a group of thinkers, such as Alfarabi (c.870–950) and Avicenna (980–1037), who 'have entirely cast off the reins of religion through multifarious beliefs'.[36] 'The source of their unbelief', Al-Ghazali goes on to argue, 'is their hearing high-sounding names such as "Socrates [469–399 BC]," "Hippocrates [c.460–377 BC]," "Plato," "Aristotle," and their likes'.[37] The author's appointed task is 'to show the incoherence of their belief' in such matters as the nature of the universe, God's attributes, the uniformity of nature, and the nature of the soul.[38] What all the philosophers being attacked have in common, in Al-Ghazali's opinion, is that they underestimate God's power. Some have argued for an eternal universe, whereas for the devout it is necessary to accept that it was created in an act of will by an omnipotent God. God also had the power to alter the course of nature if he chose, meaning that belief in nature's uniformity was tantamount to heresy, as was any denial of bodily resurrection after death.

Al-Ghazali's attack on the Aristotelian tradition in Islamic philosophy is damning, and as one of his translators has noted, '[i]t brought to a head the conflict between Islamic speculative theology and philosophy'.[39] Averroes responded with a work entitled *The Incoherence of the Incoherence*, but Al-Ghazali's theology-led approach exerts a considerable appeal within Islam. If one puts the theological bias to one side, however, one has some very powerful arguments against metaphysical claims. Difficult though it may be to ignore the theology, it is still worth emphasising sceptical attitudes wherever one finds them within the Islamic system.

If Al-Ghazali's encounter with philosophy was decided in favour of religion, then the dialogue with Greek classical philosophy within Islam prompted several thinkers of the same period to start questioning the claims of religion instead. Ibn al-Rawandi (c.910?), for example, rejected the concept of prophethood and even queried the authority of the Koran: 'even if we grant that he [Mohammed] exceeds all the Arabs in eloquence, what compelling force will this have where Persians, who do not understand the [Arabic] tongue are concerned, and what probative evidence can he advance?'[40] Philosophy-inspired free thought led to such iconoclastic sentiments as those expressed by the poet Abul-Ala al-Maarri (973–1057) on religious strife in the Islamic territories:

> Each party defends its own religion
> I wonder in vain where the truth lies![41]

Abu Isa al-Warraq (active early eighth century) argued that neither Christianity nor Judaism could be considered to have any validity because many of their doctrines broke the rules of Aristotelian logic (al-Warraq himself was accused of Zoroastrian leanings by his Islamic contemporaries). Even if, as Majid Fakhry has noted, most theologians, like Al-Ghazali, ultimately 'reacted violently' against the impact of Greek philosophy on their culture, scepticism was capable of making its presence felt in the Islamic world none the less.[42]

Scepticism is always going to be in a dialectic with theology in Islam, but that dialectic needs to be given as much encouragement as it can, such that it can be seen as intrinsic to that cultural tradition rather than a Western imposition signalling yet another round of colonial imperialism. At the very least the potential for scepticism is present in every culture. Doubt is a universal phenomenon, one that creeps into everyone's mind at some point or other, and we can draw hope from that. Regardless of whether it is conceived of as disease or cure it is something to build upon.

Scepticism in Other Philosophical Traditions

Scepticism can be found in other non-Western philosophical traditions, such as the Indian. India, as the eminent historian of religion Ninian Smart has pointed out, 'has been a laboratory of religious doctrines' (Hinduism and Buddhism in particular), and is therefore particularly fertile territory for the study of the philosophy of religion.[43] In classical Indian philosophy, which has a heritage going back well before the Greeks and the beginnings of Western philosophy, scepticism takes the form of questioning the authority of the sacred Vedas, on which the classical tradition itself is based (as Smart also notes,'there is no escaping the fact that the main determinants of systematic metaphysics in India have been religious in character'[44]). Such scepticism is particularly identified with the school known as the Carvaka materialists, who made use of the circular reasoning and infinite regress objections so popular with the Pyrrhonists. Their sceptical attitude is clearly signalled in the only surviving work of the school, the splendidly named *Lion Assaulting all Philosophical Principles* (*Tattvopaplasimha*, seventh century AD).

The Carvaka School also flouted Indian tradition by denying the doctrines of karma and rebirth, which all of India's other classical schools accepted implicitly; their materialist bias interestingly prefiguring that which led some of the major Enlightenment thinkers, such as Baron d'Holbach (whose iconoclastic views will be considered in Chapter 2), to reject religion altogether. Carvaka theorists argued that consciousness was simply the product of how certain kinds of matter were organised (and all objects were made up of material elements for this school); that consciousness varied so much between species that one could not sensibly speak of it moving from one kind of being to another (man to elephant, for example) as rebirth postulated; and that the self was co-extensive with the body and therefore ceased when that body died (they rejected reincarnation on the basis that we had no memory of a previous existence). Such overt materialism is regarded by many within the Buddhist tradition in India as 'coarse-grained' and lacking in spirituality.[45] The Carvaka school died out in medieval times, but it represents an interesting example of iconoclasm within the Indian religious tradition.

Scepticism nevertheless flourishes within Buddhist philosophy, as in the Madhyamika (Voidism) school and its most famous exponent, Nagarjuna (c. AD 150–200). Nagarjuna advocates something like a Pyrrhonist suspension of judgement in advocating that silence is the best response to metaphysical questions.[46] He believes in the emptiness of all things, which involves a reinterpretation of key Buddhist concepts: 'His central concern was to express the Middle Way so as to aid others in losing their attachment to illusion.'[47] Instead of being a path between existence and non-existence, the middle way was for Nagarjuna 'a slipping between and away from the binary categories of existence and non-existence. . . . the "and/or" which is *between* the "and/or" of existence and non-existence, identity and non-identity, causality and non-causality'.[48]

Nagarjuna's dialectical method of thought pictures a state of flux in which there are no fixed categories to fall back upon for analysis, hence his recommendation to refrain from becoming embroiled in metaphysical enquiry in the first place:

Never are existing things found to originate
From themselves, from something else, from both, or from no cause.

If an element (*dharma*) occurs which is neither real nor non-real nor both
    real and non-real,
How can there be a cause which is effective in this situation?[49]

Despite the explicitly spiritual motivation, there is nevertheless a sense of philosophical scepticism about Nagarjuna's dialectical arguments, where concepts and propositions are pitted against their opposites (also a problematisation of the link between cause and effect). We are left with a series of contradictions that prevent answers being reached or judgements made: hence the commitment to silence about all matters metaphysical. As Frederick J. Streng points out,

> emptiness is used by Nagarjuna to express the religious insight that living beings are 'saved' from their own selves and the claims of existence by appreciating the interrelatedness of everything in existence. The skepticism of every ultimate claim is an affirmation that man (and every living creature) exists in dependence on others in the most fundamental way.[50]

Given such a view of the self and its interdependence with all other existence, there would be no position from which to make claims or judgements:

> All things prevail for him for whom emptiness prevails;
> Nothing whatever prevails for him for whom emptiness prevails.[51]

As another commentator, Karl Potter, has succinctly put it: 'That is the clue to Madhyamika – it doesn't try to explain.'[52]

Although the cultural traditions are very different from those of the West, the examples above suggest that the impulse to challenge the authority of belief systems from within is well nigh universal. While it may not have developed to the extent that it has in the West, where it has an essentially non-religious heritage to draw upon from classical Greece, philosophical scepticism, or something analogous to it, can be found in some form in most other cultures. The sceptical consciousness can arise and flourish anywhere, even within elaborate religious frameworks such as are to be found in India. We are not imposing Western values on other cultures by encouraging those traditions to develop that consciousness further. If unquestioning belief is to be confronted on a global scale, that has to be the way forward, and it will be all the more effective if it is being challenged from the inside in the case of religions.

Super-Scepticism Before the Postmodern

A few remarks about the 'medieval Hume', Nicholas of Autrecourt (c.1300–69), should dispel the notion that only postmodern philosophers are capable of espousing super-scepticism. By the standards of his day Nicholas well merits the super-sceptic tag, as the following assessment of his philosophical career would indicate:

> If Anselm of Canterbury represents the medieval high-water mark in the claims made for reason, Nicholas of Autrecourt must come very close to representing the low-water mark. It is not only the dogmas of the faith which he finds to be indemonstrable, including the existence of God, but also the very foundational doctrines of philosophy itself. . . . As Hume did with a later tradition, he simply showed what follows if one insists on consistency to a professed principle.[53]

Nicholas refused to accept as true any statement, proposition, or observation which could not be reduced to the law of non-contradiction ('either A or not-A'; 'either alive or not-alive', etc.), the 'first principle'of knowledge as this was considered to be in scholastic philosophy. This was a particularly stringent requirement to make for evidence, so stringent it could hardly ever be met, and in his *Letters to Bernard of Arezzo* (c.1338) his insistence on consistency in this respect leads Nicholas to extract some very radical positions indeed from the philosophical ideas of his correspondent:

> And so, bringing all those statements together, it seems that you must say that you are not certain of those things which are outside of you. And thus you do not know if you are in the heavens or the Earth, in fire or in water; . . . Just as you do not know whether the Chancellor or the Pope exists, and whether, if they exist, they are different in each moment of time. . . . Further, your position seems to lead to the destruction of social and political affairs, because if witnesses testify of what they have seen, it does not follow, 'We have seen it, therefore it happened.' Again, I ask how, on this view, the Apostles were certain that Christ suffered on the cross, and that He rose from the dead, and so with all the rest.[54]

It should come as no surprise that in raising such alarming possibilities Nicholas fell foul of the church, and was sentenced to burn his writings publicly in Paris. The authority of the church would be in tatters if doubts about the crucifixion and the resurrection were to be acknowledged – never mind casting doubt on the existence of the pope (a point that would take on even greater resonance later in the fourteenth century when a schism within the church led to there being competing popes in Avignon and Rome). Epistemological scepticism to that degree could never be countenanced by such a militantly dogmatic institution as the medieval Catholic church, particularly with that sting in the tail of 'and so with all the rest'. Would anything at all be left of belief or the Christian system if one followed Nicholas? This is scepticism as heresy, and it is typically brave of a sceptic to be so iconoclastic.

From a non-religious perspective what is more interesting is that, as Hume was later to do with an even greater sense of conviction, Nicholas has broken the link between cause and effect. This can never be established with any sense of certainty in his philosophical scheme: 'From the fact that some thing is known to exist [effect], it cannot be evidently inferred, by evidence reduced to the first principle or to the certitude of the first principle, that some other thing exists [cause].'[55] Neither inference nor observation will lead us to necessary connection, and to argue this is the mark of the thoroughgoing sceptic (the implication being there in the work of Nagarjuna too, as we saw earlier).

One of the major commentators on Nicholas, Julius Weinberg, prefers to dub him a critic than a sceptic, but also concedes that Nicholas's 'attack on the pretensions' of past authority meant that he 'was moving towards a conception of investigation which is similar to our own'.[56] Given the points raised in the *Letters*, however, it does not seen unreasonable to me to claim Nicholas for the cause of scepticism.

Bishop Berkeley (1685–1753) flirts with super-scepticism too, in managing to call into question the existence of matter itself. That is certainly a radical step to take, making the efforts of later super-sceptics seem somewhat tame by comparison, given that they are in the main only challenging conceptions of authority, meaning, and identity. Berkeley's meditations on the nature of our sense perceptions led to the implication that matter comes and goes out of existence depending on whether it is being perceived or not. In the *Three Dialogues Between Hylas and Philonous* (1713), the latter character articulates Berkeley's own position to a companion whose initial objections – 'the most extravagant opinion that ever entered into the mind of man'[57] – give way eventually to a grudging acceptance of the broad outlines of the argument:

> retain the word *matter*, and apply it to the objects of sense, if you please, provided you do not attribute to them any subsistence distinct from there being perceived. . . . *Matter*, or *material substance*, are terms introduced by philosophers; and as used by them, imply a sort of independency, or a subsistence distinct from being perceived by a mind: but are never used by common people; or if ever, it is to signify the immediate objects of sense.[58]

Interestingly enough, Berkeley himself feels that his arguments constitute a refutation of scepticism, with Philonous being absolutely convinced of the rightness of his position: 'How cometh it to pass then, Hylas, that you pronounce me a *sceptic*, because I deny what you affirm, to wit, the existence of matter?'[59] Sceptics are on a par with atheists in this scheme of things, creatures beyond the pale. The attitude towards the philosophical mainstream, who stand accused of believing in the independent existence of matter, is, however, resolutely sceptical: that they have no basis for their belief. We might, too, detect a note of Academic scepticism in Philonous's certainty that no such basis ever will be found.

Once again, however, theology comes to the rescue. Berkeley turns to God as a guarantee of the continuing existence of the world and everything in it, thus drawing back from the very brink of super-scepticism:

> I conclude, not that they have no real existence, but that seeing they depend not on my thought, and have an existence distinct from being perceived by me, *there must be some other mind wherein they exist*. As sure

therefore as the sensible world really exists, so sure is there an infinite omnipresent spirit who contains and supports it.[60]

Although philosophically this is a very disappointing move to make, Berkeley is a good example of just how far sceptics are willing to speculate in their pursuit of 'consistency to a professed principle'. By the time the theology kicks in, a climate of doubt has been created in the reader's mind that will have a very different effect on the non-religious. Scepticism benefits from being pushed to extremes on occasion in this manner, and it is all the better when theology finds itself excluded from the exercise altogether. Then, the sceptic has to develop tactics to cope with the ensuing problems of relativism – but that is far more philosophically honest than playing the God card with all its dogmatic overtones. Divine intervention makes for poor philosophy, as it does poor science too (we'll pick up on that latter point when we look at the theories of creationism and intelligent design in Chapter 4).

Scepticism in Contemporary Philosophy

Philosophers have gone on wrestling with scepticism in contemporary philosophy, and have come up with some ingenious arguments to keep the problem at bay, while striving not to succumb to dogmatism in the process. For Ludwig Wittgenstein, our methods of enquiring into the truth of our knowledge and belief have a background that we can depend upon with what amounts to certainty. There is a 'scaffolding' that 'stands fast' for us in such cases, making enquiry possible in the first instance:[61]

> All testing, all confirmation and disconfirmation of a hypothesis takes place already within a system. And this system is not a more or less arbitrary and doubtful point of departure for all our arguments: no, it belongs to the essence of what we call an argument. The system is not so much the point of departure, as the element in which arguments are made.[62]

There are limits to scepticism, in other words, which in Wittgenstein's view ought to restrict some of the method's wilder excesses. These are sentiments which will go resolutely unheeded by the super-sceptics, however, whose reflex will be to probe away at what constitutes the 'scaffolding' and to be unsatisfied by any insistence that they can, or should, go no further than that.

It seems to be a characteristic of contemporary mainstream philosophy (the analytical tradition) to try to neutralise scepticism as a philosophical position, calling into question its assumptions and methodologies. As one notable defender of the sceptical outlook, Barry Stroud, has put it,

> scepticism in philosophy has been found uninteresting, perhaps even a waste of time, in recent years. The attempt to meet, or even to understand, the sceptical challenge to our knowledge of the world is regarded in some circles as an idle academic exercise, a wilful refusal to abandon outmoded forms of thinking in this new post-Cartesian age.[63]

Stroud, as we shall see below, strongly disagrees with this negative assessment. Yet the anti-sceptical impulse is nevertheless commendable enough in its way, being concerned to prevent philosophy from collapsing into arguments about the grounds for argument, in which case the subject is not addressing all the other problems in the world around us – problems of ethics and politics, for example. Finding flaws in the sceptical position is also a way of arresting a slide into relativism – something that any socially conscious mainstream philosopher is generally keen to avoid, with its implications of an anarchic 'anything goes' approach to ethics and politics (a charge frequently made against the super-sceptics).

Hyperbolic doubt in particular comes in for very close scrutiny, with its basic premises being strongly challenged. Such doubt can go the extent of questioning the very existence of the external world, and here contemporary anti-sceptics have been particularly critical, offering several counter-arguments to what they consider to be an untenable, and certainly socially unhelpful, position. One way of posing the problem is to suggest that rather than a body in the world you might just be a 'brain in a vat', connected up to a very powerful computer by some evil scientist such that you are given the impression of bodily existence. Hilary Putnam, however, argues that a brain in a vat could not have such a thought itself, and that 'the supposition that we are actually brains in a vat . . . is, in a certain way, self-refuting'.[64] Brains in vats simply could not have the same experiences that human beings with bodies do: 'one cannot refer to certain kinds of things, e.g. *trees*, if one has no causal interaction with them, or with things in terms of which they can be described'.[65]

Scepticism comes to seem a wilfully wrong-headed way of looking at things to Putnam, who dismisses the relativism that can come in its wake on the grounds that it could not be consistently held: 'To say this is not to deny that we can rationally and correctly think that *some* of our beliefs are irrational. It is to say that there are limits to how far this insistence that we are all intellectually damned can go without becoming unintelligible.'[66] Reasonably enough, it is the dogmatic tendency within scepticism that Putnam is most concerned to undermine: the tendency to universalise from particular instances. This proves to be something of a recurrent theme amongst contemporary anti-sceptics.

Robert Nozick takes particular issue with scepticism in his book *Philosophical Explanations*, which, as the title indicates, wants to move the emphasis of philosophical enquiry away from proof to explanation. This immediately distances him from philosophical sceptics, who invariably want to question and raise doubts as to how certain things are possible – how do we know there is an external world or other minds, that we are not a brain in a vat, etc.? – rather than seek an explanation for them. Sceptics traditionally want to leave us with problems, not answers. Instead of setting out to refute scepticism, Nozick looks for ways to bypass it: 'to formulate hypotheses about knowledge and our connection to facts that show how knowledge can exist even given the skeptic's possibilities'.[67] The intent is to be positive rather than negative, with Nozick arguing that a philosophy based on explanation is 'morally better' than its rivals (Nagarjuna would disagree); even though he concedes the value of scepticism in prompting non-sceptics to re-evaluate their belief system on a regular basis. The message is that in small doses scepticism is good for you.[68]

Nozick postulates a clear link between knowledge and belief. We believe what we know to be true, and we do not believe what we know to be false: 'I am writing on a page with a pen. It is true that I am, I believe that I am, if I weren't I wouldn't believe that I was, and if I were, I would believe it.'[69] Our beliefs 'track facts', as Nozick describes it, and scepticism in no way affects this practice or how we reach judgements about whether particular beliefs are justified or not.[70] If not entirely refuted, scepticism is, in Nozick's opinion, at least a much reduced problem by the end of his analysis of its claims: a useful corrective to philosophical complacency, if not much more than that perhaps.

Despite such attempts to neutralise the force of scepticism, some philosophers still regard it as a source of intractable problems for the philosophical enterprise. Stroud, for example, argues that it is a deeply significant element of philosophical thought, claiming that '[b]y examining philosophical scepticism about the external world I hope to bring into question our very understanding of what a philosophical theory of knowledge is supposed to be'.[71] Far from being a barrier to our understanding of the world, scepticism holds the key to it for this thinker and he wants to see it play a larger role in mainstream, analytical philosophy than it is currently doing (Stroud does not engage here with the burgeoning continental tradition of super-scepticism). Stroud's argument is that scepticism leads us back to the problem itself, and that we need to re-examine how and why the problem arises. While it is perfectly reasonable to think that our senses could deceive us, as patently sometimes they do, it is altogether more questionable to generalise from this observation to say that they are therefore totally unreliable as a source of knowledge about the external world:

> If my own sensory experiences do not make it possible for me to know things about the world around me they do not make it possible for me to know even whether there are any other sensory experiences or any other perceiving beings at all.[72]

Stroud proceeds to look closely at our methods of assessing claims to knowledge, and puts forward a series of what he calls 'platitudes', observations that all of us would accept about the world and our understanding of it and that work against the more extreme, even dogmatic, forms of scepticism vying for our attention:[73] platitudes such as that we do not think it unreasonable to act in some situations even if we do not have absolute certainty about what the outcome will be, or that sometimes we find it reasonable to subject our beliefs to challenge and other times we do not (and that not a lot necessarily hangs on each particular decision either way). The platitudes Stroud outlines derive initially from sceptical enquiry, meaning that, for this philosopher, scepticism becomes the source of our proof of the existence of the external world. Whereas most mainstream philosophers seek to undermine scepticism in the process of reaching this conclusion (seeing the scepticism itself as the problem), for Stroud it reinforces scepticism as a mode of thinking. As long as commonly accepted methods of proof exist, then the independence of the world lies beyond reasonable doubt. Scepticism invites us to keep scrutinising our knowledge, and deciding whether it is justified or not: 'The force we feel in the sceptical argument when we first encounter it is itself evidence that the conception of knowledge employed in the argument is the very conception we have been operating with all along.'[74] The very fact of being able to frame sceptical questions indicates that we do have a basis from which to test our knowledge claims, rather like the notion of scaffolding in Wittgenstein: we can rely, Stroud maintains, on 'the familiar assessments of knowledge we know how to make in everyday life'.[75] We need to have a sense of the independent existence of the world, in other words, in order to cast it into doubt.

The benefit of philosophical scepticism for Stroud is that it forces us to examine what lies behind all those 'familiar assessments', and this encourages a high degree of rigour in our reasoning. Where scepticism becomes problematical is when there is overgeneralisation from particular cases, as Putnam also notes. It is only when this occurs that the more extreme claims can be made about the lack of proof for the existence of the external world, and it is such claims that have brought scepticism into disrepute – both inside and outside the realm of philosophy. 'What *use* are such claims?', is a common objection from professional and lay-person alike. Stroud does think that some generalisations can be made from particular experience, however, arguing that, '[i]t could not be shown that when the philosopher generalizes from his particular assessment to a conclusion about human knowledge in general he inevitably denies or withdraws one of the presuppositions that make it possible for his challenge to work as it does in the particular case'.[76] It is that possibility that prevents mainstream philosophy from dismissing scepticism out of hand; the latter, carefully handled, continues to pose awkward questions for the traditional philosophical models of how we come to have knowledge of the world. To that extent we can describe it as philanthropic in Sextus' sense of the term.

Stroud manages to show how scepticism sometimes overstates the case, while never quite altogether losing credibility as a philosophical position: it is integral to philosophical thinking in this reading. Things are left interestingly open at the end of his book *The Significance of Philosophical Scepticism*, but scepticism plainly has not been defeated by its adversaries, and Stroud has made us very aware of the positive role it can play within philosophical discourse – and potentially in everyday life. We need to keep Stroud's stricture about overgeneralisation in mind in our own sceptical project, ensuring that scepticism remains an open-minded approach rather than an aid to dogmatism, but recognising, too, that it holds out the *possibility* of generalisation in certain situations (enough for the sceptic to go to work on).

A somewhat similar approach to scepticism can be found in the work of Christopher Hookaway, who recognises the force of sceptical arguments, while not wanting to accept their more pessimistic conclusions: 'it is argued that sceptical arguments question our ability to participate in the activities involved in enquiry without feeling that our ability to take responsibility for our actions is compromised'.[77] Even though Hookaway suggests there are several ways to overcome scepticism, he still sees it as a valuable part of philosophical enquiry, as long as we are careful to ameliorate some of its more extreme claims and projections:

> a position which despairs of answering sceptical challenges but describes the ways in which we evaluate beliefs and assertions, suggesting that we

can recognise their value without being able to defend them against sceptical onslaught, may be placed in a different perspective when it is seen as the epistemic counterpart of soft determinism: soft scepticism, as we may call it.[78]

('Soft determinism', by the way, is the position that we can still consider ourselves to be free agents, even though we have to accept the restrictions placed on us by the laws of physics: 'Freedom and responsibility are compatible with physical determinism.'[79]) Soft scepticism invites us to keep testing our 'cognitive goals', while not denying our claim to be rational and autonomous agents in doing so.[80] In effect, this is scepticism without the traditional drawbacks from the perspective of the mainstream philosopher.

One senses that both Stroud and Hookaway would be happier were scepticism never to arise, but feel at least bound to accept its presence within the philosophical enterprise. The virtue of scepticism in making us realise the contingent nature of much of our knowledge and belief is fully acknowledged by both these commentators, however, and that is a first step in the campaign to combat dogmatism.

Nowhere has scepticism thrived more in contemporary philosophy, however, than in later twentieth-century France. There, poststructuralism and postmodernism have generated a large and enthusiastic school of super-sceptics who have rejected all attempts at neutralisation of the sceptical impulse – and not from the measured position of someone like Stroud or Hookaway, both of whom want to keep dialogue with scepticism firmly within the philosophical mainstream. The determined move away from the mainstream that super-scepticism represents will be dealt with in Chapter 3.

Curing Philosophical Pretension

Scepticism is a normal and natural part of philosophical thought, therefore, wherever this is being conducted, in whatever culture; an all but inescapable stage in disputation about the basis for truth, knowledge, and belief. Even those committed to the grand narrative of religion cannot avoid scepticism's attractions on occasion (no matter how repressive the religion in question may be), try though they might to steer clear of the 'malady'. I would rather see scepticism as a cure for philosophical pretension, a permanent internal critique of philosophical discourse, tactically geared to thinking the unthinkable, and saying the unsayable, about all grand narratives, in open opposition to the latter's guardians. It is in the conflict with the world's grand narratives that scepticism performs its greatest service for philosophy, raising doubt about the grounds on which claims are made, systems organised, authority assumed, and power wielded. It becomes a critique, in other words, of the drive towards certainty. Grand narratives, in philosophy as elsewhere, will always strive to give that outward appearance of uncontestable authority, and that is what scepticism is concerned above all to unpick. As the Pyrrhonists insisted, there can be no position that is beyond the sceptic's challenge – and that is all to philosophy's good. We need to construct a 'little narrative' based on the virtues of suspension.

We turn next to look in more detail at an era when scepticism came into its own in general cultural terms – the Enlightenment; the age that dared to reduce religion to the status of mere hypothesis in order to dispense with it altogether. Given that the *philosophes* at the heart of the French Enlightenment, from where the rest of Europe took much of its intellectual lead, have been described as 'anti-philosophers', it seems appropriate to deal with them separately from the history of philosophical scepticism.[81] They complement rather than extend that latter tradition.

2
Enlightenment Scepticism: A Campaign Against Unnecessary Hypotheses

Scepticism played a critical role in Enlightenment thought, in particular in the campaign waged against superstition and tradition. Religion was one of the areas that attracted most attention from the leading Enlightenment theorists, whose concern was to liberate humankind from arbitrarily wielded institutional power serving its own interests – the oppressive *ancien régime*. For the more iconoclastically inclined *philosophes* (Denis Diderot (1713–84), Claude-Adrien Helvétius (1715–71), and Baron d'Holbach, for example), religion was to be turned into a private rather than a public matter. The state and religion were to be kept separate, with the latter ideally to be written out of the political process entirely. With varying degrees of success, that has become a goal of most modern nation states. Eventually, God was written out of scientific research entirely too by the more radical thinkers in that area, such as the scientist Pierre-Simon Laplace (1749–1827), notorious for his observation that God was an unnecessary hypothesis for his cosmological theories.[1]

The fact that creationist doctrine has been reintroduced onto school curricula in America and Britain in recent years, through the determined efforts of Protestant fundamentalists in each country, represents a direct challenge to the modern scientific enterprise, which most of us would regard as one of the great success stories of post-Enlightenment life; although as we shall go on to discuss in Chapter 4, science and technology are increasingly classifiable themselves as an empire of belief in their own right, wielding their own formidable institutional power to considerable effect. Once paradigms establish themselves they can be notoriously difficult to dislodge, proceeding to build-up protective mechanisms, and science in many ways is *the* intellectual paradigm of our age. There is also the interesting point to note that, thanks to Big Bang theory, God has now come back into the scientific quest in a major way: but the 'return of the hypothesis' is a story we shall reserve for fuller treatment in Chapter 4.

This will be a very brief encounter with the Enlightenment, a vast topic in its own right going well beyond the parameters of this study, and I will be concerned only with establishing its encouragement of scepticism with regard to traditional authority. Margaret C. Jacob has made a persuasive case for a pan-European 'radical Enlightenment' existing before the more moderate *philosophes* movement (which ushered in the 'High Enlightenment' of the later eighteenth century), tracing both back to England as 'the intellectual heirs of the mid-century [seventeenth] English Revolution'.[2] This radical Enlightenment is republican, pantheistic, philosophically materialist, and anti-religious in its sympathies, and helps to set the tone for the political radicalism of the later eighteenth century, with its various national revolutions and concerted challenge to the *ancien régime*. The radicals developed Freemasonry, which became a context where they could express 'an entirely new religion of nature', and which certainly represented a threat to the established religious order.[3] Jacob notes ideological correspondences between Freemasonry and the *Encyclopédie*, the monumental enterprise under the general editorship of Diderot designed to present and classify all human knowledge and learning within its seventeen volumes of text and eleven of illustrations (published 1751–72). That is not to say, however, as some contemporaries did, that the *Encyclopédie* was a Masonic project, part of a conspiracy to undermine the existing socio-political system.

What becomes clear from Jacob's study of the various networks of radicalism operating throughout the period is that Enlightenment is by no means merely an elitist phenomenon, and that scepticism against authority emerged on many fronts throughout Europe from the English revolution onwards. It is not just a matter, she insists, of 'the Parisian salons and the great *philosophes*'; there was a host of less celebrated individuals working towards dismantling traditional political and religious hypotheses for some time beforehand.[4]

D'Holbach and the 'Errors' of Religion

What marks Enlightenment scepticism out most distinctively is its deep dislike of authority, whether religious or political. The work of Baron d'Holbach is exemplary in this regard, with *The System of Nature* (1770) coming to be dubbed the 'Atheists' Bible'. So dangerous was the work considered to be that it was publicly burnt in the year of its publication under instructions from the Parlement de Paris (along with other works of d'Holbach's, such as the incendiary *Christianity Unveiled* (1761)).[5] D'Holbach was at the centre of a group of freethinking intellectuals who met regularly at his Parisian residence and country chateau, mixing there with a wide range of upper-class French society. Although he was not an original thinker as such, d'Holbach's work synthesises most of the radical ideas circulating in the mid-eighteenth century on the subject of religion, and he is one of the first thinkers of modern times to make an explicit argument for atheism.[6] To quote one commentator, d'Holbach 'does not mince his words on sensitive matters as most of his contemporaries felt it necessary to do'.[7] Even today, *The System of Nature* retains something of its radical edge as an all-out attack on organised religion as it has operated throughout the ages – to the detriment of humankind, as the author makes abundantly clear.

The preface immediately identifies d'Holbach as uncompromisingly anti-authoritarian in his outlook, and is worth quoting at some length to get the flavour of his contempt for the abuse of power he witnesses taking place all around him:

> To error must be attributed those insupportable chains which tyrants which priests have forged for all nations. To error must be equally attributed that abject slavery into which the people of almost every country have fallen. Nature designed they should pursue their happiness by the

most pefect freedom. To error must be attributed those religious terrors which, in almost every climate, have either petrified man with fear, or caused him to destroy himself for coarse or fanciful beings. To error must be attributed those inveterate hatreds, those barbarous persecutions, those numerous massacres, those dreadful tragedies, of which, under pretext of serving the interests of heaven, the earth has been but too frequently made the theatre. It is error consecrated by religious enthusiasm, which produces that ignorance, that uncertainty in which man ever finds himself with regard to his most evident duties, his clearest rights, the most demonstrable truths. In short, man is almost everywhere a poor degraded captive, devoid either of greatness of soul, of reason, or of virtue, whom his inhuman gaolers have never permitted to see the light of day.[8]

The author sets himself the task of rescuing humankind from those many errors and leading it from ignorance to rationality, the true source of human happiness. Religion is dismissed as consisting of 'reveries either useless or dangerous' or mere 'chimeras', setting the tone for a vicious indictment of the phenomenon in its institutionalised form and the unquestioning belief it demands of followers.[9] Various hypotheses are about to be discarded quite unceremoniously by this notably iconoclastic thinker, for whom our current condition, thanks to the close alliance of church and state, is one of 'slavery'.[10]

D'Holbach's contention is that humankind has lost touch with Nature, allowing 'depraved governments' to step into the breach and exert control over humankind by keeping it ignorant of its real character and capacity for happiness.[11] Only by returning to our natural being shall we overcome this state of affairs where we are oppressed so unjustly – and so effectively that most of us meekly submit. Religion can have no claim over us either, since it is based on a series of false premises. The soul, for example, 'is purely material', simply the product of 'certain modifications of the body'.[12] At a stroke much of the foundation of Christian belief is denied – and with that goes much of the power of the church to hold us in thrall. Considering the soul to be something mysterious is just one of the multitude of errors into which humankind has unfortunately fallen, and which some have taken advantage of to exploit their fellows with ever since. Once we rid ourselves of such beliefs the way is open to construct a society based on *'mildness'*, *'indulgence'*, and *'tolerance'* rather than prejudice.[13] The more humankind comes to know of Nature and its place in it, the less humankind will be susceptible to superstition and those who trade on it.

D'Holbach is totally scathing about organised religion, which he argues proceeds mainly on the basis of instilling fear in the individual, and then playing on this state of mind for all it is worth to keep the individual subservient to religious authority:

> Men, in all countries, have paid adoration to fantastic, unjust, sanguinary Gods, whose rights they have never dared to examine. – These Gods were everywhere cruel, dissolute, and partial; they resembled those unbridled tyrants who riot with impunity in the misery of their subjects, who are too weak, or too much hoodwinked to resist them, or to withdraw themselves from under that yoke with which they are overwhelmed. It is a God of this hideous character which they make us adore, even to the present day.[14]

Christianity, therefore, is no better than any other religion – a radical notion for the time – and has no greater claim on our support. It is the religious impulse itself that d'Holbach wishes to overcome, and only when that has been achieved can we speak of human enlightenment. If some individuals wish to maintain religious belief then it will have to be done within a framework where there is no pressure for others to conform: religion is to be shifted towards the personal, with its public, and certainly its political, face disappearing entirely. Religion goes beyond reason, and if one feels obliged to go there, one should not make a fuss of it nor proselytise on behalf of one's beliefs: 'If he must have his chimeras, let him at least learn to permit others to form theirs after their own fashion; since nothing can be more immaterial than the manner of men's thinking on subjects not accessible to reason.'[15]

It is an avowedly anti-clerical argument designed to ruffle the authorities, promoting scepticism rather than belief and demanding wholesale political reform in its train. Both religious and political authority – which are very much intertwined in the *ancien régime*, of course, to the advantage of an absolute monarchy – are seen to be, in the most literal sense, unnatural; developments against human-kind's best interests that have to be dismantled if we are to realise our full potential for happiness and freedom. It is the dogmatic char-acter of such power that d'Holbach most objects to. As Maurice Cranston remarks, '[h]e preferred the haphazard oppression of familiar, confused, and divided authorities, a situation in which a clever man could find freedom in the interstices' – which is proba-bly as close to pluralism as one could get under the circumstances prevailing in d'Holbach's lifetime.[16]

Christianity Unveiled represents an even more direct attack on the Christian religion, with d'Holbach arguing that it has no redeeming features that he can identify:

> Let us penetrate back to its source. Let us pursue it in its course, we shall find that, founded on imposture, ignorance, and credulity, it can never be useful but to men who wish to deceive their fellow-creatures. We shall find that it will never cease to generate the greatest evils among mankind.[17]

The point is hammered away at that Christianity is to the detriment of humankind, and that is about power, not spirituality; power held by a priesthood over rulers and ruled alike. D'Holbach asks scathingly why we should be expected to go on following a religion whose God 'has created most of the human race only to damn them eternally'.[18] Patently, he thinks it is time to stop believing in this oppressive grand narrative.

Religion and the old political order also come under attack by several others in the d'Holbach circle, with the same intent to create doubt in the minds of readers as to authority's ultimate justification. Helvétius, for example, an occasional member of the coterie, incurred the wrath of the church for his work *De l'Esprit* (1758) and was forced to recant his views, only narrowly escaping imprisonment because of the intercessions of influential friends. What worried the church authorities most was the author's 'sensationalist' philosophy, where the senses were taken to be our only source of knowledge: 'I say, then, that the Physical Sensibility and Memory, or, to speak more exactly, that Sensibility alone, produceth all our ideas, and in effect Memory can be nothing more than one of the organs of Physical Sensibility.'[19] This led to a determinist model of human nature which clashed with the church's commitment to free will, raising doubts as to the validity of doctrines such as the Fall.

Helvétius is careful to discriminate between religious 'fanatics' and 'men truly pious', with the former being accused of holding back the moral improvement of the human race: 'they judge virtuous not what is done, but what is believed; and the credulity of men is, according to them, the only standard to their probity'.[20] There seem to be few of the truly pious around, and organised religion is criticised for failing to live up to its founding ideals: 'Jesus Christ did no violence to any man. He only said, Follow thou me: but interest has not always permitted his ministers to imitate his moderation.'[21] Such interest leads to persecution, and Helvétius implies it is rife within the Christian church. He sees little difference between Christianity and Islam in terms of their imperialistic ambitions: 'If we cast our eyes to the north, the south, the east, and the West, we every where see the sacred knife of religion held up to the breasts of women, children, and old men.'[22] Such sentiments alone would be enough to alarm the Catholic church, but religion in general comes very badly out of *De l'Esprit*.

Scepticism was carried to something of an extreme by one of the more regular members of the d'Holbach coterie, Friedrich-Melchior Grimm (1723–1807), who summed up his philosophy as follows: 'I conceive nothing of the existence of God; I understand nothing of the principles and first causes of the universe; I do not know what matter is, nor space, movement and time: all of these things are incomprehensible for me.'[23] This sounds like an extreme version of Academic scepticism rather than the more public-spirited scepticism of d'Holbach: perhaps an example of what has been called 'ontological nihilism'.[24]

Riddle, Enigma, Mystery, Sick Man's Dream

Although at its most developed and influential in France, the Enlightenment is now acknowledged to be a much wider European phenomenon, and we have observed in particular the substantial debt it owes to post-revolutionary English culture, whose most radical thinkers started to chip away at the conceptual basis of religion. It is worth reminding ourselves again just briefly of the views on the subject of David Hume, one of the leading lights of the Scottish Enlightenment. We noted Hume's antipathy to religion in Chapter 1, with his arguments that monotheism was an unfortunate development in human affairs and that religion had a largely negative impact on public morality, being more concerned with maintaining its power over the masses than more spiritual matters. Hume's conclusions to The *Natural History of Religion* leave us in no doubt as to the depth of that antipathy, with the author asserting uncompromisingly that, '[t]he whole is a riddle, an aenigma, an inexplicable mystery. Doubt, uncertainty, suspence of judgment appear the only result of our most accurate scrutiny, concerning this subject.'[25] Hume effectively washes his hands of most of humanity in this respect, making a personal 'escape into the calm, though obscure, regions of philosophy';[26] his exasperation getting the better of his belief that sceptics should live and converse with their fellows in the real world. Religious principles are dismissed as 'sick men's dreams', a sentiment which neatly sums up the radical Enlightenment position.[27]

Defending Enlightenment

If the Enlightenment introduced a note of general scepticism about official authority into Western culture, it has not gone without criticism. In the postmodern era the Enlightenment project has been called into question by many thinkers, for whom it is the source of some of the most unpleasant aspects of Western society, generating the super-scepticism that was mentioned earlier in consequence. The arguments for and against that super-scepticism form our next consideration in Chapter 3, but before going on to these it is worth putting forward a few words in defence of Enlightenment thought. When one reads the work of such as d'Holbach one is struck with admiration for someone prepared to voice sentiments of such unmistakably counter-cultural intent to the dominant ideology (even if the author was careful to maintain anonymity, for which we cannot really blame him in such a society as the France of the time, where imprisonment without trial was a common fate of radical thinkers). It is unreasonable to hold d'Holbach responsible for all the abuses that have occurred in post-Enlightenment Western society; his focused attack on religion and the arbitrary exercise of political power seems as relevant now as it did in his own day. Enlightenment values constantly have to be reassessed and revised, but they still deserve our respect, and we have to remember what they helped to overcome. One other recent defender speaks of 'its universal assault on privilege and prejudice' as the Enlightenment's major bequest to us, and that is certainly not inconsistent with postmodern ideals.[28]

Figures like d'Holbach are still a source of inspiration to anti-dogmatists, since the evils he identifies remain with us – even if they have undergone some transformation in the interim. The church has learned new ways of working through the political system (a point we shall consider further in Chapters 5 and 6), despite the apparent separation of church and state in the aftermath of the Enlightenment in most of the leading Western nations. The democratic system has created new political elites who are at least as interested in retaining power over the masses as the *ancien régime* ever was, and find subtle ways of minimising dissent and opposition in order to do so. Dogmatism, attractively packaged, can still find wide popular support, as anyone surveying the global political scene at the moment can readily observe: terrorism and prejudice are still a blight on our lives (7/7 in London bringing this home yet again). We follow the lead given by our Enlightenment forebears in campaigning against such evils, and doing our best to undermine the appeal they continue to exert.

One commentator, Daniel Brewer, notes that 'the discourse of Enlightenment . . . confronts a crisis of its own making' in 'the issue of whether Enlightenment in fact ungrounds all knowledge'.[29] He goes on to suggest that much of the work of the leading Enlightenment thinkers, such as the *philosophes*, can be regarded as an attempt to circumvent this issue by the production of 'systematic knowledge' that signals the triumph of the rationalist outlook they are promoting, but that the crisis remains in trying to assess the value of their efforts.[30] While this can be made to seem a weakness in the Enlightenment project, from our perspective it becomes a strength, since one of the main effects of the ungrounding of knowledge is the ungrounding of belief. This calls for a far greater degree of pragmatism in the construction of systems thereafter, and also encourages the development of a sceptical temperament (which Brewer sees as a characteristic of Diderot's thought). We can continue to build on that legacy in confronting the unquestioning belief of our own time with a revitalised scepticism.

On that positive note we can now turn our attention to the world of postmodern super-scepticism, where iconoclasm can be observed to reach new, and often quite dizzying, heights.

3
Super-Scepticism: The Postmodern World

Scepticism has been central to postmodern thought, to the extent that we can speak of the development of a super-scepticism by leading postmodern thinkers such as Gilles Deleuze, Michel Foucault, Jean-François Lyotard, Jacques Derrida, Jean Baudrillard, Luce Irigaray (and the poststructuralist and deconstructive movements in general). Super-scepticism involves a rejection of almost all possible grounds for truth, which is about as radical as one can be in the cause of scepticism – radical to the point of self-defeating in the eyes of its critics. Whatever is suggested as a basis for belief or knowledge will fail to measure up, and such thinkers make it clear that it would be an illusion to pretend otherwise. The fact that this illusion is so widespread simply makes them all the more determined to unmask it and bring the rest of us to our senses. The roots of such super-scepticism can be traced in Friedrich Nietzsche and then the Frankfurt School's critical theory, both of which called for an overhaul of our methods of arriving at value-judgements. Its clarion call is Lyotard's claim in *The Postmodern Condition* that, 'We no longer have recourse to the grand narratives.'[1] Neither authority nor ideology is to be accepted on its own terms; instead they are held up for disdain from their target audience.

While this postmodern-poststructuralist super-scepticism is problematical in many ways, it represents nevertheless a principled attempt to undermine authoritarian modes of thought and behaviour in Western culture. It deserves to be recognised as such, despite the criticisms levelled at it by its detractors (of which there are many, it has to be conceded, and vociferous ones too). Its commitment to pluralism is implicitly subversive of current power structures around the globe, particularly of Western imperialism, although this does lay it open to charges of relativism. The dialectic of pluralism and relativism in postmodern thought will be explored in this chapter, and the general problem of relativism itself addressed.

Other criticisms levelled against the postmodern movement – from such thinkers as Jürgen Habermas – that it represents an unwelcome turn towards irrationalism, also need to be given due consideration.[2] The excesses of postmodern thought, such as its frequent tendency towards a form of nihilism, have to be acknowledged, and I will by no means be offering it unqualified support; that would hardly be in the spirit of my overall project. At its best, however, postmodern thought will be seen to constitute an extension of the Enlightenment project to free us from authoritarianism and the suppression of difference and diversity this inevitably entails. It may go further than it should, and it may strain credibility on occasion, but it is on the right road all the same. Scepticism is always a tactical position (since sceptics are arguing against the possibility of absolute grounds for belief), and, carefully deployed, postmodern super-scepticism can be a valuable tool in countering the claims made by the various empires of belief that they are in possession of absolute truth. Relativism is not necessarily an impediment to a critical theory, particularly one of tactical intent. Better relativism, I intend to argue, than true belief which wants to eliminate all other perspectives and the mere possibility of dissent. On that basis, let us examine the nature and concerns of postmodern super-scepticism.

Precursors of the Postmodern: Nietzsche and the Frankfurt School

Arguably the greatest source for super-scepticism is Friedrich Nietzsche, in particular his demand that we should engage in a full-scale revaluation of all our systems of belief: 'We stand in need of a *critique* of moral values, *the value of these values itself should first of all be called into question*. This requires a knowledge of the conditions and circumstances of their growth, development, and displacement.'[3] Nietzsche went on in the same spirit to call into question our entire concept of truth, claiming that truth was merely a set of conventions that, rather lazily, we had come to accept over time:

> What, then, is truth? A mobile army of metaphors, metonymies, anthropomorphisms, in short a sum of human relations which have been subjected to poetic and rhetorical intensification, translation, and decoration, and which, after they have been in use for a long time, strike a people as firmly established, canonical, and binding; truths are illusions of which we have forgotten that they are illusions, metaphors which have become worn by frequent use and have lost all sensuous vigour, coins which, having lost their stamp, are now regarded as metal and no longer as coins.[4]

Nietzsche's iconoclastic approach to cultural value has resonated throughout the postmodern movement, finding many admirers there. Such grand gestures have their part to play in reinvigorating the sceptical enterprise, which thrives on the iconoclastic temper. Iconoclasm and scepticism do seem to have a natural affinity; indeed, the one plus the other might be said to define super-scepticism.

The Frankfurt School, particularly Theodor W. Adorno and Max Horkheimer (both influenced by Nietzsche), also provide an important source of inspiration for the development of postmodern relativism. The 'critical theory' they devised encouraged a thoroughgoing critique of the assumptions lying behind all systems of thought – including Marxism, their initial inspiration. These two thinkers attacked the phenomenon of modernity, as proceeding from the Enlightenment, holding it responsible for such events as the rise of fascism in European culture, the Nazi campaign against the Jewish race, and the Second World War: 'the fully enlightened earth', they proclaimed boldly in 1944, 'radiates disaster triumphant'.[5] The intensity of their dislike of modernity has made them into icons for the postmodern movement, drawing criticism in turn from those opposed to super-scepticism. Habermas for one saw Adorno and Horkheimer's critique of modernity as a move towards an extreme scepticism, arguing that, 'they surrendered themselves to an uninhibited scepticism regarding reason, instead of weighing the grounds that cast doubt on this scepticism itself'.[6] Behind this move on Adorno and Horkheimer's part was the fear that the entire world was being turned into a bureaucratically controlled society where individuals, as well as difference and diversity, were being sacrificed to the political system in power. Adorno and Horkheimer saw little difference between the capitalist and the communist blocs in this regard, with both demanding ideological conformity from their citizens. Anyone who objected to this state of affairs soon found themselves accused, as did Adorno and Horkheimer in their turn by the Marxist establishment, of a 'deviant sectarianism', and punished accordingly.[7] This was a world obsessed with the notion of control, and willing to go to great lengths to maintain it. The Cold War that soon developed in the aftermath of the Second World War only served to entrench these positions further: a situation which did not really change until the 1980s.

Adorno was a particular critic of the notion of totality, which for him was where Marxist and communist theory went drastically wrong. Marxist theory posited a social totality which could be both known and controlled, and it was the communist party's destiny to be the prime agent of control as the vanguard of the masses. Such a mind-set encouraged authoritarian practices and the creation of repressive regimes, as marked out the Soviet system throughout its seventy-year history. Adorno devised the theory of 'negative dialectics' to counter classical Marxist thought with its commitment to totality. In Adorno's version of the dialectic there was never any complete resolution; what dialectics revealed was 'the untruth of identity, the fact that the concept does not exhaust the thing conceived'.[8] Since Marxists believe in there being a dialectic of history which is working its way towards the eventual socio-political triumph of the proletariat, to question the dialectic as provocatively as Adorno does is to question the very basis of Marxist thought, and certainly its viability as a political system.

In classical Marxism's theory of dialectical materialism, every thesis gave rise to its antithesis, and the conflict between the two was resolved into a new thesis. In terms of social development, this pattern would repeat itself over the course of history until the currently most exploited class, the proletariat, overcame its exploiters, and took over the running of society. At that point we would have reached Marxist utopia and the end of history. For Adorno, the contradiction that a thesis generated its antithesis revealed that it was not, and never could be, a totality. There could never be any complete thesis, since by giving rise to an antithesis it proved that 'the concept does not exhaust the thing conceived'; it was always in the process of undermining itself, of becoming something else. Totality was an illusion; in this case an illusion that it was in the interests of a powerful political elite to claim existed. Adorno's goal, on the other hand, was to create an 'anti-system' to Marxism – from our perspective, the basis of postmodern super-scepticism, which proceeds to become even more 'uninhibited' (in other words, iconoclastic) in its attitude towards reason, much to the dismay of thinkers like Habermas, who adopts a much more pragmatic attitude to social and political discourse.[9] For Habermas, super-scepticism renders politics all but unworkable, and it is an argument that continues to rage in the theoretical community.

Poststructuralism and the Rejection of Pattern

Poststructuralism is, as its name suggests, a reaction against structuralism, for some time one of the main paradigms of thought in the twentieth century (particularly in Western Europe). If one had to sum up the difference between the two movements, it would be as follows: structuralists see patterns everywhere, poststructuralists see patterns nowhere. The positions are mutually exclusive and adherents are not really interested in reaching an accommodation with each other. In fact, the poststructuralist line is that the structuralist obsession with order is indicative of an underlying authoritarianism in modern Western culture, which it is a poststructuralist's duty to bring to our attention and so help destabilise: the claimed patterns are not just false, but part of a network of repression that we should be doing our best to escape from. There are ideological impli-cations to be found in the structuralist ethos: this will prove to be more than just an esoteric philosophical debate.

No one was more assiduous in mapping out the multiple patterns to be found in the culture around us than Roland Barthes. In works such as *Mythologies* (1957) and *The Fashion System* (1967) Barthes applied the structuralist method systematically to an impressively wide range of cultural phenomena, seeking to establish the under-lying grammar operating in each case. There, we can find the worlds of wrestling, cooking, advertising, and fashion, to take just a sample, all being subjected to structuralist analysis, as in the following instance dealing with detergents:

> As for foam, it is well known that it signifies luxury. To begin with, it appears to lack any usefulness; then, its abundant, easy, almost infinite proliferation allows one to suppose there is in the substance from which it issues a vigorous germ, a healthy and powerful essence, a great wealth of active elements in a small original volume. Finally, it gratifies in the consumer a tendency to imagine matter as something airy, with which contact is effected in a mode both light and vertical[.] . . . Foam can even be the sign of a certain spirituality, inasmuch as the spirit has the repu-tation of being able to make something out of nothing.[10]

The advertising of detergents, therefore, evokes a predictable res-ponse in the consumer through its manipulation of a series of images which communicate particular, culturally agreed, meanings. Both sides understand the grammar that is being deployed in the exercise; which is to say, the patterns. As far as Barthes is concerned, almost any area of our culture will reveal a similar set of underlying patterns at work, and his gaze takes in a very wide variety of these. The world is asking to be read; as Barthes reminds us in another of his essays, '[t]he narratives of the world are numberless' – and every narrative is struc-tured by a grammar.[11] On our behalf, the critic deciphers those various grammars to extend our understanding of the world.

Ironically enough, it was also Barthes who was among the first to sound structuralism's death knell. In his famous study of the Balzac novella *Sarrasine*, *S/Z* (1970), Barthes moved firmly away from the structuralist ethos by embracing a poststructuralist commitment to difference and diversity, describing literary texts as sites of infinitely renewable games of interpretation:

> To interpret a text is not to give it a (more or less justified, more or less free) meaning, but on the contrary to appreciate what *plural* constitutes it. Let us first posit the image of a triumphant plural, unimpoverished by any constraint of representation (of imitation). In this ideal text, the networks are many and interact, without any one of them being able to surpass the rest. This text is a galaxy of signifiers, not a structure of signifieds; it has no beginning; it is reversible; we gain access to it by several entrances, none of which can be authoritatively declared to be the main one; the codes it mobilizes extend *as far as the eye can reach*, they are indeterminable (meaning here is never subject to a principle of determination, unless by throwing dice); the systems of meaning can take over this absolutely plural text, but their number is never closed, based as it is on the infinity of language.[12]

It is important to note that Barthes still allows patterns to be deciphered in a text; 'the systems of meaning can take over' the material, as he puts it, but their interpretations can never be considered definitive; just some few amongst an infinite number of possibilities. (Later, more radical, poststructuralists would find even this too much of a concession to the structuralist ethos.) No authoritative reading can be constructed because, as Barthes goes on to insist, 'there is never a *whole* of the text' (rather as Adorno had claimed there was no 'whole' of a concept[13]). Other readings are constantly adding something to the text's existing store of meanings. Barthes himself proceeds to organise *Sarrasine* into a series of five codes in an exercise of considerable intellectual ingenuity, but with the preliminary warning to us that he does this 'to obtain . . . not the *real* text, but a plural text: the same and new'.[14] Barthes is notorious for having questioned the authority of the author in his 'death of the author' concept, but here, quite evenhandedly, he invites us to question the authority of the critic as well.[15] We can never reach a final verdict about a text; other interpretations are always possible – and not just possible, but highly desirable.

The younger generation of poststructuralists went much further than Barthes in their rejection of structuralism, in their iconoclastic stance treating the very notions of structure and pattern as authoritarian impositions on the reader by the critic, and thus to be resisted. The act of interpretation itself was even claimed to be authoritarian in the radical analyses of Jacques Derrida:

> Shall we leave this text on its own power? We should neither comment, nor underscore a single word, nor extract anything, nor draw a lesson from it. One should not, one should refrain from – such would be the law of the text that gives itself, gives itself up, to be read.[16]

The entire critical enterprise was held by Derrida to be founded on an illusion: the illusion that one could pin down the meaning of a text, confident in language's stability. In Derrida's view there could only be 'readings', each one different from its predecessors – necessarily different. There was no 'original' meaning we could refer back to for clarification; in ultra-Pyrrhonist fashion, Derrida could see only infinite regress wherever he looked. This was super-scepticism in action: truth was an illusion for Nietzsche, totality was for Adorno, now it was the turn of meaning to be unmasked. Iconoclasm is well to the fore in each instance.

Gilles Deleuze and Felix Guattari's concept of nomadism is a logical extension of this critique of fixed meaning. It was deployed by the two over their two-volume collaboration *Capitalism and Schizophrenia*. The two parts, *Anti-Oedipus* and *A Thousand Plateaus*, dismantled the standard concept of personal identity as a unity, provocatively arguing that schizophrenia provided a better model for the development of the individual, being more expressive of the difference and diversity within each of us ('each of us was several', they comment about the beginning of their collaboration, 'there was already quite a crowd'[17]). Building on that, they argued that we should turn ourselves into nomads, recognising no fixed location or governing system in our lives. Nomadism came to represent an ideal whereby we could escape, in theory at least, from the authoritarian attentions of the nation state and big business. In the manner of all the nomadic peoples throughout history, we would have only the loosest allegiance to central authority, and would wander wherever our desires took us, both intellectually and physically.

Over-romanticised and historically problematical though this notion was (nomadic cultures have their own internal hierarchies of authority, for example), it did capture very well the wish to evade control that motivated so much of the poststructuralist movement. At the time of the project's publication in the early 1970s, French intellectuals were ostentatiously turning their backs on Marxism as much as on bourgeois society, and there was a generally iconoclastic air to much of the philosophy and cultural theory that was being produced. Old authorities were being rejected wholesale in the aftermath of the 1968 *événements* in Paris, when the French communist party was felt by many to have compromised its revolutionary credentials by siding with the state against the alliance of workers and students rebelling against the government of President Charles de Gaulle. In that heady environment scepticism was being pushed to what were for some commentators absurd limits.

Super-scepticism certainly informs the work of Deleuze and Guattari, who decide to call into question the entire psychoanalytic profession and its role in Western culture in *Anti-Oedipus*. They see that role as part of the mechanism of control, whereby we are forced as individuals to conform to social norms by curbing our desire: 'there is no fixed subject unless there is repression', they insist, and it is fixed subjects that 'Oedipus' (their word for all the forces that go to make-up the dominant ideology) is concerned to construct.[18] For Deleuze and Guattari, we are above all 'desiring-machines', and the point of psychoanalysis is that it 'presupposes a fantastic repression of desiring-machines' on behalf of the dominant ideology and the ruling class.[19] Desire ought to be allowed to flow freely, but Deleuze and Guattari identify what they call 'territorialities' that are designed to tame the flow of that desire, such as the family and the state.

Within those territorialities there are even more sinister entities, 'bodies-without-organs', that appropriate desire for their own purposes. A body-without-organs produces nothing itself, being described as 'the unproductive, the sterile, the ungendered, the unconsumable';[20] instead, it takes over the production of others, exploiting them quite mercilessly in the process, rather like a parasitical organism. One key example of this is capital, which is regarded as the body-without-organs of capitalism – an essentially exploitative system where it comes to human labour. The authors argue that desire must be 'deterritorialized' in order to set us free, with nomadic existence being put forward as a model for how we should conduct our social and political lives instead. It will only be when we succeed in liberating ourselves from the power of teritorialities and bodies-without-organs that we shall manage to eradicate what Michel Foucault described as 'the fascism in us all', and thus create a truly free society.[21]

The reflex reaction to authority of a thinker like Deleuze is to dissent and resist. He is a natural iconoclast, never happier than when he is rejecting systems and those who defend them. Writing on his own elsewhere he suggests that,

> every time we find ourselves confronted or bound by a limitation or an opposition, we should ask what such a situation presupposes. It presupposes a swarm of differences, a pluralism of free, wild or untamed differences; a properly differential and original space and time; all of which persist alongside the simplifications of limitation and opposition.[22]

Unquestioning belief is just such a simplification, as would be the opposition between competing systems of unquestioning belief or fundamentalisms. In each case difference is being suppressed, and with it the opportunity for dissent.

Foucault is another key thinker of this period to encourage the development of a deeply sceptical attitude towards authority – any and all authority, Foucault being another natural iconoclast. The scepticism is directed in the first instance against Marxist theories of history, which assume a series of class conflicts ending in the dictatorship of the proletariat, the most exploited class of our era. History, in other words, is not random; it has an underlying motor, or dialectic, that is pushing it in a certain direction and towards a certain goal. From this perspective, to join the communist party was to become part of historical necessity and to play one's part in speeding up the process – not to join was to become an impediment to humanity's progress. Foucault disagreed quite profoundly, and was one of several French intellectuals in the aftermath of 1968 – Deleuze and Lyotard being prominent others – to reject the notion of a dialectic of history, and with it Marxism and communism (strong forces in French culture for some time before that). History was instead for Foucault really about power, and he came to distrust whoever held this, on the grounds that their desire for control would always lead to a marginalisation of those who did not conform to the norms that were set; that is, the different. This is what had happened in the seventeenth century in the 'Great Confinement', when the authorities decided to institutionalise the insane in order to exert greater domination over society.[23] Whereas beforehand the insane had been tolerated and allowed to exist in ordinary society (even granted a certain protected status in medieval culture as 'innocents' created by God), now they were classified as different and abnormal, even dangerous, and locked away in special institutions run on the lines of prisons.

Foucault contended that the same method was soon extended to cover the sick and the criminal. A 'discourse' was created in each case which established what was and what was not deemed by the authorities to constitute appropriate behaviour, whether resident in prison or in hospital. Other minority groups, such as the homosexual community, were similarly at risk in a culture so oriented towards regimentation and surveillance. Foucault himself went on to trace how sexual behaviour had come to be standardised since classical times, such that homosexuality eventually was regarded as a form of sexual deviancy from heterosexual 'normality', and in many cases criminalised for being so (as it still is in several countries around the globe, such as most Islamic societies and many others in Africa).[24] As usual in authoritarian contexts, conformity is prized above all, in whatever area of human activity. Foucault's own somewhat eclectic collection of personal causes – prisoners, Islamic fundamentalists, gays – reflected his commitment to the marginalised who had been excluded from the dominant discourses of our time. As an iconoclast he was always attracted to those who did not fit in, and were made to suffer for their 'failure' to do so.

The attitude towards authority in Foucault is resolutely sceptical, and he had a keen eye for how society tended to set up codes of acceptable and unacceptable practices across a wide range of human activities such that the different were soon exposed – and all too often exposed to scorn. Discourses were there to be challenged and destabilised in his opinion, and we could do so by encouraging difference and diversity of conduct wherever they were to be found: the more of these there were, then the harder repressive systems would find it to operate. Again, this was super-scepticism in action, with authority being cast in an almost entirely negative light as a barrier to individual freedom of expression. In the realm of poststructuralist theory at least, authority had no role at all to play in human affairs, and unquestioning belief in it was to be despised. Justifiably or otherwise, all authority was deemed to be authoritarian, with no redeeming features to be noted.

Jean Baudrillard's super-scepticism is designed to eliminate not just value-judgement but all the systems of meaning and interpretation it operates within. He goes so far as to recommend in his book *America* the 'extermination of meaning', which amounts to a plea to have experiences without analysing them – decipherment ceases to be an objective of the cultural commentator.[25] There will be no searching for patterns, and an almost wilful refusal to find any order or design in the world around us. Baudrillard's journey through America becomes a series of disconnected impressions which fail to make-up a coherent narrative; a kind of anti-travelogue. He is happiest in the desert where existence is reduced to its basics, and there is a minimum of distraction or opportunity to make connections: 'No desire: the desert. . . . [Y]ou are delivered from all depth there – a brilliant, mobile, superficial neutrality, a challenge to meaning and profundity, a challenge to nature and culture, an outer hyperspace, with no origin, no reference-points.'[26] There is no grand vision to be articulated by the author; events happen randomly and we should not bother to question why. Such an outlook is the very antithesis of structuralism.

Elsewhere, Baudrillard rejects wholesale all theories of knowledge: 'In truth there is nothing left to ground ourselves on. All that is left is theoretical violence. Speculation to the death, whose only method is the radicalization of all hypotheses.'[27] Language is to be destabilised, its authority ruthlessly dismantled. Baudrillard has even cast doubt on the notion of reality, arguing that we live in a world of simulations with nothing real to measure them against any more. He is notorious for claiming that film, television, and Disneyland are more 'real' to most Americans than reality itself – 'hyperreal' in Baudrillard's terminology (although he can sound ambivalent about this development on occasion, even talking somewhat melodramatically about 'the murder of reality' in contemporary culture[28]). We could not even trust that the First Gulf War (1991) had taken place; it came across in the West, Baudrillard argued, as if it were a mere simulation for television. It is a consequence of a world where we are bombarded by simulations in this manner that 'history as such ceases to exist'.[29] Baudrillard certainly qualifies as one of the more iconoclastically minded of an already notably iconoclastically inclined movement.

Feminist Super-Scepticism

Second-wave feminism has also developed a super-sceptical side, as can be seen in the work of such continental thinkers as Luce Irigaray, who has made use of deconstructive techniques in the cause. The authority that is being called into question in this case is patriarchy, the very basis for Western culture in the view of the feminist movement. Patriarchy is a belief system which, like all others, ultimately depends on received assumptions, and super-sceptical feminism is asking us to suspend judgement on these too. As the researches of Irigaray and her peers indicate, such assumptions will not stand up to any very close scrutiny and rely for their continued influence on dogmatic assertions of masculine superiority calculated to inhibit any awkward questioning. Convention alone is what maintains this power, and convention can always be opened up to debate. Patriarchal dogmatism is to be destabilised, therefore, and the feminist project accordingly advanced.

Irigaray's book *This Sex Which Is Not One* puts forward the idea that women cannot be contained within masculine notions of logic. Their 'meaning' as individuals, as it were, cannot be pinned down with precision, any more than meanings in language in general can: 'For if "she" says something, it is not, it is already no longer, identical with what she means. What she says is never identical with anything.'[30] What marks women out is the property of difference they possess, whereas patriarchal culture insists upon the notion of fixed identity since it makes individuals easier to police. Rather in the manner of Hume before her, Irigaray denies that such stability is ever possible – when it comes to the female subject, anyway:

> It is useless, then, to trap women in the exact definition of what they mean, to make them (repeat) themselves so that it will be clear; they are already elsewhere in that discursive machinery where you expected to surprise them. They have returned within themselves. Which must not be understood in the same way as within yourself. They do not have the interiority that you have, the one you perhaps suppose they have. . . . And if you ask them insistently what they are thinking about, they can only reply: Nothing. Everything.[31]

This is 'difference feminism' in full cry, with its claim that women cannot be 'known', or their thoughts predicted, with any degree of certainty. As such they escape any attempt by the representatives of patriarchal society to exert domination over them. In pointing up the limitations of male power, Irigarayan super-scepticism calls for a complete reassessment of gender roles as well as the concept of personal identity. Women become living examples of deconstruction: their identity constantly changing from second to second, having no fixed point or essential features.

It can be argued against Irigaray's super-scepticism that it is operating on the basis of another belief system, in which there are implicit assumptions being made, this time about female superiority. She is often accused of biological essentialism, since men cannot achieve the condition of difference that is held by her to be natural to women. Irigaray bases this difference on the structure of the female body, with its 'plural' sexuality: *'woman has sex organs more or less everywhere* . . . the geography of her pleasure is far more diversified, more multiple in its differences, more complex, more subtle, than is commonly imagined'.[32] Perhaps there is a more focused super-scepticism in operation here than usual, but in terms of its tactical goals – the destabilisation of an overweening authority jealously guarding its power base against outsiders – it deserves to be included in any culturally wider sceptical project such as the one we are propounding.

Authority is certainly being held up for ridicule by such thinkers: this is super-scepticism with an explicit political dimension – a cure by argument for the rashness of dogmatic patriarchalists everywhere. Patriarchalism is revealed to be no more than a mental attitude, one that women as well as men can be schooled into adopting – always to their own disadvantage. Difference feminism offers the former group a new mental attitude that excludes the old with its self-imposed conventions of female inferiority.

The concept of *écriture féminine* builds on such ideas, with Hélène Cixous similarly emphasising the factor of sexual difference: 'a woman's instinctual economy cannot be identified by a man or referred to a masculine economy'.[33] Women's writing will be qualitatively different to men's, since neither can have experience of the interior world of the other: 'woman must write woman. And man, man.'[34] Again, there is a refusal to accept that the authority traditionally vested in the male has any validity whatsoever: it is at best a convention which can, and should, be overthrown. And, in the best spirit of scepticism, no effort is being made to substitute another authority in masculinity's place. Each side of the binary opposition is to be left free to develop in its own particular way, according to its own perceived interests. Patriarchy as a belief system is comprehensively rejected, with each sex being asked to suspend judgements on the other (the onus being more on the male side, of course, given its long record of oppression of the female). For quietude read separate, but equal, development.

The Problem of Value-Judgement

Super-scepticism is an extreme form of relativism, and that gives it problems with making value-judgements (even if these are implicit in difference feminism, in terms of an existing belief system being rejected). At first glance, it would seem impossible to make value-judgements at all if one espouses such a position. There would be nothing on which to base them, no ground we could all trust – essentially the line taken by Jean Baudrillard, as we have just seen. If there were such a ground, consistency would require relativists to reject it as the product of faith rather than reason. Yet super-sceptics are just as concerned as the rest of us to be engaged in politics, and by no means do they find all political viewpoints equal – or congenial either. There is a general 'leftish' bias to be noted to postmodern thought (although there are some exceptions to this rule, and postmodernists in general are often accused by critics of being implicitly neoconservative). That means its practitioners would wish to exclude some forms of political discourse from the public forum – fascism, most obviously, and also most emphatically. How you manage to justify the value-judgements involved in condemning ideas like fascism is the central problem facing the postmodern thinker, and it calls for a certain ingenuity. But the philosophical difficulties encountered in doing so should not disguise the fact that such value-judgements do get made none the less. Whatever its critics may say, super-scepticism is not an 'anything goes' position that would condone any action at all.

No one has been more taxed with the problem of value-judgement in postmodern thought than Jean-François Lyotard, who certainly refuses to accept that fascism is in any way an acceptable political position to adopt. No one in the postmodern movement has wrestled more purposefully with the restrictions of relativism either, in an attempt to retain a moral bias to postmodernism and thus keep it politically credible. Moral positions may be fluid in postmodern thought, certainly too fluid for its critics, but they do exist and postmodernists have their sticking points like anyone else – none more so than Lyotard, especially when it comes to fascism.

Lyotard attacks fascism head on in his book *Heidegger and 'the Jews'*, where he wants us to identify with the cause of the Jewish race over time, arguing that their vulnerability to mass movements like Nazism calls for our unqualified support: ' "The jews", never at home wherever they are, cannot be integrated, converted, or expelled. They are always away from home when they are at home, in their so-called tradition, because it includes exodus as its beginning, excision, impropriety, and respect for the forgotten.'[35] The Jews, those perpetual outsiders of Western culture, become a test case for our humanist beliefs, and that does involve an act of value-judgement on the part of all of us. To accept or reject Judaism is to accept or reject the right to be different, to resist the social norm – and Lyotard proceeds to use the Jews as a model for cultural difference, a model which can include any other fringe group which feels its identity is under threat from the dominant ideology. Any of us might find ourselves in the position of the Jews if ideological circumstances conspired against us: minorities are always vulnerable, always dependent on the goodwill of the mass of the population. Prejudice, regretfully, is an ever-present threat.

Western culture demonstrates a tendency, not just to marginalise, but to forget the Jews; a desire to wipe them from memory, most notoriously evident in the Nazi 'final solution'. It is a tendency well engrained within our culture, as the following musings by a fictional character, the amateur crime detective Kinky Friedman (named after, and loosely based on, his creator), provocatively bring home to us:

> When Hitler's aides suggested to him that the world would never let him get away with murdering so many millions of Jews, he'd asked a simple question: 'Who remembers the Armenians?' he'd said. I did. But the Turks had massacred over a million and a half Armenian men, women and children, and, like that pesky dental appointment, most of the world had forgotten it.[36]

Totalitarian theories cannot abide things which do not fit into their system, especially if that system claims, as fascism notoriously did, to represent the purest expression of humankind – the 'master race' mythology. Difference is an affront to such a belief, which wants to mould the world to its image and to control every last aspect of it, with no exceptions whatsoever to the rule. The Holocaust becomes the grimly logical response to ensuring that desire is fully satisfied. Lyotard wants to make it clear that the Holocaust cannot be explained away on the grounds of moral relativism. To forget is to share in the guilt for the actions taken against the forgotten, and this applies to the fate of the Armenians no less than that of the Jews – not to mention any other victims of genocide since (in our own day, Rwanda is another shocking example that most of the world conveniently has forgotten[37]).

Encouraging such forgetting is a criticism Lyotard levels against the eminent German philosopher Martin Heidegger, whose phenomenological philosophy had come to exert a powerful influence on the post-Sartrean generation of French intellectuals – including Lyotard himself in his early career. Heidegger's Nazi sympathies were exposed and condemned in a book published in 1987 by Victor Farías, entitled *Heidegger and Nazism*.[38] This created a stir amongst the French intellectual community, and Lyotard soon was contributing to the heated debate that became known as the 'Heidegger Affair'. Heidegger's concern with the concept of 'authenticity' in his philosophy is for Lyotard an example of how the exclusion of the Jews from German life could come to be justified, and even take on an air of intellectual respectability. Heidegger spoke of a nation's people, the *Volk*, as having a destiny of escaping from inauthentic existence, which for Lyotard had distinct overtones of a commitment to racial purity. The Jews, as non-Aryans, could only be seen as inauthentic in the German context, and thus as an impediment to the German *Volk* in the realisation of its manifest destiny.

There was also a worrying sublimation of the individual to the collective *Volk* that was implicitly totalitarian, meaning that dissent was not an option that could be exercised without risk of severe retaliation. Under those circumstances 'forgetting' those outside the *Volk* could come to seem not just natural, but almost a cultural duty. Since Lyotard defines a philosopher as someone who refuses to engage in the 'politics of forgetting', and who strives '[t]o bear witness' to the plight of the oppressed wherever they are to be found (trying to help them find a voice in which to make public their complaints about their ill treatment at the hands of the powerful), Heidegger therefore stands accused of failing to fulfil his philosophical obligation to humankind, of surrendering instead to 'the fascism in us all'.[39]

Although many French intellectuals defended Heidegger vigorously, arguing that his philosophy ought to be kept separate from his politics (and there was little real dispute about the latter), Lyotard saw the philosophy as leading inexorably to the politics – almost preparing the ground for it in its emphasis on the collective will over difference.[40] When Heidegger speaks of the individual as being 'grounded in that original possession of your existence like a member of a people . . . and being conscious of yourself as co-holder of the truth of the people in its state', there is no room left for scepticism of the official state ideology;[41] which of course is just the way totalitarian systems want the world to be. Heidegger is effectively preaching obedience to a higher power, precisely what the sceptic will always take issue with, in politics as elsewhere. For Lyotard, Heidegger's credibility as a philosopher was called into question by the synergy between his philosophy and fascist politics: and for Lyotard there was no accident about this. Heidegger stands revealed as a fascist to the core.

Lyotard's dislike of fascism is plain to see, and he is anything but morally relative about it as a form of politics. Fascism was, is, and always will be, unacceptable. Whether his commitment to 'not forgetting' and 'bearing witness' can be worked up into more general moral principles is perhaps more doubtful, but at least worth consideration. In some ways these notions might be regarded as the basis for a sceptic's charter. 'Not forgetting' means that we must never allow a political theory or ideology – a 'grand narrative' in Lyotard's terminology – to explain away, or cover up, events that do not fit into their scheme of things. In other words, they are to be scrutinised constantly on the assumption that, given half a chance, they will most probably abuse their authority. Philosophers are being asked to become the conscience of humankind; to bear witness on everyone's behalf to all breaches of justice that occur in the world and make sure these are included for all time in the public record. This is what Lyotard calls a 'philosophical politics', and it demonstrates his very high-minded conception of the philosopher's social role.[42] Philosophers are supposed to act in such a manner as to put a check on authority and unquestioning belief, not to reinforce these, as was the case with Heidegger. It is Heidegger's silence on the issue of the Jewish question that Lyotard condemns most of all, arguing that the German philosopher 'has lent to extermination not his hand and not even his thought but his silence and nonthought. . . . [H]e forgot the extermination.'[43]

The Anti-Holocaust Lobby

Neither should we grant any credibility at all to Holocaust sceptics, who have become quite a vocal lobby in recent years, particularly in Britain, France, and the USA (Lyotard attacks French examples in his book *The Differend*[44]). Such figures are invariably historical revisionists, whose main concern is to rehabilitate the fascist cause by querying the proof for its worst excesses, such as the Holocaust – the agenda rarely varies much. In the words of the Holocaust historian Deborah Lipstadt, those who deny the event 'seek not to illumine but to deceive' by their subtle manipulation of the evidence.[45]

The British historian David Irving is a leading figure in the denial movement, having spent his career constructing what is in effect a counter-history of the Nazi era, where the regime is portrayed in a far less negative light than we would expect from a British perspective. Thus in one of his most controversial works, *Hitler's War*, we find Irving trying to play down Hitler's role in the Holocaust (not a term Irving uses): 'While Hitler's overall anti-Jewish policy was clearly and repeatedly enunciated, it is harder to establish a documentary link between him and the murderous activities of the SS "task forces" (*Einsatzgruppen*) and their extermination camps in the east.'[46] The Holocaust is reduced to the actions of some zealots exceeding official orders rather than being attributable to Hitler himself, 'a less than omnipotent Fuhrer' in Irving's opinion, who did not always know what was being done in his name.[47] The systematic nature of the Holocaust is denied in this reading.

Irving subsequently achieved further public notoriety when in 1996 he sued Penguin Books and Deborah Lipstadt, claiming that her book *Denying the Holocaust* libelled him. Lipstadt had described Irving there as 'one of the most dangerous spokespersons for Holocaust denial. Familar with historical evidence, he bends it until it conforms with his ideological leanings and political agenda. . . . [H]e is most facile at taking accurate information and shaping it to confirm his conclusions.'[48] In his 'Witness Statement' at the subsequent trial, Irving spoke of there being 'a concealed conspiracy' against him which put his reputation as a historian at risk, with the Lipstadt book serving to promote the interests of this group.[49] Although Irving lost his libel suit, the setback has not deterred him unduly, and he continues to publish and lecture in the same vein as always despite widespread public condemnation of his views (and his books still sell despite that disapproval).

The work of such historians as Irving is not scepticism as we understand it, but, as we have noted before, the consequence of unquestioning belief in yet another authority. Holocaust denial is designed to clear the name of the Nazi party – or at the very least to make it less odious than the general perception has it these days. The ultimate goal is to remove the stigma from fascism, rendering it a politically acceptable position that can then move to re-enter the cultural mainstream – as it keeps trying to do throughout Western Europe (with occasional limited success). But neither sceptics nor super-sceptics are going to accept that line of argument. Just about the only positive point one can make about Holocaust deniers is that they have roused super-sceptics like Lyotard to demonstrate that they do not, as so often charged by critics, sanction an 'anything goes' approach to philosophy and politics. The difference is that super-sceptics remain aware of the precariousness of their own position in making claims, recognising that their own philosophical base can never be totally secure. Lack of security, however, does not prevent them from having moral principles – their anti-fascism alone would be proof of that.

Justifying Super-Scepticism

Super-scepticism remains very contentious within the philosophical world, and for many there it will represent an unfortunate, and unwelcome, blend of the worst features of the Academic and Pyrrhonian positions. It can be made to appear simultaneously nit-picking and nihilistic by opponents, thus the enemy of philosophical discourse – the very opposite of Robert Nozick's ideal of 'explanation'.[50] 'Self-defeatingly, perhaps even pointlessly, extreme' would be one way of summing up the traditionalist response to the super-sceptical enterprise. It will seem too extreme as well to most of the general public, for whom such relativism can be very alienating, representing philosophy at its least appealing. The majority of us will refuse to accept that the world is quite as unknowable as super-sceptics can make it seem (with reality 'disappearing', etc.), even though we might agree that it is perhaps less knowable than we might once have thought. But super-scepticism does succeed in putting unquestioning belief on the defensive, and that is the point of the whole exercise, to make that position look untenable; that is super-scepticism's source of justification. If super-scepticism overstates the case, there is nevertheless still a case to be made: Holocaust denial alone proves that. Whether unquestioning belief in science and technology can similarly be placed on the defensive is our next topic for examination.

4
Science and Technology as Belief Systems

Cience and technology have taken on the dimensions of a belief
system in recent times, and increasingly they set the agenda for
how our culture is developing. Most of us have bought into
their mystique and can hardly conceive of a society in which science
does not play a leading role, providing the basis for our control over
the natural world and with that the key to further improvements
in the quality of life (still the official goal of most Western societies,
and the basis of much of its politics, for all the sentiments voiced by
the authorities about the need for conservation). As stated earlier,
science is arguably *the* intellectual paradigm of our time. Certainly,
science has an immense authority in our society, and can comman-
deer vast resources, both public and private, for its operations. In
serving the demands of the market on the one hand, and the seemingly insatiable appetite of national governments for ever-more
sophisticated military hardware on the other, scientific research does
very well for itself and is likely to continue to do so (although it has
to be noted that not all scientists are happy, or even prepared, to
work on the latter).

Fears have been expressed by thinkers like Jean-François Lyotard
that techno-science – by which he means the alliance between the
multinationals and the scientific community – is creating an
'inhuman' society, in which system efficiency is prized above all other
considerations. As a case in point, the degree to which Western society

is dependent on computer systems is a warning of how we might become subservient to our technology, and to those who own it. The move towards an inhuman society could be at least as insidious a development as fundamentalism has proved to be, since it is no less concerned with enforcing its will on humankind at large: dissent is not approved of in either case.

Various recent scandals in areas such as GM crops and genetic engineering indicate the dangers that an aggressive techno-science poses, especially when it manages to work through governmental bureaucracies. As Sue Mayer, the director of Genewatch UK, and her colleague Robin Grove-White have pointed out, despite 'pervasive lack of confidence in official approaches to the handling of techno-logical risk' amongst the general public, European commissioners nevertheless have granted marketing licences for GM maize, these critics complaining that '[t]he bureaucracy stepped in and forced through a particular outcome, despite continuing political disagree-ment across the EU'.[1] In a warning which acknowledges the power and reach of the techno-scientific establishment, they state that '[t]his now looks set to become a growing pattern'; growing, and worrying in its disregard of public opinion, which is still very divided about the supposed benefit of GM crops despite the propa-ganda campaign being mounted on their behalf. Then there is medical science in general, which exerts no less of a hold over the public consciousness, given that all of us are asked to put our trust in its recommendations at various points in our lives.

Interestingly enough, science is an area that regularly under-mines itself, as theories are repeatedly overturned and particular paradigms are consigned to oblivion – as has so often been the case in physics of late, with Einstein eclipsing Newton (1642–1727), then quantum physics Einstein, and M-theory latterly edging into the sequence with its alarming claims that the speed of light may not be constant throughout the universe. To the general public this is all very bewildering, especially given the aura of authority which attaches to science. The extent to which such developments might promote scepticism – of scientific authority as much as anything else – deserves to be explored. There ought to be much more public scepticism of the scientific – and particularly technological – enterprise. Unquestioning belief in the value, methods, and objectives of science is all too prevalent amongst the general public, which will generally extend the benefit of the doubt to scientific practitioners. Science needs to be placed under permanent critique, otherwise it begins to take on a quasi-religious status that is inimical to the cause of pluralism – and science's own ideals, it should be emphasised, which are certainly well worth defending. Sometimes, admittedly, this scrutiny can be misguided, as in creationist 'scepticism' of evolutionary and geological theories; but this only points up the value of the *real* scepticism being promoted here (we'll return to this issue later in the chapter).

Medicine and the Authority of Evidence

Recent medical history provides us with an interesting example both of the virtues of scepticism, and of the triumph of scepticism being transmuted into a new form of unquestioning belief with its own protective establishment. Clearly, that is not where we want scepticism to lead; it loses its entire *raison d'être* at that point, and the case therefore calls for investigation. The culprit is evidence-based medicine, which has moved in quite a short space of time from being the scourge of traditional practices to a paradigm which in its turn resists dissenting voices. Not for the first time in cultural history, the critic *of* authority has turned *into* the authority – that's why we need scepticism to be there in our culture on a permanent basis, to offer a challenge to each new paradigm as it asserts itself. Evidence-based medicine was developed to challenge traditional medical practices, which were often based on nothing more substantial than the reputation of the doctor who devised the practice in question (hence the mocking term used by opponents, 'eminence-based medicine').

The new style of medicine, as the term suggests, was to be structured on actual evidence derived from clinical trials. It was to be scientific rather than relying on respect for reputation (as rife in medicine as in most other professions, which can be very hierarchical in this respect). The main principle lying behind the theory was randomised controlled clinical trials, in which treatments could be rigorously tested; this was to become the gold standard for the evidence-based creed. The resulting data then formed the template for future practice, which could always be further refined as new methods for accumulating and sorting data came into play. Evidence-based practitioners saw themselves as the new wave who would put medicine on a firm scientific footing, and they waged a campaign to this effect through the leading medical journals. The campaign has been successful, and evidence-based medicine is now the norm within the profession, having successfully seen off the old guard (death and retirement always work to the benefit of new paradigms, removing troublesome opposition from the fray eventually).

Counter-arguments still surface in the medical press periodically, however, suggesting that the paradigm has not convinced quite everyone, although those voices have to struggle to be heard. The issue of randomised controlled trials lies at the heart of the controversy, and these are taken by evidence-based advocates, the new medical establishment in effect, to be an infallible guide as to how well the various forms of treatment available for any given condition will work. Success rates can be given in percentage terms, and the patient is invited to choose which one they prefer after weighing up the respective advantages and disadvantages of each – the process known as 'informed consent'. Dissenters question the assumption of certainty in the method, with its statistical bias. The doctor and author Colin Douglas has argued that it has its limitations in geriatric medicine, an area that 'remains uncomfortable territory for perfectionists', as he pointedly remarks.[3] For evidence-based practitioners this is anathema, with a colleague chastising Douglas after a presentation at a meeting for his failure to adhere to the paradigm: 'That's all very well so far as it goes, Colin, but where's your perfect randomised controlled trial?'[4] Douglas takes refuge in a saying of Aristotle: 'It is the mark of a civilised man, and a hallmark of his culture, that he applies no more precision to a problem than its nature permits, or its solution demands.'[5] The sceptic can only agree, regarding the search for perfection and certainty, and with them authority, as the source of much of our culture's stock of unquestioning belief.

Another doctor, Peter Davies, similarly bemoans the pressure on doctors to produce perfect diagnoses and treatment regimes:

> The current threshold for diagnosing medical illnesses is too low, and too many doctors and patients are ensnared (wittingly or unwittingly) in a mad dance, chasing phantasmagoria of possible diagnoses because no one will now tolerate doubt, uncertainty, or the existential angst that is part of the human condition.[6]

Unquestioning belief in this instance is placed not in religion but 'on the altar of high tech scanners'.[7] Medicine is seen to conform to 'the common problem solving paradigm in the West – a linear process of problem identification, problem definition, and then problem solving'.[8]

Whether evidence is always transparent is another interesting issue. There is, as even devotees admit, a problem with the sheer volume of evidence available for consultation:

> We still often need to search large databases such as Medline to find original research data because reviews may not cover our questions, may be out of date, and may not be relevant enough to real clinical problems. Databases of primary research are staggeringly large (there are more than 12 million citations in Medline, and 7 million in Embase). . . . Finding evidence can often seem easy, but those searching may either be blissfully unaware that they have not found the best evidence, or might suspect that there is still better to be found.[9]

When certainty becomes a matter of trying 'to find the needle in the haystack', as the above author pictures the process of data searching, we may begin to wonder about evidence-based medicine's claims.[10] Certainty can come to seem an all but unreachable condition.

The general public has an odd role in this controversy about methods and procedures, because, as Davies indicates, in the main it wants to believe in medical authority and its mastery of the problem solving paradigm. Most of us feel very vulnerable when being treated for any serious medical condition, and do not really wish there to be any significant degree of doubt about the course of treatment being recommended. 'Informed consent' may appear to empower the patient (that is the intention, anyway), but it is just as likely to be passed back to the doctor for 'expert' advice. Few patients will feel qualified to make such a decision on their own, to conceive of themselves as one statistic amongst many, particularly in extreme circumstances. It will only be after the event that we can think about the process, and wonder about the basis of the medical authority we trusted so implicitly. It is the public as much as the profession that is responsible for medicine's obsession with certainty, and the consequent semi-deification of medical practitioners. Hence the rush to sue these days, particularly in the USA, when medicine fails to deliver as expected. We really do want to believe, we really do want the sense of security that such belief can bring. Davies' plea for doubt and uncertainty to be accepted as normal both inside and outside the profession is one that sceptics everywhere must applaud – even if they might find it hard to live up to when they become patients themselves.

I say the 'general public', but there are exceptions, such as those who use and advocate alternative medicine. Such individuals are very sceptical of the authority of the medical establishment, which they see as resistant to ideas that do not fit easily into their scientific regime (generally because the evidence for the efficacy of these ideas is sketchy, anecdotal, or clinically doubtful). There is also felt to be a mistrust in the profession for treatments derived from more traditional cultures than our own in the West. Again, however, this is not scepticism as we understand it in this study, but commitment to another belief system – often because the official one is failing to deliver the release from doubt, uncertainty, and existential angst that Peter Davies feels nearly everyone is, unreasonably enough, demanding these days. To the outsider, alternative medicine seems to be largely a matter of faith, since if its treatments were scientifically verifiable then they would be absorbed into standard medical practice. In some cases in homeopathy and acupuncture this has occurred, but a market still remains for *truly* alternative systems which trade in faith and are not reducible to scientific fact – that is the very basis of their attraction for a certain kind of customer. We enter the grey area between rationality and spirituality (it is no accident that alternative medicine often involves elements of new age mysticism), and sceptics will always be wary of finding themselves there.

Creationist Scepticism

The grey area between rationality and spirituality is even more in evidence when we turn to creationism. Creationism has seen a remarkable renaissance lately, mainly through the efforts of the religious right in America, which tends to interpret the Bible in a very literal way. Biblical chronology and scientific chronology differ substantially when it comes to the theory of Earth's creation, and fundamentalists simply refuse to accept the enormous time-spans for geological changes and the evolution of life that science standardly deals in. For fundamentalists, the Bible takes precedence over any empirical evidence, and as that states the Earth was created in a very short period, and not so long ago (around 10,000 years seems to be the current agreed figure), so creationists are obliged to make the evidence fit the biblical narrative. Various ingenious arguments are put forward to account for the Earth's geological composition, and although these lack scientific credibility they seem to satisfy what is, depressingly enough for the sceptic, a growing market – particularly in the USA.

A recent development indicates just how far the creationist ethos has infiltrated American culture, and how sensitive an issue it has become. Imax films dealing with evolution or the Earth's origins, *Galapagos*, *Volcanoes of the Deep Sea*, or *Cosmic Voyage*, for example, are being refused screening at cinemas in several states, particularly in the South, because they clash with biblical accounts. One viewer at the Fort Worth Museum of Science and History in Texas was reported as complaining, 'I really hate it when the theory of evolution is presented as fact'.[11] The director and producer James Cameron bemoans this 'shift away from empiricism in science to faith-based science', but it is clear that the latter is no longer just an obscure belief held by a few religious zealots – it has entered the mainstream and cannot be ignored. The Fort Worth Museum has subsequently withdrawn the film in question, so 'faith-based science' – which most of us would regard as a contradiction in terms[12] – has chalked up a significant victory inside the enemy camp.

The Science Museum in London, another Imax venue, is reported to find these developments 'worrying', as well it might, and one assumes that all such museums will now consider themselves to be potential targets for creationist supporters. Pressure from the latter could well give marketing directors pause for thought: Imax films are designed to be educational and to attract family audiences, not public controversy. We have a battle for hearts and minds being set up, and the creationists will prosecute this with increasing fervour if they can succeed in making public insitutions back down so meekly as they did in Texas.

A great deal of special pleading is needed to make the creationist narrative work, however, as we can see from studies such as Ralph O. Muncaster's *Creation vs. Evolution*, where the problem of the Earth's chronology is dismissed by the observation that God 'could have created things in an "aged' state".[13] The advantage to God of having done so is unclear, but for true believers it is a surefire way of closing off debate. Another effective method of wrongfooting your opponent is to reclassify science: '*All views* – evolution, Old Earth, and Young Earth – require a degree of faith.'[14] Even admitting that science works according to schemes and paradigms, which to some extent prejudge what the findings of any enquiry will be, this is still a breathtaking claim to make of an activity which has such a strong commitment to empirical research. If science is a faith, then it is a faith which has the capacity not just for change, but for very radical change, and on a regular basis – which is not a characteristic of religious faith, and especially not of the brand of fundamentalist Christianity being promoted by Muncaster. The special pleading continues when creationism is subtly moved out of the faith category, because it has the Bible to back it up, whereas evolution has nothing more than 'incredibly improbable chance', along the lines of 'winning countless lotteries in a row'.[15] And the Bible, let us not forget, is a 'perfectly accurate' historical record, which makes 'spectacular' predictions 'without ever being wrong'[16] (it is a small step from there to the notion of biblical 'codes', belief in which has generated a whole new literary sub-genre in its own right in recent years[17]).

One might think that the Old Earth/Young Earth division might be a source of embarrassment to creationist enthusiasts, and Muncaster does refer to the 'unfortunate disagreement' that exists in the faith-based science camp over chronology.[18] But even this can be sidestepped by pointing out that the Bible lies behind both positions: 'For Old Earth creation, faith is in the Bible and its consistency with the scientific record. For Young Earth creation, faith is in the importance of semantic details within the Bible.'[19] Those of us outside the field might think this is a critical distinction (religious wars have been started for less), but for Muncaster it resolves itself into a mere matter of the individual's 'choice of where to place faith'– rather like a fundamentalist version of 'informed consent'.[20] Muncaster himself manages to stay on the fence over the competing claims of science and semantics, and is clearly unwilling to undermine the Young Earth position. Pondering the discrepancy between the latter's claim that the Earth is around 10,000 years old and the existence of stars apparently billions of light years away from us, he argues that it could be resolved if the speed of light has been decreasing since creation (no doubt M-theory will be drawn into this argument before long). Objections to the introduction of this special condition are swept aside by the rejoinder that, '[a] God that could create the universe could alter physics'.[21] As to whether God chose to work within or outside the laws of physics, Muncaster triumphantly informs us that '[t]he Bible supports either' choice.[22] Evolutionary theorists simply cannot win playing this game.

The question will always remain, however, as to why scientists have gone to such extraordinary lengths to create a system so radically different from that laid down in the Bible. What could they possibly have hoped to gain from doing so? Creationists have to assume a vast conspiracy, reaching across time and diverse cultures, to explain the existence of the scientific enterprise, and that is rarely a satisfactory way of accounting for intellectual endeavour on this scale.

To Evolve or Not to Evolve?: Darwinian Conflicts

Darwinism, of course, is simply dismissed by the creationist camp, much to the fury of Darwinists like Richard Dawkins, who vents his ire on fundamentalists and creationists at regular intervals. What for the faithful are 'the fatal flaws of evolution' are for Dawkins hard scientific facts that need no religious input whatsover.[23] 'Today the theory of evolution is about as much open to doubt as the theory that the Earth goes round the sun', is Dawkins' confident assessment, even if he does agree that Darwin (1809–82) needs to be interpreted through more recent findings.[24] Creationists find no reference to evolution in the Bible, however, so they can just as confidently declaim that, 'the fossil record is an embarrassment to evolutionists. It demonstrates that transitional forms from one kind to another are purely mythological.'[25]

While Dawkins sees his work as a development of Darwinism, going so far as to insist that '[m]uch of what Darwin said is, in detail, wrong', the anti-evolutionist Hank Hanegraaff gleefully seizes on two comments by Darwin (one in a letter, the other in *The Descent of Man*) to argue that 'evolutionism is racist'.[26] Soon we are informed that 'social Darwinism has provided the scientific substructure for some of the most significant atrocities in human history', such as those committed by Nazism and communism (since both Marx and Hitler were confirmed evolutionists).[27] Against this wholly negative trend in human history stands Christianity and its simple, but timeless, truths: 'We have the inestimable privilege to share the news that nothing could be more compelling in an age of scientific Enlightenment than: "In the beginning God created the heavens and the Earth".'[28] Hanegraaff's argument is easy to refute, depending so largely as it does on guilt by association: Hitler was supported by many German church leaders when he came to power; do we condemn Christianity on that basis also? But what is important to note from our point of view is the totally uncritical reliance on the scriptural record. Biblical semantics wins again, and Darwinism is banished to the outer darkness of 'the great nineteenth century mystery religions' along with Marx.[29] For this author, you can be a Christian or a Darwinist, but not both.

Yet Darwin can also be used to reinforce Christianity, along with other religions as well, as David Sloan Wilson has argued in his book *Darwin's Cathedral*. Wilson's premise is that religion is an organism that has evolved over the course of human history, and that religious groups, through the process of natural selection, 'acquire properties that enable them to survive and reproduce in their environments'.[30] Religion becomes an adaptive process along Darwinian lines: 'we should think of religious groups as rapidly evolving entities adapting to their current environments. Religions appeal to many people in part because they promise transformative change – a path to salvation.'[31] For Wilson, religions have a 'secular utility' in enabling people to come to terms with a complex and often bewildering world, and the promise of salvation is a critical aspect of the exercise, offering a sense of purpose to human existence.[32]

Wilson's is a carefully conducted, wide-ranging analysis and his use of Darwinian theory is inventive, but he does leave many unanswered questions – and I think he gives religion far too much of the benefit of the doubt. He concedes that religion has not always been a force for good in human affairs, remarking wryly that, '[w]henever I strike up a conversation about religion, I am likely to receive a litany of evils perpetrated in God's name. In most cases, these are horrors committed by religious groups against other groups.'[33] Wilson deflects this objection on the grounds of evolution's impersonality: 'a behaviour can be explained from an evolutionary perspective without being morally condoned'.[34] If we are able to stand outside the organism in that way and recognise the problem, we might wonder why we continue with the practice that creates it. Perhaps that recognition could even be seen as part of an evolutionary process to lift the organism of humankind to a higher level, where it would not need the religious impulse with all its well-documented unpleasant side effects – holy wars, autos-da-fé, fundamentalist terrorism, etc. – to the point where we could discard the hypothesis – as so many of us would like to do? (Another point that needs explaining is why so many of us seem to have been bypassed by the adaptive process.) As Wilson points out, several theorists, such as Dawkins, have argued that religion is 'a cultural parasite that spreads at the expense of both human individuals and groups'.[35] If you are persuaded by that, as essentially I am in my role as representative sceptic, then you would hardly want to maintain it as a system. Describing religion's function does not constitute a justification for its existence.

The 'Paradigm of Doom': The Problem of Global Warning

If creationist scepticism does not deserve to be included as part of our project, then the issue of global warming provides an altogether more interesting test case for our consideration. Evidence for global warming, and all the dire consequences deemed to follow from it, is extensive; as is the evidence that the warming is primarily the result of human activity in the last century or so, since industrialisation spread across the globe, and living standards began dramatically to improve across a rapidly expanding population. The problem is easy to identify. We are simply using too much fossil fuel, creating a greenhouse effect that is potentially disastrous for all life on the planet. Humanity, in particular that part of it living in the Western world, stands condemned as playing fast and loose with the planet's future.

Somewhat belatedly the international political community has taken note of this state of affairs, and the Kyoto protocols were drawn up in an attempt to arrest the process as much as possible by placing restrictions on emissions. Unfortunately, in the interim period between those protocols first being mooted and their coming into full force in February 2005, they have tended to be honoured in the breach rather than the observance. America has even refused to sign up for them at all, which, given that it is the world's largest user of energy and almost certain to remain so for the foreseeable future, hardly inspires much confidence in the protocols' likely impact on this pressing problem.

In the opinion of most scientists working in the field, the process of global warming is proceeding largely unchecked as before: indeed, if anything it seems to be speeding up, and most forecasts for the onset of irreversible damage to the Earth's current environment have been revised downwards – sometimes quite drastically so. Since the Kyoto protocols are only asking for a 5 per cent cut in emissions in their first seven years of operation (and are unlikely to achieve even this, especially with America's non-compliance), action is still erring too much on the side of caution for the scientific establishment. A few centuries or a few generations until the 'tipping point' is reached have become a few decades or maybe even this generation's lifetime. Polar ice-sheets slide into the sea, glaciers retract, holes in the ozone layer expand (the hole in the ozone layer over the Antarctic is about to be complemented by another over Northern Europe, according to recent reports). The details are all becoming horribly familiar to the general public, who receive each new report with a somewhat fatalistic fascination. Warnings that we cannot go on as we are doing emerge from the scientific community on a regular basis, and take on an increasingly apocalyptic tone: coming soon near you, not much you can do about it. The outlook can be made to seem very grim: as one expert has put it,

> By the end of this century it is likely that greenhouse gases will have doubled and the average global temperature will have risen by about 2°C. This is hotter than anything the Earth has experienced in the last one and a half million years. In the worst case scenario it could completely alter the climate in many regions of the world. This could lead to global food insecurity and the widespread collapse of existing social systems.[36]

Within the scientific community itself, however, the catastrophists have met with some opposition, and global warming scepticism is now a recognisable phenomenon which is beginning to assert itself more forcefully through the media. Unlike the creationists, however, they do have a scientific basis for their scepticism, and their arguments succeed in revealing some weak points in the theories of global warming. As one commentator on the debate, Fred Pearce, has put it in the pages of *New Scientist*:

> Sceptics have attacked the findings [on the cause of climate change] over poor methodology used, and their criticism has been confirmed by climate

modellers, who have recently recognised that such proxy studies systematically underestimate past variability. As one Met Office scientist put it:
'We cannot make claims as to the 1990s being the warmest decade.'[37]

Pearce endeavours to give these sceptics the benefit of the doubt:
enough uncertainty exists in terms of the computer models being
used, and the actual data from the past available for researchers to
model on, to raise the spectre that the sceptics may after all 'possibly
be right' in their analyses.[38] Other causes of climate change leading
to global warming are put forward by such sceptics, such as solar
cycles. The argument goes that sunspots are more likely to be
responsible for the increase in temperatures in the last 150 years,
with a change in the pattern of volcanic eruptions also being identified as a key factor in the creation of the greenhouse effect we are
now experiencing. Sceptics can also point to dramatic fluctuations in
the Earth's temperature in the past (sometimes the very dim, distant
past when humankind could not have been a factor) proceeding
from entirely natural causes. Glaciers almost reached the equator at
one stage in Earth's history, whereas Britain may well have had a
tropical climate at others. It could be argued, and is by the sceptics,
that global warming is just a normal, natural part of the Earth's life-
cycle, and that gloom and despondency are being unnecessarily
spread amongst the general population by the catastrophists.

The increasing interest in the supervolcano underneath Yellow-
stone National Park in Wyoming, which if it erupted would have
globally devastating effects well past current projections of what
global warming would do, is an indication of the threat we face from
purely natural causes, and that is to the benefit of the sceptics' argument. So is the evidence that there is a serious risk of more tsunamis
after the major one in the Indian Ocean in late 2004 (other earthquakes
have already been occurring, creating considerable unease throughout a large geographical area in consequence). 'We need to get these
things in proportion' is the message which is being relayed. Nature
can always outdo humankind on the disaster front, just as it can on
the terrorist front: in the words of a leading virologist commenting
about superbugs and such like, 'nature is the ultimate bioterrorist'.[39]

More radical sceptics in this area question the projections made from global warming as to the likely consequences, arguing that other factors may temper the more dire of these (such as that large parts of the planet will be become uninhabitable, with agriculture collapsing, leading to large-scale social breakdown, etc.). In fact, the evidence for global warming itself provides one such possible example. One of the more alarming projections of global warming is that the Gulf Stream may shut down, possibly very suddenly, meaning that the Northern Atlantic will become colder rather than hotter – a scenario exploited to some effect by the 2004 Hollywood film *The Day After Tomorrow*. The effect on the British Isles and Northern Europe would be to lower the temperature very significantly, with a dramatic impact on our way of life. Currently, at similar latitudes elsewhere in the Northern and Southern hemispheres without benefit of the Gulf Stream or any similar phenomenon, temperatures are significantly lower: think Labrador with its barren wastes rather than the British Isles. It is only through the agency of the Gulf Stream that Northern Europe enjoys the relatively mild climate that it does.

That raises the possibility, however, that a dramatic rise in average annual temperatures courtesy of global warming could be countered by a dramatic drop courtesy of the disappearance of the Gulf Stream: a point duly made by global warming sceptics. The answer back tends to be that the fall triggered by the Gulf Stream will probably not be enough to offset the rise engendered by the greenhouse effect; but it would have to be conceded that all the projections involve a very large degree of uncertainty. It depends on the data being used, and the model that delivered that data. Either side may be right, or wrong; or have failed to take other factors into account which could affect their conclusions. As Fred Pearce somewhat drily summarises the situation: 'We might still get away with it: the sceptics could be right, and the majority of the world's climate scientists wrong. It would be a lucky break. But how lucky do you feel?'[40] (If you feel unlucky, you might like to ponder on *The Day After Tomorrow*, whose producers gave us an instant ice age in the northern hemisphere.)

Pearce also makes the salient point that global warming has turned into the new geophysical paradigm, and that those who are in any way sceptical of the paradigm can find it difficult to be taken seriously within the profession – or even to get their views published, especially in academic journals edited by global warming proponents. Peer review of submissions for such journals ensures that the 'paradigm of doom', as it has been dubbed, remains the dominant voice on the topic.[41] In that sense the paradigm-dissenters may be deemed to be proper sceptics, up against an establishment which only wants to hear reinforcing evidence for its theories and is dismissive of anything to the contrary. The supporters of paradigms invariably close ranks when challenged, and those of global warming are no different: they will not entertain other interpretations of its data. To persist in such interpretations is to put one's academic credibility at risk – no small matter for consideration in such a competitive field. A form of scientific fundamentalism takes over at such points, with 'true believers' vigorously defending their orthodoxy against supposed heretics. From that perspective, global warming sceptics are performing a public service in pointing out the gaps, and they certainly do exist, in the global warming case.

So are we dealing with proper scepticism here after all? That is, with a genuinely open-minded, public-spirited, critique of an authoritarian paradigm more interested in protecting its power base than in upholding genuine scientific rigour? Although it can seem that way superficially, one further line of enquiry may make this interpretation of events more questionable, and that is to ask who or what the sceptics in question represent. At that point things can start to look very murky. Many of the most vocal arguments for scepticism on this issue come from organisations or think-tanks sponsored by the big oil companies, with ExxonMobil a particularly enthusiastic contributor to this project. That alone ought to generate some suspicion, since fossil fuel suppliers have the most to gain from encouraging scepticism over global warming. It should also make us suspicious that many of these anti-warming arguments are coming from economists rather than scientists; although that it is not necessarily conclusive evidence of bad faith (these things cannot always be left to the 'experts' alone, and interdisciplinarity is the name of the academic game these days).

There are scientists in this camp as well, and Pearce identifies several high profile examples: Patrick Michaels from the University of Virginia, Richard Lindzen from MIT, and three British figures, Philip Stott, the TV personality David Bellamy, and Martin Keeley.[42] The latter, a noted palaeogeologist, has been stinging in his criticism of the paradigm, claiming that 'global warming is a scam, perpetrated by scientists with vested interests'.[43] Unfortunately for the credibility of his forthright views, however, Keeley has his own vested interest to be declared as an oil exploration consultant. Scepticism in the service of big business surely has to be treated with a certain degree of caution. Turkeys do not vote for Christmas, and no more do big oil companies vote for an end – or even a significant reduction – to the use of fossil fuels: profit comes first and foremost, therefore the more consumption of the product the better. The Bush administration's rejection of the Kyoto protocols shows the oil companies in their true colours in this regard, those companies having been amongst Bush's most enthusiastic backers, financially and otherwise. Big backers always expect a pay-back, and they are now receiving it.

When global warming scepticism proceeds from a genuine dispute over data or projections made on the basis of these it has a certain credibility, and will be granted this by the more open-minded of global warming proponents. The weight of evidence that is accumulating in favour of the global warming paradigm is compelling, yet there is still room for debate on interpretation. But the rationale for that debate has to remain scientific rather than market-driven, and it has to be said that, scientifically speaking, it is becoming more and more difficult to sustain the sceptical interpretation. It will only remain scepticism as long as there is something to remain sceptical about. The multinational energy companies, however, only accept the science that fits with their commercial agenda. Align yourself with that position and your sceptical credentials will be irredeemably tarnished.

Lyotard and the Rise of the Inhuman

Big business, in the form of 'techno-science' (the alliance between the multinationals and the scientific world, which can also involve big government), has been the focus of Jean-François Lyotard's doom-laden predictions of what a science-engineered future could look like if current trends were allowed to continue unchecked. Lyotard speculated that the increasing obsession with computer-oriented system efficiency would eventually lead to the demise of the human as we know it. An 'inhuman' destiny awaited us if the techno-scientists were allowed to have their way. What was motivating this particular line of development, Lyotard claimed, was the desire to find a means of prolonging life past the ultimate end of the solar system (some 4–6 billion years into the future, although on current projections life would most likely have disappeared long before then). Whereas humanity could not survive this event, machines arguably could. The ability of space probes to survive on the surface of formidably inhospitable planets such as Mars, or Saturn's moon Europa, is an indication of their potential. It was therefore worth devoting an ever greater amount of resources to improving these to the point where long-term survival became a real possibility. This would be the future when the sun shut down.

Clearly, Lyotard was assuming that some sort of artificial life (AL) or artificial intelligence (AI) would be the means of breaching this physical barrier, and these are fields in which techno-science is investing heavily. Very large claims are being made for AL and AI in terms of how they will alter the world and our perceptions of it. New life-forms are already assumed to have been created, and the AL-AI lobby is excited by the prospect this opens up. One expert suggests that robots, for example, 'will be our heirs and will offer us the best chance we'll ever get for immortality by uploading ourselves into advanced robots', and all of this occurring within our own century.[44] The rest of us might be more wary of the supposed benefits of such research. Computer viruses also count as a new life-form, and they are not exactly beneficial to the human race – especially when they start to mutate, thus frustrating existing anti-virus programs. Robots may prove to be just as capricious and oblivious of human projects and plans.[45] Nevertheless, this is an area of research which can only go on expanding: the weight of techno-science, and with that a wealth of funding, is firmly behind it. One commentator in the field has remarked recently on 'a reawakening of interest in AI the world over', after some lean funding years caused by lack of really substantial progress.[46] 'Uploading' is at least someone's vision of the future, inhuman though it may sound to many of us.

The great virtue of machines for techno-scientists is that they are, so far, both predictable and obedient. Programs are followed, commands implemented without question, the system is all. Assuming the equipment is not damaged, those space probes just mentioned do what their programs tell them to: no more, no less, indifferent to their surroundings or the politics involved in putting them there in the first place. Software is efficient in a way that human beings neither could be, nor in a general sense probably would want to be – at least, not indefinitely. None of us lives our life on an entirely rational basis; that's part of what it means to *be* human, to be a complex mix of reason, emotion, and instinct. Computer-directed machines lack the messiness of the human mind and human consciousness; they do not indulge in dissent, they do not rebel against authority, nor do they ask awkward questions about their tasks or complain about their environment. In short, they never aspire to be sceptics. The problem of infinite regress never arises for them. They are in fact the perfect elements for an authoritarian-minded system to work with; performance-oriented above all else – until they develop minds of their own anyway, at which point all bets are off, with humanity losing control of the program.

The move towards such system-efficiency at the expense of all other considerations was for Lyotard a move into a world of the 'inhuman', and he called for a campaign of resistance to be drawn up against it. There was an air of urgency about this call too, because he saw the inhuman as a factor that was already creeping into our lives in various insidious ways (even if some cultural theorists quite liked the idea of enhanced human-machine interaction, as in the much-touted 'cyborg' concept[47]). Recent developments in genetic engineering are just the sort of thing that Lyotard is asking us to question. In other words, we were being pushed into adopting inhuman attitudes in order to smooth the way for the expected triumph of the techno-scientific ethos. Every advance in computer technology that took over what were previously human functions and created a further level of dependence of the human on the system was yet another stage in the process of our progressive 'inhumanisation'; raising the possibility of a new master–slave relationship developing, reversing the traditional balance of human and machine. It is a point worth making that we are probably far more dependent on such systems in the West than most of us in the general public either realise, or would probably care to admit. We have ceded a great deal of our control over our environment to such systems, and that is a development which can only become more widespread since it is manifestly to techno-science's benefit for that to happen. Inhumanisation means profit, and profit, as we know from long experience of living in a consumer society, only too easily succeeds in suspending moral considerations.

Lyotard's great fear is that at some point the systems will have taken over altogether and humankind effectively will be at their mercy: 'what if human beings, in humanism's sense, were in the process of, being constrained into, becoming inhuman . . .? And . . . what if what is "proper" to humankind were to be inhabited by the inhuman?'[48] It is yet another catastrophist vision, and the worst-case scenario may never happen, as it may not where it comes to global warming either. But the vision does have a certain degree of credibility – how lucky *do* we feel here? – and it does provoke a sceptical view of the entire techno-scientific enterprise, which may not be as benign nor as humanitarian in bias as it likes to pretend to be. Techno-science is not, Lyotard is warning us, beyond politics. In characteristically postmodernist fashion, he asks us to treat all systems with a high degree of suspicion; to assume that all of them will become imperialist after a certain stage of development, and thus antagonistic to the liberal humanist outlook with its commitment to difference and diversity. In the broadest sense of the term that is what we are being asked to defend (allowing for the fact that there are many shades of liberal humanism, not all of which Lyotard could agree with): that is our primary legacy from the Enlightenment movement. Difference and diversity are precisely what the forces of techno-science are trying to eradicate, since they can only inhibit the total efficiency that is being sought through its increasingly sophisticated systems. From a techno-scientific perspective, homogenisation is what is wanted, and homogenisation is what it will pursue with single-minded zeal.

Lyotard has other interesting observations to make about the operations of techno-science, especially when it comes to the issue of gender. Machines are ungendered, but gender is an inescapable part of being human, and if machines are not forced to include this aspect in some manner then we cannot be seen to be projecting human life past the end of the universe: 'The human body has a gender. It's an accepted proposition that sexual difference is a paradigm of an incompleteness of not just bodies, but minds too.'[49] Gender involves difference within the realm of the human rather than the homogeneity that marks out the machine world, and as always difference is to be treated as an impediment to performance efficiency by the techno-scientific establishment. 'Incompleteness' is never going to be an acceptable state in a context where the closed system is the norm. A system without gender characteristics is by definition inhuman as far as Lyotard is concerned, and even if gender could be 'uploaded' it is difficult to see what its utility would be to the system. And it is not just gender that is abolished by computer technology; it is time as well. Computer programs simply unfold according to encoded instructions, which in Lyotard's view destroys time consciousness:

> if one wants to control a process, the best way of doing so is to subordinate the present to what is (still) called the 'future', since in these conditions the 'future' will be completely predetermined and the present itself will cease opening onto an uncertain and contingent 'afterwards'.[50]

Again, we come back to that vexed issue of control: the holy grail of authoritarian systems. Such control is free of doubts concerning its objectives, and hostile to those who express any: it wants certainty, it will not permit contingency.

In making it sound like one vast conspiracy Lyotard is no doubt overstating the case against techno-science in *The Inhuman*; things are rarely quite that simple. What he has succeeded in doing, however, is alerting us to the latent authoritarianism of much scientific research, especially when it is backed up by the vast resources of the multinationals or imperialist-minded governments, as well as to the power that the techno-scientists can exert over the general public. There is still a tendency to be so awed by the achievements of techno-science that it is usually given the benefit of the doubt when it comes to its research programmes. Very often, by the time that awkward questions start to be asked, it is too late to stop the momentum of the research in question even if its value to humankind is becoming more and more doubtful. Try reversing global warming, or the holes in the ozone layer, disposing of nuclear waste, or dismantling nuclear weapons – and, increasingly, try preventing GM crops experiments from being conducted. The ideological triumph of science has had some deeply worrying side effects that look as though they will be with us indefinitely. If that is not a cause for scepticism, then I do not know what is. Techno-science cannot be trusted not to put its programmes before the interests of humanity.

Intelligent Design: The Return of the Hypothesis

Another way of accounting for technological progress is to conceive of it as part of a process of intelligent design. This is an idea which has been found very attractive by many scientists of late, as well as by certain elements of the religious community: the 'return of the hypothesis' as I dubbed it earlier. Intelligent design is a more sophisticated form of what used to be called the 'argument from design', much bandied about in eighteenth- and nineteenth-century European culture, by figures such as the English clergyman and theologian William Paley (1743–1805). Paley famously argued that if while out walking on a heath he found a watch lying on the ground, then he would assume that it was a manufactured product rather than something that had come about by sheer chance:

> when we come to inspect the watch, we perceive . . . that its several parts are framed and put together for a purpose[.] . . . This mechanism being observed . . . the inference, we think, is inevitable, that the watch must have had a maker: that there must have existed, at some time, and at some place or other, an artificer or artificers who formed it for the purpose which we find it actually to answer.[51]

In other words, faced with such a complex artefact with so many interlinked mechanisms we would assume consciously engineered design. Working back from the fact of our world and human civilisation in a similar spirit, we would have to assume a creator for a system of a staggeringly higher order of complexity than a mere watch: 'for every indication of contrivance, every manifestation of design, which existed in the watch, exists in the works of nature; with the difference, on the side of nature, of being greater or more, and that in a degree which exceeds all computation'.[52] For Paley, it was stretching credibility to absurd lengths to suggest that this could be put down to chance either.

Contemporary conceptions of intelligent design proceed from much the same basic notion: that our development is part of a definite pattern and has been engineered that way. One of the leading lights in this movement, the biochemist Michael J. Behe, recalls Paley in his insistence that life's 'irreducible' complexity can only be explained by design:

> The simplicity that was once expected to be the foundation of life has proven to be a phantom; instead, systems of horrendous, irreducible complexity inhabit the cell. The resulting realization that life was designed by an intelligence is a shock to us in the twentieth century who have gotten used to thinking of life as the result of simple natural laws.[53]

It is no accident, therefore, that we have the forms of technology we do, nor that we are continuing to make progress in that area in exerting dominion over our environment: this was meant to be. Intelligent design presumes an intelligent designer. From that perspective, the forces of techno-science demand our unqualified support, rather than the criticism meted out to them by Lyotard. Albert Einstein once remarked that 'God does not play dice', and a similar belief informs those arguing for intelligent design.[54] Alexander Pope's confident assertion that, 'Whatever is, is right', might be the motto of this line of enquiry, although this time around it has a substantial body of scientific data to back up its claims rather than just a metaphysical notion.[55] A more scientific rendering would be:

> A total of more than two hundred known characteristics of the Milky Way galaxy, the solar system, and Earth required fine-tuning to prepare the planet for the arrival and survival of life – and ultimately human life. The infinitesimal probability of all these factors coming together goes beyond coincidence.[56]

One might remark that where there is 'infinitesimal probability' there is still hope, and that by its very nature coincidence is always going to appear improbable, but the way the case is presented here hardly admits of debate. We shall return to the work of the authors in question, Fazale Rana and Hugh Ross, both Old Earth Creationists, later.

Sceptics may well want to question this theory, since it locks humankind into a predetermined pattern of development: yet another authoritarian scheme suggesting we have no effective say in our destiny – or even the *right* to have a say. We become little better than glorified robots under such a dispensation, and are simply carrying out our allotted programs as predestined by a higher power. Sceptics may also want to raise the possibility that God might indeed play dice (taking 'God' in an abstract sense as whatever motivating force might lie behind phenomena such as the Big Bang). There is no contradiction involved in such a suggestion; supreme beings can choose to do whatever they want. Gambling is an almost universal human trait, after all – maybe that derives from the predilections of the assumed creator?

The Big Bang is increasingly being put forward as conclusive proof of intelligent design in the universe, with the Catholic church happily accepting the notion on the grounds that something must have created the Big Bang, and that something must be the most powerful force imaginable. God, the ultimate intelligent designer, easily slots into that latter category for the Catholic hierarchy, and is at least a plausible assumption, if philosophically still rather questionable. That something caused the Big Bang to happen does not prove that something was God, just an unknown something (or set of processes; it need not be a being as such). But for Pope Pius XII, speaking in 1951, the Big Bang was just what the church had been looking for to confirm its theology once and for all and leave sceptical secularists without a case to argue:

> present-day science, with one sweeping step back across millions of centuries, has succeeded in bearing witness to that primordial *Fiat lux* [let there be light] uttered at the moment when, along with matter, there burst forth from nothing a sea of light and radiation, while the particles of chemical elements split and formed into millions of galaxies . . . Therefore, there is a Creator. Therefore, God exists![57]

Again, it is a big leap from the *Fiat lux* to a Creator, and an even bigger leap from a Creator to God as pictured by the Christian religion, but one can understand why the Catholic church seized on this theory with the enthusiasm it did (significantly choosing it over the rival Steady State theory, which still had a great deal of support at the time[58]). Looking at the Big Bang from the standpoint of intelligent design, then it can seem as if everything has worked out specifically to create life as we now know it; that it is unlikely that life would have developed purely through some series of chance factors (God doesn't play dice, etc.). For the believer in intelligent design, everything – from sub-atomic level right up to the macro-level of the entire universe – fits together far too neatly for it to be accidental. If precisely that set of circumstances is required to generate the conditions by which life and a sustainable environment become possible, then there must be a larger-scale pattern lying behind the scenes dictating how events unfold; it cannot be arbitrary. Complexity theory, with its commitment to a process of repeated self-organisation to higher levels of sophistication by organisms and systems, trades on just such ideas.

It is a seductive vision, and it is not hard to see why the Catholic church would be so keen to embrace it; if science can be made consistent with theology then the credibility of the latter is given a significant boost. Never mind techno-science, religio-science would be a formidable opponent with an immense weight of authority behind it that would be very hard to contradict. Creationists, of course, are less susceptible to this vision's attractions, even if this does not quite turn them into true sceptics in our sense. They prefer to take the Bible as their source, rather than cosmological physics.

A recent study outlining the intelligent design argument from a staunchly religious perspective, Fazale Rana and Hugh Ross' *Origins of Life: Biblical and Evolutionary Models Face Off*, is worth exploring in more depth. The authors are both scientists and devout Christians (one a convert from Islam), and their concern is to demonstrate 'how nature's record, embodied in the latest scientific discoveries, integrates with the Bible'.[59] They reject the simplistic accounts of the Young Earth creationists, but not the element of the supernatural: 'Scripture shows how God began with an amazing vision nearly 4 billion years ago when He spawned first life. He then hovered over early Earth like a mother eagle brooding over her young to preserve this life under hellish conditions.'[60] Everything about life on Earth – and they can envisage none elsewhere; we are taken to be the result of a unique divine experiment – points towards intelligent design for these authors, who argue that '[s]ystems and structures produced by intelligent agents typically possess characteristics that distinguish them from those produced by natural processes'.[61] This is Paley updated, and their RTB model – RTB standing for 'Reason to Believe', the name of an organisation to which both belong[62] – is designed to provide incontrovertible proof for intelligent design in the name of what Rana and Ross call 'science apologetics'.

The authors have very high aspirations for the model, which will only be justifiable for them if it proves to be *better* than all other purely science-based models in terms of its explanatory power and predictions: in effect, the basis of a new scientific paradigm. Their aim is to generate answers for all the unresolved problems left in the standard models – and there are many, as even the most committed supporters have to concede. The Bible becomes *necessary* to completing the scientific account.

The RTB model is based on the following eight premises:

1. Life appeared early in Earth's history, while the planet was still in its primordial state.
2. Life originated in and persisted through the hostile conditions of early Earth.
3. Life originated abruptly.
4. Earth's first life displays complexity.
5. Life is complex in its minimal form.
6. Life's chemistry displays hallmark characteristics of design.
7. First life was qualitatively different from life that came into existence on creation days three, five, and six.
8. A purpose can be postulated for life's early appearance on Earth.[63]

Behind those principles lies the need to pack everything about the appearance of life into the six days of creation as described in Genesis, and for there to have been reasons for God to proceed in the way he did (possibly this is delving further into the mind of God than any human beings have the right to do, but we'll let that quibble pass for now[64]). Accept these premises and the model makes sense from then on. It is the basic creationist account plus the standard scientific time-scale for the Earth's existence, and the latter helps to fend off many of the obvious objections from the scientific side. It is on the question of chronology that the creationist account is at its weakest after all, and most in conflict with the scientific establishment. RTB sidesteps that hurdle neatly enough, and is a good example of Old Earth creationism.

But what of the other main assumption lying behind the model – the conjunction of design and purpose? Admittedly, design and purpose in life on Earth or the universe at large cannot conclusively be disproved; the Big Bang remains a mystery (or at least what precedes it does). That is not, however, the same thing as saying that the proferred explanation is true. The mere continued existence of something does not equal purpose as such, nor does it necessarily lead to a scientific theory. As Massimo Pigliucci for one has pointed out, intelligent design 'is simply the statement of a possibility and cannot really be pushed any further than that.'[65] The assumption also raises some very intriguing questions about the nature of God, which are not necessarily very helpful to the RTB cause overall. The image of an omnipotent being brooding fretfully over an experiment whose outcome seems doubtful is rather odd. Surely omnipotent beings are in control of physics, both before and after the creation of the universe? '[A] God of creation could have operated outside the laws of science', as another enthusiast puts it.[66] So why the 'hellish conditions' which God has to protect nascent life from? It rather sounds as if God is working within certain constraints – a heretical thought, no doubt (Al-Ghazali would certainly have thought it so). If God is less than omnipotent, as the human 'experiment' suggests, then design is a far more problematical notion: perhaps it went wrong somewhere along the line? (Which would be one way of explaining why design has included so much natural disaster, war, and human suffering along the way to our present condition; with the 2004 Asian tsunami raising such issues very forcefully yet again.[67])

Perhaps we are still struggling against the hellish conditions and their aftermath even today? In one sense we are, because we have the end of the solar system to look forward to, a few more billion years ahead (and the end of life well before that, possibly in as little as thirty million years or so, with the system becoming unbearably hot as the sun burns up). Even this unwelcome event can be turned to account by the authors, who somewhat blithely conclude that this is why life must have evolved so early, in order not to waste any of the available time for its development. Life was, as they put it, from the very beginning 'racing the solar clock'.[68] Again, this sounds as if at least part of the process is outside of God's control. Omnipotent beings presumably have all the time available that they want – time to waste as well as time to use. Putting them in a race against the clock seems a curious way to set about impressing us with their power and farsightedness; unless the race is self-imposed, of course, but in that case it loses much of its sense of drama, as what was self-imposed can be self-unimposed (especially by the omnipotent). The

more one tries to plumb the depths of God's design and God's purposes the more such conflicts emerge. Although that does not seem
to deter the devout from working back from where we have reached
now, developmentally, to an apparently benign creator (although a
failed experiment on the part of the latter is at least a possible verdict
on the human condition). Whatever was, really was right for this
constituency; doubt just does not arise.

Rana and Ross certainly put considerable effort into making their
RTB model work, and demonstrate some ingenuity in integrating
science and religion – if you give them the biblical creation span of
six days to start with. Yet the question does come to mind: what if
one does not need that hypothesis? In real terms it is the religion that
requires the apologetics, not the science. Drop religious belief and
most of the problems disappear – even if that does still leave the
issue of what caused the Big Bang unresolved. But sceptics have no
difficulty living with such metaphysical uncertainty; not enough to
project them into unquestioning belief anyway. We find similar situations arising throughout the history of science, with ever more
baroque modifications being put forward to save theories, rather
than switch the perspective and devise new theories with less
ideological baggage. Ptolemaic astronomy, for example, evolved
complex systems of epicycles to explain why stars did not appear
where they were supposed to do under its cosmological scheme
(based on perfectly circular orbits, and an Earth-centred universe).
In the later days of the theory these were, to put it mildly, extremely
unwieldy, to the point of credibility ebbing away from the cosmological model being used. Eventually the discrepancies became
glaring enough to encourage a radical rethinking of the model and
its hypotheses, with the theory being scrapped in consequence in
favour of the new Copernican system of cosmology.[69]

Then we must remember that Christianity is not the only world
religion with a sacred book claiming to explain creation and the
purpose of life: would we have to construct a different science apologetics for every other claimant? If we did, and multiculturalism
surely demands no less, it would be most unlikely they would all
agree, setting the scene for yet another 'face off' to be conducted.

How would one find criteria by which to judge such a face off, I wonder? Sextus Empiricus' objections still hold good in this respect. For Rana and Ross it is enough that 'the shared imagery and theological connection of the Luke, Deuteronomy, and Genesis passages suggest that God worked on early Earth to bring forth life's "seeds" ', but why should that persuade those proceeding from a totally different religious starting point?[70] Linking intelligent design so closely to Christianity merely succeeds in extending the range of one's dogmatism – and the same would apply if any other religion were substituted for Christianity.

At the core of the authors' ostensibly scientific enquiry lies unquestioning belief: reason to believe, but only to believe as we do. In the words of Rana's 'Epilogue' to the book: 'in its [the Bible's] pages I encountered not only the Creator but also a Savior, and to this day I continue to discover the rewards of knowing Him'.[71] There is simply no arguing with that: no scientific evidence will shake such faith. The scale of the problem we face as sceptics becomes all too evident at such points.

Sceptics for Science

The argument here has been that scientific paradigms can all too easily take on the character of unquestioning belief, although that is a distortion of the scientific enterprise and its ideals which scientists, of all people, should not engage in. Those ideals certainly need to be preserved, so this is not to be construed as an argument against science; rather it is against the misuse of science, by practitioners as well as politicians and other figures of authority outside the scientific field *per se*, as a way of establishing power over others. It is science as politics, serving the interests of an elite – and it is against such elites that sceptics will always line up. Scepticism is, in fact, in the best interests of science: without the sceptical temperament there is always the danger that science will lapse into dogma. Unless paradigms are prevented from suppressing or even silencing their detractors, unless new paradigms keep coming on stream on a regular basis, then science will not be doing its job properly. Not all of those detractors have a case to be answered – the creationists patently do not, and intelligent design's assumptions at the very least call for very close examination – but all of them deserve their chance to question scientific authority and its accompanying mystique (as long as they acknowledge the right to be questioned in turn, and for others to question the paradigm as well).

Political authority also attracts its share of dubious detractors and quasi-sceptics, but as we shall go on to discuss in the next chapter, the full spectrum of opposition has to be given its due there too.

5
Towards a Sceptical Politics

hat might a sceptical politics look like? Or at the very least, a sceptical approach to politics? Scepticism is being put forward here less as a system of thought than as a permanent internal critique of systems of thought – as it has tended to operate traditionally within the discipline of philosophy, keeping the discipline on its toes, so to speak. Its value lies precisely in its ability to raise questions about existing methods of organising social phenomena like politics, rather than in the provision of specific answers to political problems. It may be negative, but it is nevertheless extremely valuable: politics, too, must be kept on its toes. The concept of 'agonism', as developed in the work of Chantal Mouffe and William E. Connolly, for example, calls for further exploration in order to consider its potential as the basis for a sceptical politics. The adversarial quality of these thinkers' agonism is particularly congenial to the sceptical temperament, although it shares the disadvantage of all sceptical thought in being open to charges of relativism. Again, the tactical aspect of scepticism needs to be emphasised, and I would argue as before that relativism is preferable to dogmatism. You can conduct a debate with a relativist; you cannot really with a dogmatist. And debates are what we desperately, and constantly, need if we are to make inroads into the power base of the various empires of belief.

In their controversial book *Hegemony and Socialist Strategy* Ernesto Laclau and Chantal Mouffe supported the idea of resistance to authoritarian political systems by the variety of 'protest movements' that had been springing up around the globe in the latter part of the twentieth century.[1] Since they did so in 1985 the range of protest groups has grown considerably, to embrace such phenomena as the anti-capitalist and anti-globalization movements that have created havoc at so many World Trade Organisation meetings in recent years. When combined with breakaway socialist groups in several Western countries, and the increased interest being shown in Ecocriticism (across the political spectrum), there is the basis for a sceptical politics to be noted. It is at least clear that there is a strong undercurrent of resistance to the current political systems in the West, which are under considerable strain. We shall now evaluate the scope of this network of resistance to initiate a more pluralist political system than at present applies.

Just to show that scepticism can cut across traditional party-political lines and take a variety of forms, the phenomenon of Euroscepticism in Britain will also be examined. Such right-wing scepticism – as in the case of the United Kingdom Independence Party (UKIP) and certain sections of the Conservative Party – considers itself as no less in conflict with an overbearing belief system, the European Union this time around, than its left-wing counterpart does. This is often for what I would take to be extremely dubious reasons (in effect, the defence of a very traditional version of the status quo), but it can nevertheless be seen to have a role to play in a pluralist critique of political authoritarianism even if its motives are suspect. Although scepticism is a broad church, not all scepticism is defensible (especially when it is scepticism on behalf of special interests); however, all scepticism deserves to be investigated. We have already seen how scepticism over theories of global warming, although problematical in many ways, nevertheless has succeeded in raising awkward questions about both the methodology being applied and the conclusions being drawn from its findings.

The close links between religious belief and politics demand analysis too, in order to demonstrate what a sceptical politics is designed to confront. American fundamentalists have used the political system quite shamelessly – although, as even the representative sceptic would have to admit, also quite adroitly – in an attempt to impose their ideology on the rest of that society (and with some success, many states passing socially regressive legislation in consequence). Then there is also a strong theocratic tradition within the Islamic world which is becoming increasingly powerful and gaining greater respectability there, where it is generally presented by supporters as Islam's true destiny. Similar programmes in other areas such as economic theory and nationalism deserve to be unpicked as well.

To Be or Not to Be a Sceptic

When is scepticism not really scepticism? I would say the answer is: when it is in the service of an authoritarian cause. Creationism was one such example we dealt with in Chapter 4, and Euroscepticism, as practised on the right of British politics, is another which repays closer attention. There is an argument to be made for Euroscepticism. The European Union is a huge organisation – and one continuing to expand as it takes in new members every few years, with more in the offing – which in many ways has replaced national government throughout the continent. This state of affairs has its good points, as national governments are traditionally self-interested and national self-interest only too easily leads to conflict in the wider political domain. European history in particular provides a host of examples of this phenomenon, with the twentieth century's two world wars the product in the first instance of the collision of national self-interests in the European arena. It was the desire to avoid a repetition of this history that drove the pan-European ideal in its earliest stages in the aftermath of the Second World War, with Britain significantly missing from the project, and many still subscribe to that ideal now. In the sense that its member nations have not been at war with each other since it was founded, the EU can be considered a success. A European consciousness has been fostered that has helped to defuse petty disputes between nation states, and that has to be considered a good thing for the continent's inhabitants at large. Expansion ought to have the same positive effect on the new members, and that too is surely to be welcomed, although it has not been without opposition from within the original community itself.

In its sheer size and scope the EU poses a threat as well. The larger an organisation grows, the more authoritarian it tends to become; the more power it gains, the more it generally wants – this practically has the status of a natural law. Individuals soon come to feel disenfranchised when confronted by such a huge bureaucracy, which all too often is unresponsive to local needs, detail becoming lost in the overall policy. At some point, it could be argued, the EU will become too big to be truly democratic, being too far removed from everyday life, and that is one of the fears that Eurosceptics give voice to – if not always from liberal democratic or humanitarian motives, as we shall go on to discuss. It has to be admitted, however, that there are Eurosceptics on the left as well as on the right, so we cannot necessarily fall back on the anti-democratic charge: this is a complex debate with many shades of opinion within it, and many subtle political nuances. There is Euroscepticism, and there is Euroscepticism; fairness demands that we weigh up the pros and cons of each type.

Yet when we turn to far-right Euroscepticism, we do not find a context where scepticism as it is being promoted in these pages can flourish. This is the territory of the little Englander, who puts greater store in symbols than the political realities of a rapidly changing world; symbols such as the pound, the monarchy, and the assumed superior quality of the British Parliament over all other national and international political bodies. This kind of Eurosceptic does not want Europe: he or she wants the past, preserved in aspic as it were. Britain is very much an offshore island from this viewpoint – Europe starts at Calais. The scepticism is very narrow, directed against Europe only; when it comes to traditional British culture, unquestioning belief replaces scepticism – almost as a reflex. Somewhat paradoxically perhaps, mistrust of the EU coexists with reflex obedience to institutional authority – the authority that represents the British past, replete with all of its traditional symbols. It is scepticism in the service of the status quo, in other words: conservative – or reactionary, if one wants to be more critical.

The weakest point of Euroscepticism is that it trades on a notion of national identity which no longer has any real purchase in a world of globalization. Whether you like it or not, globalization cannot be uninvented (although it can be made more equitable and less exploitative of vulnerable nations, and should be[2]), and it has rendered the nineteenth-century version of national self-interest all but obsolete. We are all connected together now, and no nation is immune to developments elsewhere, whether in the social, political, or economic domains (inasmuch as these can be differentiated any more in a global culture). When America sneezes, the world catches a cold, as the saying goes; but increasingly it works in reverse order too; even the US is not immune to events elsewhere. Far right Euroscepticism is at best romantic, at worst anachronistic – it also has an unfortunate tendency, well documented in the pronouncements of UKIP, to be virulently racist. Traditional British life of the most insular kind is generally what is being celebrated, and whatever criticism may be made of *real* scepticism, it cannot be called insular. The UKIP brand of Euroscepticism (which draws tacit support from a significant proportion of the British public, enough at least to gain the party significant representation at the European Parliament in Strasbourg after the 2004 elections) is based on prejudice; scepticism as I understand it, on a questioning mind. They could hardly be farther apart: I certainly cannot envisage a scepticism which included racism as part of its outlook.

It is entirely possible to be sceptical about the EU without being a Eurosceptic of the kind just discussed, however, and it is also a defensible position. Bureaucracy is the enemy of my type of scepticism, and always will be, since bureaucrats invariably end up on the side of true belief, defending the system against scrutiny, maintaining the status quo and all the various privileges that attach to it. As things stand in British public life, however, it is the more extreme kinds of Euroscepticism that catch the public attention – and that of the media, which is only too prone to pander to the lowest prejudices on this issue. No British newspaper ever lost readers by attacking the EU, even if it had to manufacture its scare stories itself (as several have, quite shamefully): there is a ready readership for this. Yet the

EU certainly needs a dose of scepticism, and a sceptical politics has to provide the means for this. Let's consider how it could do so. We return to the concept of agonism, which would have to be a feature of EU life for it to defuse the cruder forms of Euroscepticism.

The Argument for Agonism

Chantal Mouffe's major complaint against standard democratic politics is that it lacks real opposition. As practised in most Western countries (take the UK or USA, for example), it is based on a system of collusion between the main political parties, whose ideological difference from each other is seen to be more apparent than real. The ruling class, in other words, includes both the government and the ostensible opposition, who are quite content collectively for power to circulate amongst themselves. There is, Mouffe claims, a cosy consensus in operation that marginalises true dissent: 'This is the typical liberal perspective that envisages democracy as a competition among elites, making adversary forces invisible and reducing politics to an exchange of arguments and the negotiation of compromises.'[3] She wants to replace this consensus with a more radical form of politics, where compromise with one's opponents is studiously avoided and the system is kept under stress at all times. This is what she calls 'agonistic pluralism', and it works on the basis of 'confrontation between democratic political positions' and 'real debate about possible alternatives'.[4] The emphasis on confrontation is designed to disrupt the political system and keep it in a state of permanent tension. For Mouffe, this is the only way to break the monopoly the elite holds on political life, and her vision of what constitutes democracy is very different to what we are used to seeing in the average Western nation state, where compromise is a way of life.

We need to consider what politics would look like if Mouffe's prescriptions were adopted. It has to be said immediately that they do not appear to be very well suited to parliamentary politics, where at least some degree of cooperation between the parties involved, government and opposition, is necessary for any semblance of system to work at all. The spectre of anarchy looms if oppositional forces do not accept the validity of a government's mandate to act, or are unwilling to accept defeat – whether in debate or election – with something approaching good grace. The parliamentary system does not exhaust the political process, of course, and perhaps Mouffe's ideas describe that wider context of organisations and media that go to make-up what can be called the informal political process. These latter need to keep stating their oppositional views, and providing a focus for dissent against the dominant ideology in their society. The question does arise, however: just how far do they go in their non-cooperation with that dominant ideology? Is it simply a case of keeping debate going? Or is anything more sinister implied? In other words, just how agonistic do we become? If it just a case of keeping debate going, then we have the basis for such a system already. While the media is often collusive with the political establishment in societies such as ours, it is not totally so (unless you're a card-carrying conspiracy theorist). It is still possible to publish or broadcast anti-consensus views somewhere or other, and also to argue the case against compromise.

Mouffe carefully distinguishes between 'politics' and the 'political', with the latter described as 'the dimension of antagonism that is inherent in human relations', and the former 'the ensemble of practices, discourses and institutions which seek to establish a certain order and organise human coexistence in conditions that are always potentially conflictual because they are affected by the dimension of "the political" '.[5] The antagonism found in the political realm, where the special interests of groups and individuals regularly clash, means that we are confronted by an array of enemies there, and this hostility often spills over into institutional politics. Agonistic pluralism is an attempt to locate a mid-point between the poles of antagonism and consensus, neither of which is felt to be a condition congenial to a true democracy. Instead of mutual hostility, in agonistic pluralism we have mutual respect between opponents, now reclassified as 'adversaries' with whom we can enter into spirited debate. Although an adversary is still to be considered an 'enemy', he or she is now 'a legitimate enemy, one with whom we have some common ground because we have a shared adhesion to the ethico-political principles of liberal democracy: liberty and equality. But we disagree concerning the meaning and implementation of those principles.'[6]

In similar vein, we find Connolly arguing for the need to shift our political focus from antagonism to agonism:

> One response, suitable for some issues on certain occasions, is to strive to convert an antagonism of identity into an agonism of difference, in which each opposes the other (and the other's presumptive beliefs) while respecting the adversary at another level as one whose contingent orientations also rest on shaky epistemic grounds. An antagonism in which each aims initially at conquest or conversion of the other can now (given other supporting conditions) become an agonism in which each treats the other as crucial to itself in the strife and interdependence of identity/difference. [7]

Identity is always a state of contingency for Connolly, which he regards as a positive aspect of human being; although, like Lyotard, he does not believe this means that 'anything goes' when it comes to ideological outlook: 'It does not open itself to a politics of racism or genocide, for instance.'[8] Connolly feels that a politics based on agonism 'disturbs the dogmatization of identity', from where much political strife derives in his view.[9] Sceptics will be happy to embrace such a project.

Mouffe goes on to claim that such differences as exist between adversaries will not be resolved by the standard kinds of political debate (parliamentary, etc.), which will usually end in some kind of compromise – uneasy or otherwise, it makes little difference to the pluralist critic. Instead, what agonistic pluralist debate strives for is 'a sort of conversion', where the adversary is won over to one's point of view, discarding his or her own in consequence (something like a courtroom case, perhaps).[10] She likens this process to a paradigm change, as outlined most famously in the work of Thomas Kuhn, for whom changing from one scientific paradigm to another constituted an act of conversion: one could believe one or other paradigm, but not both simultaneously.[11] Conversion and consensus are just as mutually exclusive, although they do share the trait of being temporary states: a new conversion is always a possibility, just as is a new consensus. In terms of the attitude of mind involved, however, they are poles apart.

The primary aim of politics, according to Mouffe (following on from Connolly's lead), 'is to transform *antagonism* into *agonism*'.[12] Only thus, she argues, will 'democratic contestation' be kept a factor in our society. Without such contestation we lapse back into a consensus which merely serves to exclude large sections of the population from the political process.[13] In such cases there is what Mouffe calls a 'democratic deficit', which in her opinion is the major cause of the dramatic rise of fundamentalism – whether 'religious, moral and ethnic' in form[14] – of late, with special interest groups resorting to increasingly more extreme means to make themselves noticed and keep their beliefs in the public eye. Consensus is always achieved at the expense of someone in Mouffe's view (there are similarities to Foucault's views of how power works), and democracy always suffers when such marginalisation occurs. The disenfranchised become embittered and unpredictable in their actions, and the democratic deficit widens. There can never be a situation in which radical dissent from the ideological norm is not justified: 'one should abandon the very idea that there could ever be a time in which it would cease to be necessary because the society is now "well-ordered" '.[15] Permanent dissent becomes the political ideal, in a much more polite version of the Trotskyist and Maoist creed of 'permanent revolution'.

Mouffe's vision of society also seems to echo the scientific notion of the 'edge of chaos', which postulates that systems work best when kept under severe pressure.[16] The threat of imminent collapse into disorder on the one hand, or a regression into a socially stultifying stasis on the other, encourages the system to greater feats of ingenuity in order to keep itself functioning and developing. Nothing is taken for granted in such a situation, and the system benefits accordingly from maintaining its precarious position balanced between atrophy and chaos, constantly vigilant about the situation around it (the 'fitness landscapes', as they are called[17]). Dissent within politics plays that kind of galvanising role in Mouffe, with antagonism and consensus the conditions to be kept at bay by constant manoeuvring. No one must become, or stay, too comfortable. Certainly, politicians must not be allowed to be so, with consensus the comfort zone they will invariably seek.

Although the gaps in Mouffe's argument need to be acknowledged (we'll come back to them in a moment), the concept of agonism is worth expanding upon. We might consider, for example, if we can apply Mouffe's principles to the 'political' as well as to 'politics'; on the grounds that contestation in this wider realm might have a significant effect on the conduct of institutional politics. Perhaps it is at least as important to move from antagonism to agonism in this informal arena as it is in formal politics. The more agonistic voices heard the better, the more contexts for that agonism to be expressed within, the better it will be too. It is in this realm, after all, where we spend most of our everyday lives, and where politics has to answer to ultimately. There is two-way traffic between the domains, and politicians neglect the political at their peril – that's where the voters come from, after all.

At this point we can call again on Lyotard's notion of the little narrative, which offers us a form of micro-politics by which to confront the dominant power structures of our society, whether these be political or economic. Multinationals are just as likely to be the targets of these campaigns as national governments. Little narratives are created by concerned individuals to address perceived abuses of power (that is how we conceived of scepticism in the Introduction, as you remember), and they can feature alliances across standard party-political divides – the 'Rainbow Coalition' notion becomes the ideal. They are issue-oriented. It is also in the nature of little narratives that they can be put together by enthusiasts – only a few are needed to get the ball rolling – at any place or any time, and in a relatively short period, with the consequence that the dominant power structures can never rest easy: opposition can always be forthcoming from unexpected quarters without warning. Again, the point is to challenge the drift into consensus.

In the ideal sense that Lyotard probably intended the concept, little narratives would be agonistic in style, working to convert adversaries to their point of view by persuasive argument (and they would certainly be striving to disturb any 'dogmatisation of identity' that might arise within the ranks). But it has to be admitted that many of the examples of little narrative we can find if we look around us in the world at the moment are better defined as antagonistic. Eco-fundamentalism provides us with one such high profile example, since at the extreme end of the spectrum this meta-morphoses into eco-terrorism. Protecting the environment and endangered species from the depredations of an uncaring or just thoughtless humankind is one thing, destroying life and property in the name of that cause something else again. The same can be said of religious fundamentalism in its more extreme manifestations: con-version at the point of a gun is not what Mouffe, Connolly, or Lyotard had in mind. Neither is sucide bombing exactly an invitation to debate the finer points of opposing belief systems. Terrorism is antagonism taken to its logical limits, and it represents a total rejec-tion of the agonistic principle: anyone who can undertake such an activity has willingly embraced the dogmatisation of their identity the belief system has demanded.

In terms of gaining any significant measure of public support, particularly from the 'floating voter' type (much coveted by all the major political parties), agonistic methods are still the best way to proceed. Indeed, agonistically minded little narratives have consid-erable potential to disrupt the status quo in whatever is their chosen area of operation. They can adopt a wide range of tactics as well; it does not always have to be standard political discourse in the stan-dard political formats. Humour can be used, even satire: the tone does not have to be serious, even if the overall aim of destabilising some overbearing authority might be. The arts can be as effective a site as any for undermining power structures; the media in general can be deployed productively as well. A proliferation of such little narratives is a highly desirable social outcome. Neither do they have to be quite as transitory, or single-issue minded, as Lyotard himself felt was necessary to prevent them from hardening into political institutions in their own right, and thus being absorbed into the status quo. As long as dissent within is fostered, then little narratives could flourish to fight several campaigns – as magazines or news-papers can, for example, or certain radio and television pro-grammes. Politics has to take account of the political – that is where it must look to for support of its policies – and the more agonistic cri-tique there is emanating from the latter then the harder it will be for the former to drift into, and maintain, a deadening consensus.

As to those gaps mentioned earlier, however, we might wonder at what point conversion becomes consensus. We might also wonder just how far agonistic opponents will be allowed to wander from the centre of the liberal democratic ideal that Mouffe is concerned to protect. Liberty and equality can be interpreted in widely divergent ways: 'liberty from' and 'liberty to do', for example, often can cancel each other out. Political philosophers have wrangled over just this problem for centuries, if not millennia, and the emphasis can change quite markedly from generation to generation within a given culture ('liberty to do' currently is in the ascendancy in the West). Equality is no less contentious an issue, and one wonders just how much lati-tude there could be in contestation over this. Is equality of opportu-nity possible without equality of wealth, for example? Establishing the 'common ground' a liberal democracy requires for agonistic plu-ralism to work may be even more problematical an exercise than Mouffe envisages.

Returning to the realm of politics: how can agonism be made to work here? Or perhaps the question really is: *can* agonism be made to work here in an effective and democracy-affirming fashion? Wouldn't a really thoroughgoing agonistic politics lead to the frag-mentation of political parties as those organisations are constituted now? In a two- or three-party system, such as is the norm in a country like Britain, and most other Western democracies, the parties tend towards the 'broad church' model; which is to say that they generally seek to achieve an internal consensus for a wide range of views which at the extreme ends of the spectrum can often overlap with those of other parties. Mass parties want to appear before the electorate as divided in belief or policy, and take great pains to give an appearance of unity (even if it is at times no more than an appearance, masking considerable internal turmoil). Were

Mouffe's views to be taken at face value, however, there would have to be a significant amount of agonistic infighting occurring within each party at any given time, which in current terms of reference would seriously undermine the party's effectiveness if it were publicly visible. Think of how parties exploit such divisions when they do become apparent in their opponents, arguing that the voters cannot put their trust in a group that cannot even agree amongst themselves.

One answer to the dilemma would be to encourage breakaway groups from the large parties, and to aim for a multiplicity of small parties instead, where it would be easier to present a united front. As the political philosopher Thomas Hobbes (1588–1679) once famously noted, the fewer individuals involved at the centre of a power structure, then the less likelihood there is of disagreement. Following his own logic to its obvious conclusion, Hobbes himself favoured one only, an absolute sovereign – the ultimate in indivisibility.[18]

A multiplicity of competing parties only increases the need for compromise and consensus to be constructed, however, if anything like a working administration is to be created. Such a situation is usually the recipe for behind-the-scenes negotiations and shady deals between the participants, which is hardly in the spirit of agonism, where everything must be open to public view. This might well be an interesting alternative to the boredom and predictability of the two-party system as we know it (even if this is three-party in some instances, it is usually the case that the third is relatively weak, and so adds little in the way of agonistic content to the general process). Yet it might also lead to a lack of stability, with short-term government succeeding short-term government in something of a blur – as already happens in some systems. Modern Italy has had a history of the latter, for example; not necessarily to its benefit. Fragmentation would have the effect, however, of significantly decreasing the power of the mass political parties, which many would see as no bad thing at all. Mass political parties almost inevitably become authoritarian in manner over time, and are notoriously loath to embrace innovation and new ideas, especially if they are unsure what impact this will have on their main sources of funding – vested interests abound in such cases, no matter where on the political spectrum the party lies.

There are, of course, many small parties on the fringe of British politics as it is (and equivalents in all the major Western societies), and these might be said to be serving an agonistic function. To focus on one such in the UK, there is the Socialist Workers' Party (SWP), a long-established Trotskyist-inclined group with a widely available newspaper, the *Socialist Worker*. The SWP has a small but loyal following, and it has survived the recent collapse of communism as a force in world politics with apparent equanimity (since it was more often than not just as critical of the communist as the capitalist bloc, this is perhaps not altogether surprising). It has no representation in Parliament, and looks unlikely to achieve any in the immediate future. Nevertheless, it continues to snipe away from the sidelines at nearly everything the British political establishment does, as if this were a meaningful activity on its part. From this position there is no real difference to be noted between the main political parties, which are viewed, Mouffe-style, as one consensus-oriented entity.

It is easy to be dismissive of groups like the SWP and to regard them as irrelevant to the political process. Their national profile is minimal, never mind the international profile they consider themselves to have. Yet they clearly speak for a definite constituency, small though it is, and just as clearly strive to maintain their own ideological purity in the manner that we would expect true agonists to do. Although they are prepared to join with others in short-term, broad-front campaigns, conversion is their primary objective and they go about their task with a single-minded zeal. In that respect they do meet a real need amongst the political nation, giving voice to an unease about the motives of the establishment.

The SWP may be perceived by most of the electorate as no more than a minor irritant in the political system (when perceived at all), but that is what agonistic pluralism demands: irritants that keep the mass parties on their toes, having to justify their policies to non-believers from outside the consensus circle. We may well find some of the SWP's policies to be dismaying. As I write they are supporting the insurgency in Iraq on the grounds of its anti-Americanism, although one can hardly imagine the insurgents themselves, with their roots in either Islamic fundamentalism or Saddam Hussein's old ruling party the Ba'athists, reciprocating. But such stances make us think, and, just occasionally, see things in a different light. The main political parties can become very predictable in their attitudes, as well as in their debates with each other, and new perspectives are always to be welcomed. Sometimes those perspectives even reveal contradictions within the establishment's policies that it would rather keep hidden, and there is real value to the general public in that happening. The SWP can be relied upon to adopt an antithetical position to whatever the establishment does, and thus to offer a real alternative to consensus. (I say all of this realising that such sentiments will please neither the SWP nor its detractors: it will be neither fulsome enough for the former, nor critical enough for the latter. Perhaps that is the ultimate agonistic position, to fall foul of *all* one's opponents?)

On the minus side, we have to note yet again that this is agonism in the service of a universal theory which is anything but sceptically inclined. While the SWP might be acting in an agonistic manner in terms of the current political system, that does not mean they are supporters of the concept of agonism itself. Far from it: agonism has been thrust upon them by circumstances, rather than chosen by them as a preferred mode of political being, and they would undoubtedly dispense with it if they could. In the broad sense of the term they are a totalitarian grouping, and no friends to dissent: they have a party line and members are required to stick to it. The far left has never been comfortable with dissent, either within its own ranks or within society at large when it has come to political power. Dissent tends to be regarded as implicitly treasonous, as witness the reaction of the Soviet communist party throughout its history to even the hint of opposition amongst its membership. This was invariably terminated, very often with extreme prejudice to those brave souls who challenged the party's authority. The perils of authoritarianism become glaringly apparent in such cases, and the arguments for agonistic pluralism all the more urgent.

One of the more problematical aspects of Mouffe's theory of agonism is that it would seem to demand the existence of a viscerally far-right presence in politics, in order to maintain the political balance. There would need to be pressure on the centre from both sides if consensus were successfully to be kept at bay, since the centre could hardly persuade both left and right into its embrace (whereas one or the other it just might). An argument could even be made that fascism could fulfil that role. As Martin Pugh has pointed out in his book on British fascism, Oswald Mosley briefly presented a credible alternative to the National Government after the formation of the British Union of Fascists (BUF) in 1932, largely because the National Government was felt by many to represent yet another example of compromise by the old political order.[19] That order was being held responsible for the crippling economic crisis of the Depression, therefore creating the conditions for a challenge to be made to its methods and practices. There is no doubt that Mosley's intentions did not include consensus or compromise. While it could be claimed that Mosley and the BUF were really antagonistic rather than agonistic, as we've seen it is not always that easy to distinguish between the two.

Mouffe might query whether the far right are really committed to the liberal democratic project she has in mind. Fascists clearly are not, but the terms 'liberal' and 'democratic' are capable of very wide interpretation, and as long as 'conversion' remains the ultimate goal it is difficult to see how Mouffe can object. One suspects this might stretch the left's commitment to agonism to breaking point (certainly the far left's), since no love is lost between these ideological polar opposites. For the SWP to accept the British National Party (BNP) as legitimate participants in the political process – and vice versa – would require a quite extraordinary leap of faith to be made by their membership. Given that each side is more likely to demonise the other than to enter into conversion-seeking debate, this seems an unlikely event to occur.

Agonistic pluralism has its drawbacks therefore, but it does seem to provide a context in which scepticism could well thrive. If it involves the political as well as politics, then the range of dissenting viewpoints is multiplied, as are the opportunities for expressing them and generating yet more adversarial debate. There would need to be a recognition on the part of all the players involved that there could never be any final triumph for any one political project, and that consensus was strictly off the agenda, but if this agreement were forthcoming then there really would be the 'radical democracy' that both Mouffe and her erstwhile writing partner Laclau have been campaigning for so vigorously over the last two decades or so.

Whether the goodwill currently exists to move towards such a state of affairs is an altogether more contentious issue. Vested interests are unlikely to look kindly on Mouffe's proposals, and the desire to triumph conclusively over one's ideological opponents is deeply embedded in our psyche. Totalitarian regimes are historically more the norm than democracy is, even in our own age – we only have to think of China, where a quarter of the world's population lives under a one-party system, even if this less restrictive than it was in the Maoist past. As political commentators never tire of telling us, politics is a rough old trade, and its professional practitioners do not give up their hard-won privileges lightly. One imagines the spectrum of allowable dissent that the left, right, and centre, respectively, would be willing to countenance would be far narrower than Mouffe would prefer to be the case. Most political parties would be happiest if dissent went no further than slightly more extreme versions of themselves.

I've made the point before that scepticism always lays itself open to charges of relativism, and also hinted that this might be a problem for agonistic pluralism as well. In both instances we note an automatic assumption of dissent when confronted with a claim of absolute authority. But if we look at agonistic pluralism a bit more closely, then perhaps it might be seen to escape the charge of relativism. There is certainly an equality of opportunity being offered to all those articulating a political position within the liberal democratic arena, with all parties being granted the right to engage in the activity of conversion. Debate is the life-blood of this system and it is to be energetically promoted. No one position should consider itself innately superior to any other, or above being challenged by its opponents in robust fashion. This can sound like relativism, but each position is attempting to convert the others and refusing to be drawn into any lazy consensus where its own beliefs would lose their definition. Each position is under an obligation to defend itself with zeal, and truly believes what it says, but must expect to be placed under constant, intellectually searching critique; permanently on the defensive as well as the offensive, at the 'edge of chaos' where it can never relax. Everyone is holding some belief or other, rather than regarding all beliefs as having equal value and treating it as arbitrary which position one decides to embrace; everyone is committed to a particular paradigm, and to convincing others to abandon their own and join theirs. Firm belief meets bracing competition at every turn, in what looks surprisingly like an idealised version of the free market – surprising for a post-Marxist, that is. This time it is a free market of ideas, and like an idealised economic free market, it sets its face against monopoly (an ideal rarely realised, as we know). There must always be adversaries, and they must always have an equal chance to make their case.

I would argue that a plurality of competing paradigms is not the same thing as relativism, although it is also, sadly enough if we reflect on scientific history from where Kuhn drew the concept in the first place, not all that common a condition to find in operation for any length of time. As Kuhn's researches have revealed, when the condition does occur it is generally only as a temporary prelude to a new paradigm asserting its authority conclusively over the old. At which point competitors are either ridiculed, or simply ignored by the 'victors' (who proceed to rewrite history to their own advantage, further reinforcing their credibility to the new generation). Adherents to paradigms seek to dominate the scene rather than to invite challenge, and in that sense we can identify a fundamentalist streak in their make-up: they do tend to think and act in terms of believers and non-believers, with scientists proving to be as bad as anyone else in this respect. That is an obstacle Mouffe's project would have to overcome, but if it could do so then it would create a very different kind of political landscape to the one we now have, and one in which unquestioning belief would have to rethink its practices.

Agonism plus scepticism sounds to me like a good basis for undermining the empire of belief. Religion can still be in there in the thick of the struggle striving for converts, but it will have to do so surrounded by adversaries, and, more to the point, acknowledging the necessity of those adversaries being part of the ideological process. A system of competing paradigms would only work if there was questioning within each paradigm by its own supporters, and, furthermore, questioning about the fundamentals of the paradigm's beliefs. Religion is not particularly good at this, being prone instead to create fundamentals which it then sets about protecting quite aggressively against all outsiders. For agonistic pluralism to work, however, there must be no comfort zone available for believers either inside or outside a paradigm.

It is not impossible for religion to reinvent itself as an agonistic entity, but it will require a significant shift in perspective by adherents; not least to see religion as above all a form of politics. While religion clearly does become deeply involved in politics (and is so today around the world, with fundamentalists in the vanguard across the religious spectrum), it tends to regard itself as, ultimately, above politics. Generally speaking, it defends its involvement in national and international politics as a method of establishing religion's supremacy and curtailing the activities of adversaries: neither agonistic nor pluralist, in other words.

Perhaps we need to ask whether liberal democracy is itself functioning as a paradigm, and thus becoming a candidate for agonism in its turn. Looked at from outside – extreme left or right, for example – the liberal democratic ethos might appear to be a form of consensus, and Mouffe to have more in common with the views of Francis Fukuyama than might at first appear likely (and than she would ever want). Fukuyama claimed the triumph of the West, arguing in his book *The End of History and the Last Man* that liberal democracy had now become the political norm that all nations should be judged by, and that it was in fact to be regarded as humankind's manifest destiny.[20] Once there in that happy state, having seen off all possible rivals, we would have reached the 'end of history', where there would be no more need for any development of the political system, which would have achieved perfection. All that would remain to do was to protect the system against its enemies – a diminishing group of ever-decreasing credibility, in Fukuyama's reading of the post-Soviet world.

The left collectively were appalled by Fukuyama's ideas, which they saw as an insult to both the Third World, with its very different cultural outlook (including a significant dose of reflex anti-Americanism thanks to twentieth-century economic imperialism[21]), and the cause of socialism. For the left this was Western-centric thinking with a vengeance and it had to be combated, all the more so since Fukuyama's ideas were so enthusiastically embraced by the right in American politics, which was particularly taken by his sense of evangelical fervour (in the aftermath of the collapse of the Soviet empire such attitudes found a ready audience, as one might expect). Yet one wonders whether there might be an element of that same mind-set in Mouffe's theories. If liberal democracy sets the parameters of debate, even if it is a looser, more flexible concept of liberal democracy than we find in Fukuyama's work, then someone is bound to be excluded. In that case we would have a restricted pluralism – which begins to sound uncomfortably close to consensus. Once again we face the problem of just how far to the left or right Mouffe would be prepared to see agonistic pluralism extend.

Agonism and Pyrrhonism

There are still problems to be faced with agonism, therefore, and it is by no means a foolproof solution to political dogmatism. It does provide, however, a different perspective on the political process, which gives food for thought. Perhaps we might now consider how it relates to Pyrrhonism, and whether the two might usefully interact. Agonism does involve holding certain positions, and rejecting all others – while always acknowledging the necessity of continuing on in searching debate with those other positions. That debate is concerned with trying to undermine one's opponents and achieving their conversion to one's own cause. But the assumption is that the debate will be never-ending. No triumphalism is implied in the agonistic outlook, no sense that final victory is either attainable or desirable – that way lies the dreaded conditions of compromise and consensus. Pyrrhonism, meanwhile, involves trying to undermine any and all positions without replacing them with one of its own. In each case we are given reasons to suspend belief in the judgements being offered. The Pyrrhonist forces other positions to examine the grounds for their beliefs and claims, and agonism at its best does the same. In a way, the Pyrrhonist is looking for converts too – converts to doubt.

Agonists and Pyrrhonists are united in wanting to eradicate dogmatism from public life, although Pyrrhonists might well regard agonists as dogmatic in holding to the positions they do. The point has to be made, however, that agonistic positions are at best provisional, since they are always involved in debate which, theoretically at least, could lead to conversion to another viewpoint. Agonism is a contested site rather than a comfort zone. Neither is it the case that the Pyrrhonist believes in nothing at all, politically speaking. As Popkin has noted,

> The sceptic is raising doubts about the rational or evidential merits of the justifications given for a belief; he doubts that necessary and sufficient reasons either have been or could be discovered to show that any particular belief must be true, and cannot possibly be false. But the sceptic may, like anyone else, still accept various beliefs.[22]

What the sceptic will not do, however, is insist that only those beliefs are valid and refuse to listen to other points of view. The sceptic is always thrown back into debate, but willingly so, accepting that such is the nature of belief, to be defensible only up to a point. Relativism imposes such a duty on us. Mouffe's 'never-ending interrogation of the political by the ethical' always applies:[23] belief is at best a temporary resting place, where we are forever awaiting challenge from opponents. When it comes to holding beliefs themselves, both the sceptic and the agonist accept that they are inviting such a response; that they cannot fall back on the dogmatic mode they so despise in others. The intellectual comfort zone must always be avoided if credibility is to be retained.

The Politics of Dogmatism

If we consider what dogmatism has led to in today's world, then we can see why a sceptical politics urgently needs to be developed to counter its impact. In America, evangelical Christianity is a major factor in the political life of the nation, with pressure groups such as the Christian Coalition (which has at least the tacit support of the Bush presidency) helping to fund and run campaigns against liberalising legislation. Evangelicals and fundamentalists disagree profoundly with abortion and homosexuality, and do their best to ban the former and restrict the rights of those who practise the former – gay priests and bishops being a particular dislike of such activists, as we have noted (more on this issue in Chapter 6). These campaigns are mainly fought at state level, and not every state gives in to such pressure; but a significant number, largely in the 'Bible Belt' of the South and Midwest, do, spurring the campaigners on to greater efforts in other areas of public life. Restrictions have even been placed in some states on the sale of the morning-after pill, with the religious right seeking to become the moral guardians of the American populace right down to the private details of their sexual lives.

America is still far from being a theocracy (although some would disagree), and its multiculturalism is a significant barrier to such a possibility, but it is clear that the religious right sees politics as one of the most effective ways of putting their moral principles into practice by challenging and suppressing liberal trends in American life.[24] The objective is ideological domination, and pluralism can only be regarded as a hindrance. Certainly, the support of the religious right during presidential elections is eagerly sought, particularly by the Republican party, and potentially crucial in determining the outcome of the election. Faith-based voting is a characteristic feature of the current American political scene, with the Republican party the main beneficiary.

It is depressing to observe the erosion of libertarianism in America, and although there continues to be spirited opposition to the religious right (even within the Bible Belt), there is no denying that it has had considerable success in its campaigns and that it has had a dramatic effect on the national consciousness. The fact that creationism has made such a determined comeback, and won so many converts in recent years ('I really hate it when the theory of evolution is presented as fact', as the aggrieved Imax customer in Fort Worth had it), is proof of how just how deep that impact is, and also of how close the connection between religion and politics can be in America. Creationism could not have worked its way back onto so many school system syllabuses without significant political effort by the religious right, on the appropriate committees and public bodies at local and state level. Once again, we meet up with the indefatigability of the true believer. Banning pro-evolution films takes political guile as well – guile that undermines the basis for agonistic pluralism. A line has been crossed when one goes back to a sacred book like the Bible for political guidance, because it is hardly likely to recommend open-minded debate with one's opponents. The Bible is not a pluralist document, nor a source for multiculturalism. Agonistic pluralists have their work cut out to arrest such a shift towards dogmatism – but arrest it they must if real democracy is to survive. Doubt and uncertainty urgently need to be injected into any political process where the religious right are operating.

Doubt and uncertainty also need to be brought to bear in the realm of economic policy. Politics and economics go hand in glove as we know, and the economic theories adopted by national governments – especially in the West, where the world's richest economies lie – and such international regulatory bodies as the International Monetary Fund (IMF) and the World Bank, serve to shape political life on the global scale. The current economic paradigm has been defined as 'market fundamentalism', the goal of which is as unregulated a free market around the world as can be achieved.[25] This has been tirelessly promoted by the IMF and World Bank for several decades now, and they tend to insist on its implementation whenever they are asked to help bail out ailing national economies. The results are often catastrophic, with economies such as Argentina collapsing after adopting IMF/World Bank prescriptions as required in order to gain necessary aid to counter rampant inflation. Political crisis predictably followed. Other countries badly affected by the IMF/World Bank regime include most of the ex-Soviet empire and South America, as well as the relatively successful countries of South-East Asia (such as Thailand and Malaysia, for example). Many of the latter nearly went under in the late 1990s, and have taken years to return to something like their former level of economic activity, with considerable social distress being experienced in the interim.

Market fundamentalism demands that national currencies float on the open world market rather than being protected by their governments; that an aggressive programme of privatisation is undertaken (state ownership of industries or utilities is distinctly frowned upon by the IMF/World Bank authorities, as is the notion of a welfare state); that regulations on economic activity are relaxed as much as possible (no protectionist trade barriers in favour of local industries and products, for instance); and that all countries embrace the concept of globalisation, where there are no restrictions on the movement of capital or production. The ideal is one large global market without borders. The consequence of globalisation is that the major multinationals can shift production from country to country at will, seeking out the best deal in each case, regardless of the effect this can have on vulnerable economies in the Third World. It is this phenomenon as much as anything which has fuelled the rise of the anti-capitalist movement which has disrupted a succession of World Trade Organisation conferences, where the agenda is dominated by the world's richest economies (the G8 group).

Behind the IMF/World Bank/globalisation ethos lies unquestioning belief in the principles of free market, *laissez faire* economics; a belief that the same method must be employed everywhere, with cultural differences simply being ignored. Under this regime economic activity is largely divorced from national cultures, which are treated as subsidiary to the market – and many multinationals do tend to act as if national governments were irrelevant to their interests (many multinationals, of course, are richer than many Third World countries). Belief in the free market is total in such institutions, and has all the force of law, or even Scripture, to believers. Whatever situation the market creates, rather like the concept of intelligent design, must be what was fated to happen. Any debate that does take place about policy has to do so within the strict parameters of free market theory; all other theories are off-limits, and any government involvement seen as incipient socialism.

Sceptics would want to draw attention to the many failures that implementation of extreme free market policies has caused (the list is long), and also query where the conviction comes from that refuses to consider other methods of economic activity – public-private cooperation, for example, as still happens in some Western economies in contradiction of the paradigm's ideals. At the very least, a suspension of that conviction would seem called for to the committed sceptic, Pyrrhonist principles to the fore. The evidence is far from compelling that this is the only sensible way to conduct our economic life. Yet dogmatists in this area no more admit the possibility of different interpretations than they do in the religious sphere – even if such Western governments as the UK and France can be more pragmatic in practice than their pronouncements would often indicate (even America operates some protectionist measures, for its steel industry). Third World economies are not allowed this luxury, however, being treated instead like laboratory experiments by the free market dogmatists when they are called in to resolve their problems.

Another problem for the sceptic to address is nationalism, a phenomenon which has managed to survive the introduction of such supra-national bodies as the EU, and continues to be a force to be reckoned with in world politics – rarely for good. Unquestioning belief underpins nationalism as well; unquestioning belief in the superiority of one's country and its cultural heritage, generally felt by believers to be under constant threat from outsiders. Nationalism has a tendency to be reactionary in this regard and does not have much truck with doubt: fervent nationalists are quite certain of their country's virtues and the necessity of defending these from any adulteration. In extreme cases the latter can have unpleasant overtones of racial purity, as in the various anti-immigration movements that have sprung up around Europe in recent times (most notably in the UK, France, Holland, and Belgium). Although these are some-times directed against economic migrants from the countries of the ex-Soviet empire, even those now ensconced within the EU, nationalists usually reserve their deepest resentment for non-white migrants from Africa or Asia. Whether the latter are political or eco-nomic in origin hardly seems of much consequence to the aggrieved. Nationalists are implicitly anti-pluralist and critical of those within their own country who disagree with their views. Debate with plu-ralist-minded fellow citizens does not figure much in their plans either; such individuals are often taken to be traitors to the cause and vilified for their lack of 'pure' nationalistic sentiment. Sport is capable of bringing out the very worst of such outlooks, when it comes to support of national teams in particular.

It is hard to imagine extreme nationalism passing any Pyrrhonist test either – circular reasoning and infinite regress abound in its arguments, and the very idea of suspension is treated as akin to treason. Once again we are dealing with ideas which owe more to faith than reason and logic. There is an inability to appreciate the position of the other or to doubt the validity of one's outlook – the hallmarks of dogmatism, in other words.

A Network of Resistance

Taken together, there is much for the sceptic to go to work on in both politics and the political. The empires of religious belief, economic policy, and nationalism, as cases in point, all attempt to impose uni-formity on the general public, suppressing, and even demonising, alternative views. All of them have learned how to operate through the political system to realise their objectives, striving to mould that system to their own ends – and those ends are authority, power, and domination over others. They have to be pressed as to where their authority comes from, and invariably it will be seen to be based on nothing stronger than unsubstantiated assumptions which lead to circular reasoning and an infinite regress. At that point the sceptic goes into action, drawing attention to each example of circularity and regression and generating doubt about the systems subsequently based on them. The sceptic will emphasise that we have no need of those hypotheses, that political systems can be constructed on a more open, less elitist model that allows a wider range of voices to be heard (the multitude of little narratives to which Lyotard, and the post-modern movement in general, is committed).

The case for difference and diversity follows naturally in the wake of such campaigns, once central authority has been revealed to have no real basis other than convention; in Nietzsche's phrase, 'illusions of which we have forgotten that they are illusions'.[26] Scepticism, super-scepticism, agonistic pluralism, relativism, and iconoclasm are all motivated by a desire to destabilise those illusions, to keep libertarianism (or 'cosmopolitanism', as it is sometimes referred to) alive and well in our culture and the politics of dogmatism firmly at bay. The basis for a network of resistance is there.

Doubt certainly needs to be a more prevalent factor in the political process to counter all the anti-liberalising trends detailed above: trends which are a blight on post-Enlightenment culture. We need to consider now where else doubt is in evidence in our institutions, and how we might draw inspiration from its role there to extend it even further into contemporary life to create a climate inimical to the development of unquestioning belief.

6
Reasonable Doubt?

What part does doubt play in our culture? It certainly plays a key role role in areas like the legal system, and it is worth exploring how this works to see if this ethos can be expanded to take on the proponents of unquestioning belief. Such an enquiry invites dipping into the history of doubt as a cultural concept, particularly its problematical role within religious thought and practice – where it is generally regarded as a sign of weakness in the individual. The religious establishment is only really comfortable with true believers, the more devout the better, and takes it as one of its main objectives to eliminate doubt within its area of operation. For guardians of the faith, 'Doubting Thomas' is simply a candidate for conversion, and will be worked on to that end – quite remorselessly if he keeps refusing to see the light. Humanism has traditionally taken a sceptical attitude towards religion, and there are humanist trends within established religion to be acknowledged in this context. Anglicanism features some of these, for example, even if they do find themselves increasingly under attack from a fundamentalist wing opposing such phenomena as openly gay or women priests.

Doubt has to be differentiated from suspicion – such as the more than somewhat paranoid suspicion of the Islamic world that has grown up in the West since 9/11 (with the situation in post-invasion Iraq currently polarising opinion even further, as the insurgents clearly intend it to). From our perspective, doubt is a positive phenomenon, suspicion a negative one, and we have to be careful that the former does not collapse into the latter. I am advocating an open-minded scepticism rather than a closed-minded suspicion based on cultural prejudice (and it is fervently to be hoped that 7/7 in London does not generate more of the latter). Even super-scepticism should not lead to fear of the cultural other.

The role of satire across the arts and entertainment industry (film, television, literature, popular journalism such as *Private Eye*, even the comedy industry) in sowing seeds of doubt about the institutions and value-systems of our culture is also worthy of attention. Satire's impact should never be underestimated, which makes any move towards banning attacks on religion, as is happening in the UK as I write with the proposed Incitement to Religious Hatred Bill (due for passage in the current Parliament from 2005 onwards), all the more worrying. We are assured that the new regulations are designed to prevent attacks on believers rather than belief, but there is considerable uncertainty as to how these can be kept separate: indeed, *if* these can be kept separate. At the very least, there is scope for some legal wrangling here, which might well make many think twice before daring to satirise organised religion.

The fact that the creative community within Britain has risen up in opposition to such proposals indicates deep unease as to their potential effect on artistic freedom of expression. The right to satirise entrenched interests needs to be upheld; otherwise it will be open season for the advocates of unquestioning belief. If this argument is lost, then we can expect more campaigns such as the one that succeeded in having the play *Behzti* removed from the stage at Birmingham Repertory in 2004, for offending the local Sikh community with its representation of Sikh belief. Salman Rushdie's experience with *The Satanic Verses* should leave us in no doubt as to just how far unquestioning believers are prepared to go in pursuit of their religious ideals. Offence is certainly worthy of debate, and satire has to remain within some bounds. What those bounds might be we shall go on to discuss later, but mob action is hardly debate (neither is a *fatwa*), and once it becomes established as in any way acceptable as a response to satire then free speech goes out the window. We shall return to the case of *Behzti* later in the chapter.

Doubt and Legal Process

Doubt has a central role to play in the judicial system of Western democracies, with 'reasonable' doubt being one of the major criteria used in reaching judgement in criminal cases. If reasonable doubt can be fostered in the jury's mind by the accused's legal team, and they will take that to be their primary objective in prosecuting the case, then conviction should not occur. While there does not have to be certainty before moving to that latter decision, it does have to be *beyond* reasonable doubt in the minds of the jurors. Doubt takes on a positive dimension in the legal system in consequence, something we would like to encourage in almost all areas of existence. Reasonable doubt as applied to the claims of religion, for example, ought not to come up with unquestioning belief as its verdict. It is hardly beyond reasonable doubt that the Bible is literally true, for example, or that any one God is manifestly superior to all the rest.

Reasonable doubt has been defined as follows:

> The level of certainty a juror must have to find a defendant guilty of a crime. A real doubt, based upon reason and common sense after careful and impartial consideration of all the evidence, or lack of evidence, in a case. Proof beyond reasonable doubt, therefore, is proof of such a convincing character that you would be willing to rely and act upon it without hesitation in the most important of your own affairs. However, it does not mean an absolute certainty.[1]

This seems relatively straightforward, but another definition brings out a potential problem in the concept:

> Not being sure of a criminal defendant's guilt to a moral certainty. Thus, a juror (or judge sitting without a jury) must be convinced of guilt of a crime (or the degree of crime, as murder instead of manslaughter) 'beyond reasonable doubt', and the jury will be told so by the judge in the jury instructions. However, it is a subjective test since each juror will

have to decide if his/her doubt is reasonable. It is more difficult to convict under that test, than 'preponderance of the evidence' to decide for the plaintiff (party bringing the suit) in a civil (non-criminal) trial.[2]

There is a very subjective element involved in the process, therefore, and it could vary quite considerably from individual to individual – some of us are more easily persuaded than others, more inclined towards severity or leniency in our judgements. That subjectivity is balanced in the jury system, however, by the need to debate the viewpoint collectively with the other jurors (other 'reasonable individuals', as the law has it). Only if there is a majority decision either way will guilt or innocence be established. What is crucial in that system is that doubt has to be aired in a public forum against a range of other opinions: it is not enough just to have inner conviction, whereas in matters of religion it seems to be. That does leave the problematical case of a judge sitting without a jury, where the process of debate is elided – a powerful argument for the jury system, most of us might well think (Thomas Hobbes excepted, one must assume).

Reasonable doubt is an imprecise concept, and various attempts have been made to clarify it further, especially by judges in their directions to the jury. Hence the following remarks in *Regina* v. *Summers* (1952):

> If a jury is told that it is their duty to regard the evidence and see that it satisfies them so that they can feel sure when they return a verdict of Guilty, that is much better than using the expression 'reasonable doubt' and I hope in future that that will be done. I never use the expression when summing up. I always tell a jury that, before they convict they must feel sure and must be satisfied that the prosecution have established the guilt of the prisoner.[3]

Others have been critical of such attempts: 'it is a mistake to depart from the time-honoured formula. It is, I think, used by ordinary people and understood well enough by the average man in the community.'[4] Another suggestion has been to emphasise benefit of the doubt:

135

the jury should be told that the accused is entitled to the benefit of the doubt and that, when two views on any point of the case are possible on the evidence, they should adopt that which is favourable to the accused unless the state has established the other beyond reasonable doubt.[5]

While there is scope for a certain amount of interpretation, the concept seems workable enough in practice, and its demand that there must be reflection on the burden of proof is well appreciated by jurors.

Preponderance of the evidence, on the other hand, the standard for proof in civil cases, merely requires a recognisable weight of evidence either way to establish a decision: 'persuasion on balance of probabilities', as the legal commentator P. B. Carter has described it.[6] The famous O. J. Simpson case provides an example of how the difference between the two concepts can affect verdicts. Simpson, a black former American football star, was charged with murdering his white wife, but acquitted in his criminal trial in 1995. The trial turned into a national obsession in America, with Simpson's defence team successfully managing to portray their client as a victim of racial hatred on the part of the Los Angeles Police Department, which was accused of planting false evidence in an attempt to prejudice the outcome. Simpson was subsequently found guilty of wrongful death when a civil suit was brought against him by his wife's family, however, and ordered to pay $33.5 million in damages. Although civil suits incur less severe penalties, aggrieved plaintiffs can feel that moral justice has been achieved if they are successful in their prosecution, even at this lower level of the legal system.

Preponderance of the evidence has been defined as follows:

> the greater weight of the evidence required in a civil (non-criminal) lawsuit for the trier of fact (jury or judge without a jury) to decide in favor of one side or the other. This preponderance is based on the more convincing evidence and its probable truth or accuracy, and not on the amount of evidence. Thus, one clearly knowledgeable witness may provide a preponderance of evidence over a dozen witnesses with hazy testimony, or a signed agreement with definite terms may outweigh opinions or speculation about what the parties intended. Preponderance

of the evidence is required in a civil case and is contrasted with 'beyond a reasonable doubt,' which is the more severe test of evidence required to convict in a criminal trial. No matter what the definition stated in various legal opinions, the meaning is somewhat subjective.[7]

Again, the subjective element is conceded, but as with 'reasonable doubt' it generally has to be negotiated with the other jurors (cases where a judge sits without a jury excepted), so inner conviction alone is not the sole determinant of the ultimate decision: 'there is safety in numbers', as Lord Diplock has remarked, which 'serves to counter individual idiosyncrasies'.[8]

It would seem unlikely to me that preponderance of the evidence would lead to unquestioning belief when applied to religion either, especially since the evidence is generally very sketchy (mere hearsay in most cases), and often downright counter-intuitive. Think of miracles, where the balance of probabilities surely would have to lie on the side of disbelief. I say counter-intuitive, but true believers will say faith overcomes this (miracles can even be given a pseudo-scientific spin as 'singularities'). Nevertheless, the legal system would seem to discourage reliance on unquestioning belief in matters of judgement, and its emphasis on reflection is worth extending to all areas where judgement is required – especially when we come to accept just how rare a condition absolute certainty is in our lives.

Doubt and Religious History

It is not surprising that doubt has had a bad press in religious history, since it is the obverse of faith. Faith constitutes a willing suspension of doubt, and if that does not occur then religions are unlikely to build-up a mass following. Religions leave considerable scope for the growth of doubt, since most of them involve miraculous events, generally as part of their fundamental creed (virgin birth, resurrection, divine intervention, etc.; these crop up regularly across the religious spectrum). It requires faith to accept such extraordinary claims, as well as the eye-witness accounts from generations ago that claim to verify them, and doubt can only be regarded as an impediment to the process. It is characteristic of religious zealots to cast doubt in the role of the enemy that must be overcome if true belief is to triumph. We can see an interesting example of this in fictional terms in John Bunyan's (1628–88) work *The Holy War* (1682), which gives us a fascinating insight into the workings of the devout Christian mind on this topic: Bunyan being one of the most famously devout Christians in one of the most famously devout periods in British history.

The Holy War tells the story of the town of Mansoul, which is repeatedly besieged over the course of the narrative by a vast army of 'doubters' trying to conquer it and subjugate the inhabitants to its will. There are, for example, 'the *Election-doubters*, the *Vocation-doubters*, the *Grace-doubters*, the *Perseverance-doubters*, the *Resurrection-doubters*, the *Salvation-doubters*, and the *Glory-doubters*' to contend with, all of them persistent in their aims.[9] Mansoul becomes a battleground for a highly symbolic struggle between the forces of faith and doubt, with the latter being led, significantly enough, by the devil – Diabolus. The Diabolonian forces use doubt as a means of undermining Mansoul's faith in the promises of his spiritual guide, Prince Emmanuel, to receive him into heaven after his life's struggle, and they win several victories along the way (and equally, suffer several reverses as Emmanuel returns periodically to assert his assumed authority over Mansoul). At no point is it ever suggested that toleration might be an acceptable solution to the two sides. This is clearly a duel to the death in which only one can prevail: agonism is not an option for such bitter opponents. Doubt is perceived in entirely negative terms, the enemy not just to individual salvation but to good order and clean living. Thus when the Diabolonians overrun the town, Mansoul is pictured as having been reduced to the condition of a wasteland:

> And now did *Mansoul* seem to be nothing but a den of Dragons, an emblem of Hell, and a place of total darkness. Now did *Mansoul* lye (almost) like the barren wilderness; nothing but nettles, briers, thorns, weeds, and stinking things seemed now to cover the face of *Mansoul*.[10]

Bunyan's is the authentic voice of the Christian zealot, for whom absolute, unquestioning belief is the only acceptable mode of existence.[11] Doubt is taken to be evidence of the devil at work in human affairs; something we must always be on our guard against at the individual level to prevent even a shred from entering our minds and poisoning our belief system (Bunyan seems to have spent a large part of his life fighting this battle within himself[12]). Dissent from 'the truth' simply will not be tolerated. Scepticism is the mark of the unbeliever and must be destroyed wherever encountered.

Similar attempts are made by a parade of characters in Bunyan's most famous work, *The Pilgrim's Progress* (1678, 1684), to plant seeds of doubt in the mind of his hero, Christian, on his road to the Celestial City. As one Atheist puts it, 'I laugh to see what ignorant persons you are, to take upon you so tedious a Journey; and yet are like to have nothing but your travel for your paines. . . . There is no such place as you Dream of in all this World';[13] but ultimately all such attempts prove to be just as fruitless in deflecting the single-minded Christian from his desired goal. Even temporary imprisonment in Doubting-Castle is overcome by the hero, who finds 'a *Key* in my bosom, called *Promise*' that provides a means of escape from his predicament.[14] True belief will prevail; all that one needs is faith.

Humanism Within the Religious World

Humanism has made some inroads within religious belief, although increasingly these days it finds itself in conflict with fundamentalism. The current state of the Anglican church is a case in point. Anglicanism has traditionally been a church which has sought the middle way, and it has steered a course between the extremes of Protestantism and Catholicism fairly successfully over the centuries (even if radical Protestants and Catholics might disagree with such a sympathetic assessment). Anglicanism also has tended to avoid being over-prescriptive in terms of worship, and has allowed a certain latitude in this regard, with some parishes leaning more towards the Catholic, some more towards the Protestant, end of the spectrum ('high' and 'low' Anglicanism respectively). Of late, however, Anglicanism has been riven by bitter internal controversy over the issues of gay clergy and women priests; to the extent where a schism is openly being talked of by its senior officials. Fundamentalism is becoming a more common attitude within the upper reaches of the church hierarchy, and those espousing it are becoming ever more assertive in their opposition to humanist trends within the organisation. That humanism has expressed itself as support for gay clergy and the ordination of women priests, and the Anglican church has been in the forefront of change on these matters within the religious world.

It is particularly on the issue of the election of gay bishops that the split has occurred. The notorious case of Canon Jeffrey John, appointed to be bishop of Reading in 2003 and then forced to stand down after a smear campaign was mounted against him by fundamentalists (splashed all over the national press in a manner calculated to arouse latent prejudice), brought the issue to a head, precipitating arguably the worst crisis in the church's modern history. When the American wing of the Anglican church, the Episcopalians, followed suit by electing a gay as bishop of New Hampshire (Gene Robinson), the crisis deepened significantly. The American church has even been asked to withdraw from the parent organisation's decision-making bodies for a period of three years, in the hope that it will see the light and submit to the dictates of the fundamentalists who now seem to be holding the reins of power. If the Americans do not comply, then schism looms.

Just to hammer the point home, a Ugandan bishop subsequently has refused funding for Aids victims in his country – where homosexuality is a crime that can bring a sentence of life imprisonment – because the American diocese that offered it had supported the election of Gene Robinson as bishop. 'South Rwenzori diocese upholds the Holy Scriptures as true word of God', was the message from Uganda, the fundamentalist emphasis unmistakable.[15] For the humanists within the church it has all been a particularly humiliating experience, which has cast doubt over the church's very existence – and certainly its ability to adapt to contemporary mores.

Humanism is on the defensive within Anglicanism, therefore, and looks likely to remain so at least in the short term (although the

Episcopal church in Scotland subsequently has taken a brave stance on gay priests, endorsing their right to be ordained). The head of the church, the archbishop of Canterbury, Dr Rowan Williams, considered to be on the progressive wing of Anglicanism when he was appointed, has been outmanoeuvred by the fundamentalists to the extent where his supporters have even been claiming, in a notably emotive phrase, that he is 'a virtual prisoner of the religious right'.[16] Those particular supporters, Giles Fraser and William Whyte (a vicar and historian respectively), have called for an alliance between the religious and secular left to challenge that so successfully put together by Christian fundamentalists and political neoconservatives, insisting that,

> the present situation . . . demands a reassessment by the secular left of the religious left. Because only the religious left is capable of challenging the religious right with the language of faith. The secular left, in short, needs to stop sniping and start making new friends. In America, the Christian right and the neocons have grown strong by working together. Now so must we.[17]

Fraser and Whyte emphasise the religious roots of British socialism, and see this as the basis for joint action: the 'Labour learned more from Methodism than Marx' argument, harking back to the 'Christian Socialist' movement of the nineteenth century. Whether the *sceptical* left would find it possible to become involved in defending faith, even at second hand, is more problematical – and I doubt there are many 'Christian Socialists' of the kind that fuelled the rise of the Labour party left around these days anyway. But let's just say there may be scope for pragmatism here, as long as the relationship between the partners maintains an agonistic character. Cooperation should not be allowed to gloss over the fact that each side still wants to convert the other to its position, and could never reach any long-term consensus without seriously compromising its ideals and thus losing followers. That the religious left feels the need to put out such a distress call to the non-religious, however, suggests just how desperate the prospects for religious humanism have become. It is all but an admission that fundamentalism is now out of control.

Humanism is similarly on the defensive in other world religions. Catholicism has steadfastly maintained a conservative line on contentious issues such as abortion, contraception, priestly celibacy, and women priests, with the late Pope John Paul II refusing to heed the pleas of the modernisers within the church throughout his long period of office. Even the various paedophilia scandals that have come to light in the last few years across the Catholic world, trailing damaging lawsuits in their train (with many more planned to follow), have failed to embarrass the church enough for it to alter basic policy significantly. The election of Benedictus XVI to the papacy after John Paul II's death has further dashed the hopes of the modernisers, who would have wished for a more open-minded leader than his predecessor. Instead, they now find themselves faced with a doctrinal hard-liner who spent twenty-four years as head of the church's modern equivalent of the Inquisition, picking up the nickname of 'God's Rottweiler' for his uncompromising defence of orthodoxy along the way. Neither does Benedictus XVI have much time for doubt and scepticism, complaining that 'having a clear faith based on the creed of the church is often labelled today as fundamentalism. Relativism, which is letting oneself be tossed and swept along by every wind of teaching, looks like the only attitude acceptable to today's standards.'[18] Agonism does not get a look in.

For the time being Catholicism is in one of its more reactionary phases in recent history. Neither does it exhibit much sign of shifting from its line on what it takes to be fundamental issues, especially since most of its upper hierarchy, like Benedictus XVI himself, were appointed by the late pope precisely because of their conservative conception of church doctrine (we've already seen how paradigms can operate in a similarly protective way in science, with defenders of the faith there acting as gatekeepers). Reformers have been frozen out and can only watch helplessly as the church turns its back on dialogue.

The difficulty with such organisations as the Catholic church, where so much weight is put on tradition and the authority that derives from it, is that it can come to seem like an admission of defeat to change policy. Modernisers can so easily be cast as heretics under such a regime. If priestly celibacy has been right for so many centuries, how can it suddenly become wrong now? (Repeat with contraception policy, abortion, and an all-male priesthood, as required.) The church is not about to allow itself to be 'swept along by every wind of teaching' – which for most of us has the more positive connotation of being willing to listen to new ideas. While change can and does occur (Catholicism has finally absolved Galileo of heresy, for example, and even embraced Big Bang physics, as we saw in Chapter 4), the natural gravitation is towards preserving what went before and defending it to the last with all the tools at one's command. Positions are not given up lightly: the church prides itself on taking the long view of history. Galileo had to wait several centuries for his name to be cleared, after all.

In Islam, too, we note that the conservatives have been in the ascendancy in recent decades, and that humanist trends within the religion, much in evidence from the late nineteenth century onwards as an attempt to come to terms with Western colonialisation and its vastly superior technology, have been under growing threat.[19] At the very least humanism keeps a low profile within twenty-first-century Islam, as a series of countries, under considerable pressure from fundamentalist activists within their own ranks, experiment with the application of Shari'a law and the concept of theocracy (Saudi Arabia, Iran, and parts of Nigeria and Pakistan, for example; with Iraq being pushed in that direction by the anti-American insurgency movement). Islamism, as it has been called, is clearly the dominant force in the Islamic world at the moment, and it is difficult to see how a humanist dimension can be developed and maintained within such a hostile context. While such a dimension has been there in the past, it would be a brave individual or group who would argue strongly for it in Islam's heartlands at the moment: that way, repression surely lies. Although humanist overtures do still get made on occasion, it is significant that they usually come from outside the traditional Islamic world. One such example is the activist author and broadcaster Irshad Manji, based in Canada, whose book *The Trouble with Islam Today: A Wake-up Call for Honesty and Change*, has created shock waves throughout Islam – to the extent that she been dubbed 'Bin Laden's nightmare'.

The 'trouble with Islam', in Manji's view, is that it is insular, anti-semitic, resistant to new ideas, and suppresses women, leading the author to declare that 'I refuse to join an army of automatons in the name of Allah.'[20] She is unconvinced by claims of the Koran's supreme authority too, provocatively asking how we can read the book 'literally when it's so contradictory and ambiguous?'[21] Despite receiving death threats for such views, Manji has gone on to set up a campaign for the development of pluralism within the Islamic world, arguing that,

> No community, no ethnicity, no culture and no religion ought to be immune from respecting the universality of human rights. This, of course, is a controversial message in an age of cultural relativism. I truly believe we can become pluralists without becoming relativists. . . . If ever there was a moment for an Islamic reformation, it is now.[22]

This is all very encouraging, and the Bin Ladens of this world certainly deserve such nightmares, but it is being delivered from the West, and it remains to be seen how much impact it will have within traditional Islamic cultures with their tight hold on the populace's access to information and debate. Pluralism seems a distant dream there for the time being, although the existence of the Internet means that the ideas are at least there to be viewed.

It is the same problem that we find in Catholicism: a refusal to revise any practice that has been sanctioned by the potent combination of the sacred book and tradition. This is all the more unfortunate since modern scholarship, admittedly mainly Western, has begun to cast doubt on the authority for these practices. The wearing of the veil by women is taken to be one of the most fundamental requirements of Islam by the devout, and latterly the subject of a series of high profile court cases throughout Western Europe over the right to wear it (still bitterly contested in France, where it has become a big national political issue dividing the population). But a recent book by a German scholar, Christoph Luxenberg (an assumed name taken to protect himself), has argued that this may be the result of a mistranslation from Syrio-Aramaic, the most common language of the Middle East in both Christ's and Mohammed's lifetimes, into Arabic. According to Luxenberg, another possible translation of 'veil' would be 'belt'.[23] The implications of such a change for women's position within Islam could be enormous, but the current Islamic establishment is not exactly inclined to encourage such exegetical debates – tradition rules instead. Luxenberg may be wrong, of course, but we are unlikely to see his views subjected to the usual academic scrutiny. As far as the religious establishment goes, we are dealing with fundamentals in such cases and fundamentals are not open to interpretation.

Nor is this just a problem within Islam: Christianity has been bedevilled with translation problems from the beginning – most of them swept under the carpet by the authorities. It remains one of the great ironies of the Christian tradition that the Bible can be quoted with such authority, and accepted by so many believers as the unambiguous word of God and his chosen agents, when it is several times removed from its original language. The opportunity for error to creep in over the course of such a large document, compiled from such a wide variety of sources, is considerable – and most probably inevitable. The reliability of the eye-witness accounts that generated the gospels poses yet another set of problems, as even medieval theologians could admit on occasion (most notably Nicholas of Autrecourt, as we saw in Chapter 1). Such thoughts rarely cross the minds of the devout, however, who continue to believe their sacred text is a repository of literal truth to be called upon to solve any and all problems that may arise in their lives. It seems inconceivable to the sceptic that there could not be a considerable measure of doubt about the authenticity of both the original documents and their subsequent translations, but sadly that does seem to be so for a vast army of true believers for whom the Bible constitutes revealed truth.

Doubt is one of the most human of feelings, a constant backdrop to so many lives and one of the best ways most of us have for gaining a sense of proportion over our place in the world. How it is so easily excised by the faithful must remain a mystery to the sceptic.

Representing Religion

Representing Sikhism negatively had very unfortunate consequences for the playwright Gurpreet Kaur Bhatti, whose 'black comedy' *Behzti* (*Dishonour*), spurred the local Sikh community in the West Midlands area to take direct action to stop it being staged at the Birmingham Repertory Theatre in 2004. The opposition has gone as far as death threats against the author. In the play a young Sikh woman is the subject of sexual abuse by an older Sikh man, and after vociferous protests, largely by male Sikhs, the play was withdrawn from performance by an apologetic management. Sikhs are rarely represented on the British stage, and the protesters argued that it was unfair to single them out for such a negative portrayal in this instance. While there is a certain justification for the argument, minority groups being very susceptible to demonisation and rightly wary of that possibility, it does raise questions about whether censorship is the best way to deal with the issue. One could argue that the most effective way to respond would be to present a positive image in some other context; in other words, to enter into debate about cultural representation by showing the other side: there is nothing to stop such a move being made.

The response to the play raises also the dreaded concept of 'balance', as if all works of art had to present all possible viewpoints on an issue, without taking sides or exagerrating situations for dramatic effect (and to provoke debate). The notion of art as polemic is unsustainable if such demands are made – and some of the very best art over the course of history has been polemical in intent. It is not necessary to agree with such pieces; they are designed to make you think and respond – but to respond intellectually, not through violent action. Art would become very boring were it always balanced, and creative artists have to be given the licence to express minority views and to question the power relations in their society. This did not happen in Bhatti's case, and she became the victim of an overbearing belief system instead. There is more than a little irony in her comment about her personal approach to writing: 'I believe if your heart is in the right place, if you ask the right questions, if you make the right choices, anybody can write about anything.'[24] For that to be true, a respect must be shown for artistic choices, which plainly was not extended by the author's fellow Sikhs to *Behzti*.

Behzti has since gone on to win the Susan Smith Blackburn Prize, an American annual award for the best English-language play by a woman author. The author herself has put out a foreword to the play in which she eloquently defends her action in writing it, on the grounds that someone has to point out when Sikhism's ideals are not being upheld in practice:

> Truth is everything in Sikhism, the truth of action, the truth of an individual, God's truth. The heritage of the Sikh people is one of courage and victory over adversity. Our leaders were brave revolutionaries with the finest minds, warriors who propagated values of egalitarianism and selflessness. . . . Clearly the fallibility of human nature means that the simple Sikh principles of equality, compassion and modesty are sometimes discarded in favour of outward appearance, wealth and the quest for power. I feel that distortion in practice must be confronted and our great ideals must be restored. Moreover, only by challenging fixed ideas of correct and incorrect behaviour can institutionalised hypocrisy be broken down.[25]

The need for representing the bad side of human nature as well as the good has long been recognised by creative artists, but religion can be very intolerant when it is suggested that its officials are guilty of hypocrisy. In such cases, attacking believers is considered to equal attacking belief. Systems of belief in general do tend to put a lot of weight on 'outward appearance', and in Bhatti's view – one that will be shared by a majority of her writing peers, I am sure – it is the duty of the creative artist to dig 'beneath the surface of triumph' that is often presented by the guardians of any system.[26]

The protestors' refusal to allow this to be made public has even drawn condemnation from India, with the *Hindu* newspaper declaring that 'some will see the fact that the play's production has been brought to an end by this campaign of intimidation as some kind of victory. The reality is we all lose by it.'[27] While the sentiments are admirable, as I go on to discuss below they may owe as much to

India's volatile political situation, in which Sikhs and Hindus are often bitter opponents, as to any specific commitment to artistic freedom. Nevertheless, something very basic is at stake here, and yes, we *do* all lose by it eventually: the critical point being that all of us have to be given the same access to artistic freedom, and the same protection from campaigns of open intimidation. The fact that the artist is speaking from *within* the belief system being criticised ought to defuse the obvious objection of demonisation by outsiders, and inspire respect for her opinion.

In *Behzti*, the heroine, Min, is a thirty-three-year-old unmarried woman with an apparently carefree attitude, but whose family life has been marked by considerable sorrow. Her father has committed suicide, leaving her mother poverty-stricken and embittered with her lot in the Sikh community in the Midlands. The pair attend a festival at a local Sikh temple, where her mother seeks help from one of the officials, Mr Sandhu, in finding her daughter a marriage partner. Left alone with Mr Sandhu, Min is raped, after finding out that Mr Sandhu was a homosexual lover of her father. Mr Sandhu's proclivities are an open secret at the temple, and he is known to have raped young people of both sexes before. Eventually, he is murdered by Min's shocked mother and there is the suggestion that Min will recover from the ordeal and begin a relationship with Elvis, her mother's black home-care assistant. The play shifts sharply from comedy to tragedy in its closing stages, and paints a less than impressive picture of Sikh society in England in general, and Sikh manhood in particular. Min's eventual assessment of her compatriots is withering:

> Now I'm beginning to get why people walk around like they do with sallow skin and blinking eyes, not ever really looking at each other, because they can't face . . . they can't face . . . the sight. And my praising [of God], it's nothing to do with this . . . You know . . . I'm ever so glad I'm not you lot . . . cos it must be difficult, all that pretending all the time . . . Next time . . . if I still manage to praise . . . I'll tell him about you lot, perhaps he'll help. See if he can . . . yes . . . If I can . . . I'll ask him . . . for all of us.[28]

The fact that she turns away from her mother to Elvis at the end of the play is highly significant, as if she were rejecting what Sikh culture has become in England; in effect, turning her back on tradition.

Sikh activists have been involved in an even more violent protest since the events surrounding *Behzti*, this time against the Indian film *Jo Bole So Nihaal*. In May 2005, two cinemas in New Delhi showing the film, in which the Sikh hero is played by a Hindu actor, were bombed with the loss of several lives and a large toll of wounded. At one point in the film, the hero is pursued by scantily clothed women to an accompaniment of Sikh scriptures being recited. The fact that the film's title, which translates as 'those who call out to God will be blessed', is a phrase much used in Sikh temples has also angered the Sikh authorities, with the Shiromani Gurdwara Parbandhak Committee (Sikhism's highest-ranking religious council) calling for it to be altered, as well as for some offending scenes to be removed from the film. Again, the belief system has chosen to be both judge and jury when it comes to artistic representation, refusing to allow this to be a matter for the creative artists alone. Belief and believers simply conflate in such instances, with no adverse comment being permitted about either.

Granted, the politics involved is extremely complex, with Sikhism being very much a minority religion in India – 20 million adherents only out of a national population of over a billion – and having been in open conflict with the Indian government at various points in recent times.[29] But whether this excuses such hypersensitivity over the portrayal of one's religion in an aesthetic context is an altogether more contentious issue. It is hardly clear that there is much in the way of mockery going on in *Jo Bole So Nihaal* either. The Sikh hero foils an assassination attempt on the US president while in Manhattan, which only makes the episode seem all the more curious, since on the face of it this seems like a positive image to project of Sikhism (Third World anti-Americanism notwithstanding).

Christian fundamentalist groups are also not slow to bring pressure to bear against the arts community when they feel similarly offended. The televised production of Richard Thomas' and Stewart Lee's *Jerry*

Springer: The Opera on the BBC in 2005 prompted a large-scale protest on behalf of the organisation Christian Voice that gained a considerable amount of media coverage for several weeks before and after the screening. Christian Voice were objecting to the authors' portrayal of religion (Jesus as a homosexual, for example), as well as to the bad language that was prevalent throughout the production. There were 8,000 obscenities according to Christian Voice, fewer than 300 according to the BBC – the discrepancy aside, this is still a large number for television even in the latter count. As one of the protestors put it: 'There should be freedom of speech but there should never be freedom for desecration.'[30]

The scale of the protest was impressive, with 47,000 phone calls being made to the BBC in a very short period; although as one critical report put it, these days a reasonably computer-literate individual could engineer such a response on his or her own without too much difficulty.[31] One might also note that this is still a small percentage of an audience that was measured at 1.7 million. However it was done, the group did succeed in gaining a lot of publicity for their ideas, and, conversely, bad publicity for the BBC, even if they did not achieve their main objective of having the broadcast itself cancelled (and the audience turned out to be much higher than average for televised opera, apparently). Yet again, it was a clear attack on freedom of expression, which might well make the BBC think twice before taking such a risk with manifestly anti-religious material in the future. As a publicly funded institution the BBC is particularly vulnerable to such campaigns, and its political enemies are usually quick to take advantage of them: 'what is our licence fee being used for?', etc. Other broadcasting networks will no doubt have taken notice of the outcry as well.

Where such self-censorship might end no one knows. It cannot be good for the political health of the nation, however, if charges of blasphemy can still have such public resonance, with the National Director of Christian Voice, Stephen Green, portentously claiming that, 'if this is not blasphemy, nothing is' (one protestor's placard read the 'Blasphemy Broadcasting Corporation', just to ram the point home).[32] Neither is it good for our political health if the computer equivalent of a mob can constitute a significant factor in a debate about artistic expression. It is depressing to think that playing the blasphemy card can still generate such widespread support (or, and in this context this is much the same thing, at least the appearance of widespread support).

Belief, not Believers?

The government line on this, as I write, does little to dispel anxiety about the potentially damaging impact on free speech of the proposed new legislation. Fiona MacTaggart, the Home Office Minister for Race Equality and Community Cohesion, has repeated the standard mantra that it is believers not belief that will be protected, but she does so in such a way as to make one suspect the worst. Consider the following statement in a newspaper article, for example:

> The offence we propose will not prevent people from debating or ridiculing religions and beliefs as robustly as happens today. Evangelical Christians will still be free to preach the gospel and warn of the evils they perceive in other religions. We are not banning critical and offensive remarks or extending the law of blasphemy. The bill focuses on something very specific, namely the conduct of those who try to propagate hatred of people and communities because of their religion or belief.[33]

It appears that it will be acceptable for each religion to differentiate itself from other religions (even if they do regard other believers as heretics, and make this quite clear in their pronouncements): but what if one is an atheist, and wishes to reject any and all religions, indeed the religious impulse in general? There is no religious establishment or power base to hide behind or claim support from in such cases, and not much law to fall back on either, making one much more vulnerable to charges of causing offence from such organisations, which are not averse to using bullying tactics against critics.[34]

Then how is one to prove that in rejecting a belief one is *not* also rejecting believers – especially if the believers claim otherwise (and they are all but being invited to claim so under such legislation)? To criticise Islam these days in the UK is to seem to be criticising specific immigrant communities; to criticise Islamic fundamentalism is to be anti-Arab, since it is Arabs that are most closely identified with such views. And try being critical of Jewish fundamentalism without being perceived as anti-semitic; it is almost a reflex reaction from those on the receiving end (and a very effective tactic, since few will wish to have such a charge levelled against them, especially if they are on the left). Belief does not exist in a vacuum. Behind every belief is a believer capable of feeling aggrieved by attacks on their religion (such things only too easily become personal), particularly if these do descend into outright ridicule. The latter is most likely to be interpreted as blasphemy, however it is framed in complaint to the legal authorities by the offended parties. Religious critics run the risk of finding themselves being regarded as guilty until proved innocent in such a climate.

The example given by MacTaggart as to the kind of case the law specifically has been drawn up to deal with does not inspire much confidence either. Somewhat emotively, she instances the leader of a breakaway group from the National Front in the 1970s – the National Party – making approving remarks about the murder of a young Sikh by a gang of white youths: 'One down, 1 million to go.'[35] The judge ruled it was not illegal to voice such a view when a prosecution was brought against the National Party, but MacTaggart argues that, '[l]ike some of today's advocates of free expression, he [the judge] missed the point: the law does not proscribe opinions but prevents using them to create hatred of others'.[36] The particular case is a nasty one and the sentiments despicable, but the way it is presented here by MacTaggart makes it seem as if a defence of freedom of expression is also a defence of the murder that had occurred.

If one moves the issue to a more abstract realm of thought, we can ask how it can be proved that an opinion creates a particular response in others, or how one can guard against the misuse of an opinion by others. 'Hatred' is an emotive term too. One can appreciate what it means here, and agree that it is the right term to use, but be worried that any anti-religious comment at all might be interpreted this way, even if not intended to be. The distinction between ridicule and hatred might be extremely difficult to draw (another lawyer's paradise, one fears), with the addresser and addressee inhabiting different linguistic regimes. It is at the very least unclear what would count as acceptable ridicule, and if the two sides are as far apart as believers and non-believers by definition are, hard to work out how an accommodation can be reached, if ever. You say ridicule, I say hatred – stalemate.

Once again, however, the case chosen for comment puts the critic of religion on the defensive, although it is worth noting an aside from a *New Humanist* editorial regarding the British National Party and the issue of 'faith' schools: 'Here's a question for the Home Office and the Department of Education to consider: when does a belief become a faith?'[37] Quite: and one need look no further than America, and the Church of Jesus Christ Christian Aryan Nations, to see this particular combination in, deeply unpleasant, action.[38] Racism in this case has indeed been turned into a faith, with all the benefits such status brings with it in a Western democracy. If this were taken to its logical conclusion, it would become very difficult indeed to criticise the BNP or any similar extremist political grouping.

Even Satanism is now recognised as a religion by the British Navy, which after a recent test case has been forced to allow one of its sailors to worship on board ship according to his religion's demand that its believers practise excess. Where does that leave us in terms of the new legislation? Can we separate belief and believer here? At points like this we seem to have gone beyond satire, but one easily could imagine a very interesting court case being developed out of just such a situation. Once your belief is classified as a religion you can claim all the advantages this traditionally bestows on adherents (charitable status for starters); religion is still a protected species in a society such as ours. Neither is it all that difficult to start a religion in order to take advantage of the law. According to one commentator, America has become a 'divine supermarket', where religions are constantly being developed to meet consumer demand – and that demand shows no sign of decreasing.[39] If Scientology can become a religion, then surely anything can?

The Bounds of Satire

So what should the bounds of satire be? Perhaps a brief trip back into literary and artistic history might help us establish what is and what is not acceptable, and whether any rules of conduct can be drawn up for satire as a project. No one could satirise better than the eighteenth century, and no one could do it more viciously either. In the words of the literary historian David Nokes,

> The literature of the early eighteenth century, indeed the literature of the entire century from the Restoration of Charles II to the accession of George III, is dominated by satire. It would be difficult to find another comparable period of modern literary history whose tone was so firmly established by a single dominant genre.[40]

Nokes emphasises that eighteenth-century satire has specific social and political objectives, 'such as the exposure of scandal, the censure of hypocrisy, the punishment of vice or even the removal of ministers'.[41] No matter how unkind the satire may be, therefore, it has an underlying moral purpose that sustains it. In Alexander Pope's (1688–1744) summation, satire 'heals with Morals what it hurts with Wit', and as long as that can be said of it then it can be justified.[42] When it descends into personal abuse for its own sake, rather than with a larger moral or political point to make, then it loses its right to be defended. It ought to be what the person represents, rather than the person himself or herself, that is satirised. The satirised may not always be able to recognise that distinction, which is hardly surprising, but the larger audience must be. Satire is designed to spread doubt about authority, whether vested in the person or in the institution, and to mock its pretensions; that certainly fits the cause of scepticism.

Observing Pope wade into his contemporaries in works like *The Dunciad* (1728), however, can raise doubts about the purity of his moral intentions. He can be very wounding indeed, and one would not wish to be a target of his wit. The poetic establishment of the time is mercilessly mocked, relegated to the status of dunces, with first Lewis Theobald ('the Great Tibbald', 1688–1744) and then in a later version of the poem Colley Cibber (1671–1757) crowned as King Dunce by the goddess Dulness:

> High on a gorgeous seat, that far outshone
> Henley's gilt Tub, or Fleckno's Irish Throne,
> Or that, where on her Curlls, the Public pours
> All-bounteous, fragrant grains, and golden show'rs;
> Great Tibbald sate: The proud Parnassian sneer,
> The conscious simper, and the jealous leer,
> Mix on his look. All eyes direct their rays
> On him, and crowds grow foolish as they gaze.
> Not with more glee, by hands Pontific crown'd,
> With scarlet hats, wide waving, circled round,
> Rome in her Capitol saw Querno sit,
> Thron'd on sev'n hills, the Antichrist of Wit.[43]

Nokes points out that the Great Tibbald is only loosely connected to his ostensible inspiration: 'A study of the real-life Lewis Theobald would be of as much, or as little, significance as a study of John Dickens to an appreciation of Mr Micawber.'[44] Tibbald is to be regarded as an archetype of poetic dullness rather than a portrait of a specific individual, and hence a subject for the satirist of human pretension. But again, one wonders what it would be like to be on the receiving end, and whether being transferred to the status of an archetype would ease the ensuing pain and embarrassment. Pope's satire can sometimes leave an unpleasant aftertaste, with its innate assumption of superiority in both aesthetic and moral terms of reference: *he* can recognise 'the Antichrist of Wit', even if the unfortunate subject and his followers seemingly cannot.

For all its domination of the eighteenth-century literary scene, satire could also attract a great deal of criticism from contemporaries; as P. K. Elkin has noted, '[t]here was probably not a single Augustan writer who did not, at one time or other, warn against the dangers and ills resulting from its misuse'.[45] Elkin also points out that satire in the age 'served a bewildering variety of purposes', and could easily be confused in the public mind with more vulgar literary forms such as the lampoon.[46] Satirists felt compelled in consequence to defend their art, and Elkin traces the substantial body of writing produced to this end, where satirists were wont to claim the higher moral ground for their efforts. As one defender at the time put it: 'A *satire*, then, is commendable; a *lampoon*, scurrilous.'[47] Some of the claims made were, Elkin decides, 'absurdly grandiose', and ultimately he is not convinced by the vision of satire as a guide to moral correction.[48] Where its virtue lies, for this commentator, is in its ability 'to taunt and provoke' readers and make them examine their beliefs and prejudices.[49] On those grounds it is still eminently defensible.

The desire to taunt and provoke the audience is very evident in the work of Jonathan Swift (1667–1745), one of the most dedicated satirists of the age, whose *Gulliver's Travels* (1726) holds humanity's political, religious, and scientific pretensions up for savage ridicule – arguably at least as scurrilous as commendable in style. In the Laputa episode, for example, the mad experiments being conducted in the Grand Academy of Lagado into 'extracting Sunbeams out of Cucumbers' and reducing 'human Excrement to its original Food' (amongst many others) mock the Royal Society, which admittedly had some strange experiments of its own on record.[50] The conflict between the Big-endians and the Little-endians is an indictment of religious division, which in the previous century had been one of the factors involved in the English Civil War of the 1640s, and a source of considerable contention throughout the Restoration regime that followed, with nonconformists being persecuted for most of Charles II's reign (1660–85). In Lilliput, as Gulliver tells us, an edict is published by the Emperor 'commanding all his Subjects, upon great Penalties, to break the smaller End of their Eggs. The People so highly resented this Law, that our Histories tell us there have been six Rebellions raised on that account; wherein one Emperor lost his Life, and another his Crown'.[51] Then there are the disgusting, all too human-like Yahoos, so unfavourably compared to the equine Houyhnhnms. Swift's vision of the human race is deeply pessimistic: this is satire going well past the personal and the specific political circumstances of the age, and in that sense managing to transcend scurrility.

Athough it is gentler in tone – more ironic than vituperative, to use the critic Ronald Paulson's formula[52] – Henry Fielding's (1707–54) satire, like Swift's, encompasses most of humankind, who are seen to be motivated almost solely by self-interest unless their baser instincts are brought under control by a ruling elite for the common good. The main task of this elite is to prevent a collapse into public disorder, a seemingly permanent possibility in Fielding's world where few can be trusted to follow society's rules. As someone living through politically turbulent times, with the second Jacobite rebellion striking fear into the heart of the country's ruling class, Fielding's obsession with law and order is perfectly understandable. This is a nation after all which within a century had experienced a civil war (1640s), the 'Glorious Revolution' of 1688–9, and two Jacobite rebellions (1715, 1745): you did not have to look far to find large-scale public disorder.

Fielding's satire is based on a very low opinion of the human race, therefore, and does carry suggestions of assumed superiority yet again on the part of the author. The politics are conservative, and we cannot claim Fielding himself for the cause of scepticism and dissent – he is not exactly advocating a move to little narratives. Yet we can recognise the underlying moral agenda, and appreciate that Fielding can be just as satirical about his own social class of the aristocracy and landowners as he is about the lower orders of servants and peasants. Self-interest is what is being satirised, and that is a trait shared by almost all members of society – with such significant exceptions as Fielding's fictional hero Tom Jones. Tom's good nature is in striking contrast to those around him, particularly the corrupt and hypocritical world that he encounters in London society, 'the very worst of Places to be in without Money', where the aristocracy merely set a bad example by their many intrigues for the rest of the populace to imitate.[53]

It is an unflattering portrait that Fielding paints of human nature, and for all his humour and pointed wit there is a very serious objective behind his fiction: humankind must be kept in check if anarchy is to be avoided, and this is a permanent state of affairs needing to be addressed by the ruling authorities. Again, this is a satirical vision that transcends the merely personal. The author is sitting in judgement on the whole human race, and is not particularly impressed by its behaviour, nor inclined to give it much of the benefit of the doubt.

It is a striking point about so much eighteenth-century literary satire that its politics are so conservative, so often in the service of Britain's version of the *ancien régime*. The same might be said for arguably the greatest of twentieth-century British literary satirists, Evelyn Waugh, whose decidedly reactionary views – upper-class to a fault – are tempered by a willingness to attack his social peers as ruthlessly as he does anyone else. The upper class certainly do not come out well from Waugh's early fiction in particular (see *Decline and Fall* (1928) or *Vile Bodies* (1930), for example), and the author's misanthropy easily cuts across class barriers. It is that universal application that makes authors like these so useful for a sceptical project like ours. Even though they long for a world in which authority is both respected and respectable, a more 'moral' world than the one it is their misfortune to inhabit, they make it seem so unlikely that it will ever happen – given humankind's excess of failings and foibles, so gleefully catalogued by the authors in question – that authority in general is effectively discredited. Their satire has as much to say to radicals as to reactionaries – arguably even more, since the former start from an anti-authoritarian position anyway, and are keen to find reinforcement from whatever source they can. If the ruling class are such fools as they appear, then why grant them any political legitimacy? Why not just dispense with them altogether? On both sides there is a desire to amend morals, if for very different ideological ends.

However motivated, satire is an important contributor to the political in its role as the watchdog of politics and politicians. Sceptics will want to cultivate it, no matter what its underlying political affiliation may be: it spreads doubt about the basis for authority, as well as authority's justification for its actions.

Satire becomes much more personal when we move to the end of the eighteenth century and the political caricature of James Gillray (1757–1815) and Thomas Rowlandson (1756–1827). In the former's work particularly the depictions of politicians and the monarchy can be quite vicious, with scurrility often well to the fore (as one commentator has put it, Rowlandson lacks Gillray's 'savagery'[54]). The high and mighty of the period are made to appear foolish, vain, and all too human; hardly worth the public's respect at all. Gillray unashamedly invokes the personal, his art consisting of 'seizing upon a person's outstanding physical characteristic and exaggerating it to the point of ridicule. Thus if the subject has a long nose, strech it by a foot; if his belly is large, make it elephantine.'[55] This treatment is meted out to such notables of the period as George III (1738–1820), the Prince of Wales (later George IV; 1762–1830) and his circle, and the politicians William Pitt the Younger (1759–1806) and Charles Fox (1749–1806). For all the wit and humour, Gillray's work can be very dark indeed, very much the product of a man who 'scarcely knew the meaning of the word "morality", and appears to have believed that mankind was beyond redemption' (in clear contrast to his illustrious predecessor William Hogarth (1697–1764)).[56] Perhaps we have reached the very bounds of satire with this figure.

The *Guardian* cartoonist Steve Bell is a modern-day equivalent of Gillray, as little persuaded by the sincerity of politicians and the monarchy as his predecessor. His caricatures of Margaret Thatcher and Tony Blair as power-crazed beings offer a particularly jaundiced view of British public life (note the mad, staring eyes in each case), and the monarchy fare little better at his hands. While Bell can become very harsh on occasion, there is no doubt that he has been conspicuously successful in tapping into the deep vein of distrust of public figures that has grown up in recent times (one of the signs of a postmodern world, as many cultural theorists would have it, and a positive one for that constituency too). If you are on the left in Britain, then Steve Bell is certainly a critical part of the political landscape – for a while in the 1980s, with the Labour party in considerable disarray and seemingly unable to offer any realistic challenge to the ruling Conservatives, he almost felt like the official opposition.[57]

Nokes makes a point of drawing some parallels between eighteenth-century satire and more recent examples in our own times, such as *Private Eye* and *Spitting Image* (and we can add Steve Bell's efforts to that list, as just indicated), in order to show that the techniques of the former can seem less 'remote when translated into the terms of a modern mass culture'.[58] The 'satire boom' of the 1960s in Britain – *That Was the Week That Was*, etc. – can be seen to extend into our own time, and to be no less politically aware, no less concerned to spread doubt about the pretensions of authority and to effect a change in public consciousness. At its best, as in the eighteenth century, the satire of our own day seeks 'the exposure of scandal, the censure of hypocrisy, the punishment of vice or even the removal of ministers' – and is to be applauded for doing so. The long-running television panel game *Have I Got News for You*, for example, takes a very irreverent attitude towards public figures that recalls eighteenth-century practices in its robustness. In the USA, Jon Stewarts cult television programme, *The Daily Show*, has for several years now provided a running satirical commentary on the American political scene, with particular attention being paid to the Bush administration. Those in power will never like being subjected to this treatment, but it is an important element of an agonistic pluralist society none the less, as sceptics will be the first to insist.

What ought to be out of bounds is the personal, with the public role of the figures in question being the proper target for satire. Eighteenth-century satire suggests that it is not always that easy to draw the line between the two areas (and that some satirists hardly even bother to try), but it is the more generalised satire that probably survives best now rather than the historically specific. Both Fielding and Swift still have something to say to us in that regard (more so as far as the general public is concerned than Pope, for all his poetic brilliance), and do seem to be deploying their wit in the service of a moral ideal, expecting more of the human race than it is currently delivering in terms of its conduct. The most effective satire casts doubt on belief systems and ideologies rather than the individuals who subscribe to these, helping to develop a climate of iconoclasm. Having said that, it is human beings who create belief systems and put them into operation and sustain them, so this can never be the most precise of distinctions: nevertheless, we can see where the bias should lie.

Societies are all the healthier when doubt is an integral part of their systems. In the Conclusion we can go on to speculate how the university sector and the media could play more prominent roles in the production of doubt and scepticism within our culture.

Conclusion: The Sceptic Fights Back

I trust that this book has demonstrated there is more than enough justification for a concerted campaign on behalf of scepticism and reasonable doubt in our society – and that Pyrrhonism, agonistic pluralism, and soft scepticism can combine to give us the basis to wage that campaign. There is too much at stake to be lukewarm about this either, too much unquestioning belief around that seriously could erode the hard-won gains of Enlightenment and post-Enlightenment culture: personal freedom, to put it at its most basic. I will end by emphasising the key role that the university system could play in such an endeavour – and also by asking for a greater contribution from our media, which are all too often subject to manipulation by the politically and economically powerful. The media are considerably in thrall to the imperialist claims of science and technology as well – 'oh, brave new world' and all that, the basis for countless television and radio programmes and newspaper features asking us to marvel at the wonders uncovered by science.

Ultimately, the call I am making, as the representative sceptic, is for less belief and more doubt in global culture and a rolling back of the forces of both traditional authority and multinational-led techno-science. As we discussed in Chapter 4, the latter is often just as much the preserve of the true believer, and just as concerned to remove doubt from the public agenda in order to safeguard its power over us. It is time to initiate a new age of doubt and scepticism to replace the tide of dogma that is threatening to engulf us. This is taking scepticism in its widest possible sense, although excluding mere suspicion (of the other, other ways of life, etc.). There is the basis for at least a measure of cultural optimism in such a project, a new Pyrrhonism in effect, and I intend to end on an optimistic note: there is more than enough cultural pessimism around at the moment without adding to it. Let's use all the means available to promote scepticism and ensure that it is seen to be a positive, life-enhancing attitude to adopt; the natural way to act in a democracy, with the philanthropic intent of Sextus very much to the fore.

The Academy and Scepticism

How might universities promote the cause of scepticism? Universities are the natural home of scepticism, since they exist not just to disseminate knowledge but to scrutinise all claims to knowledge – and to do so as rigorously as possible. This critical function is absolutely central to the university's role in public life, and even if universities sometimes do fall into the trap of defending paradigms past their sell-by date, the ideal tends to reassert itself eventually. When it comes to the humanities and social sciences, it is arguably the case that developing a sceptical sensibility in students is more important than the subject matter that is being imparted in any individual discipline. It is often said that knowledge is power, but it might be more correct to say that *thinking* is power. Now that we have entered an era of mass higher education, this is where the academy can make a really meaningful contribution to the realm of the 'political'. The more graduates who emerge from the university system with a commitment to scepticism towards ideas (all ideas, scientific ones included), possessing an ability to think against the grain of tradition and received opinion, the less of a catchment area there will be for the advocates of unquestioning belief to go to work in. More sceptical response equals less success for authoritarianism, and that can only be to society's future good. Scepticism is an attitude of mind that can be taught, and universities provide the best available context in present-day culture for that process to take place: the response to dogmatism ought to start there if anywhere.

There are barriers to fostering scepticism within the university system, however, that need to be considered, and these are the product of a significant shift in funding mechanisms in the sector in recent years. The more that commercial principles, dragging in the free market ethos in their wake, are applied to academe, as is increasingly the case these days, the more the sceptical project is threatened and rendered subservient to ideology. This is particularly so when it comes to research. Research in the British university system is increasingly required to find external funding, and this can alter its character dramatically. To a large extent, external funding has always been necessary in the sciences, given that they often demanded extra equipment and resources that universities were financially unable to provide. Science research can be extremely expensive and has had to establish close links with industry in consequence. One unfortunate side effect of this is that a great deal of research in the science area is either directly or indirectly connected to the defence industry, which is invariably awash with money (this being a priority area for most governments). This has been a point of contention within the system itself for some time. Scientists with a conscience on this issue, and there are a significant number, can be placed in some difficult situations and face some difficult career choices in consequence.

What has changed in recent years is that the humanities have been forced to adopt the same approach, required to win external funding and even expected to show a profit on their research activities. Even more alarmingly, a whole new tier of management has emerged rapidly to deal with this new regime, and to exhort academics to comply with its demands. This hardly encourages criticism of the dominant ideology, nor of the free market principles that underpin it. The tendency instead is to speak the language of the funders, as the managers most certainly do, and so reinforce their power base. There is a real danger of highly speculative research ('blue sky') being squeezed out in favour of more obviously utilitarian projects with commercially exploitable content. When one's career prospects are directly linked to success in winning external funding, with academic promotion increasingly coming to depend on this factor, then the pressure is really on to avoid taking chances and start following the money instead.

Once the funding is dictating the character of the research, it is more likely that the researchers will be drawn into the free market net, becoming more concerned with financial outcomes than the validity, status, or cultural role of the ideas being explored. Funding soon becomes the assumed criterion of success, and many practitioners in the field suspect that it is becoming the only criterion that really matters to university managements – a new gold standard in a more sinister sense of the term. Expressing scepticism about the market fundamentalist ethos is not the way to go about attracting research funding from the private sector, and if humanities subjects in general have to curb their sceptical temper to fit in with the new regime then it merely entrenches the free market system and its hold on the popular consciousness. When universities become businesses, they can so easily cease to be truly critical voices within their culture. This is a trend which must be not just monitored, but actively resisted by those of sceptical outlook. When there are vested interests to placate, belief tends to go unquestioned (or at least *under*-questioned anyway, with prudent self-censorship kicking in), which is all to the benefit of the empire in question.

As an example of what the humanities must avoid, there is the current state of medical research to be considered. Complaints are increasingly being voiced within British and American medical circles about the role of the drug companies in this enterprise. Drug companies not only initiate and provide funding for a huge number of clinical trials, but are quite capable of suppressing findings that contradict their claims for their products or that they think in any way embarrassing to their public image. British and American medical councils and journals often express misgivings about this state of affairs, but there is a real fear within the profession that its intellectual autonomy has been badly compromised by the aggressively pursued sponsorship policies of the drug empire. Many researchers in consequence feel themselves to be engaged in a constant battle to preserve the integrity of the medical discipline within the university system.

Fostering scepticism within the research area in higher education must become a priority, therefore, for anyone concerned to challenge the insidious spread of dogmatism within Western public life. As far as possible universities should be outside the ruling establishment, constantly scrutinising and contesting authority rather than helping to uphold it through promoting the doctrine of commercialisation, or serving the interests of any particular political elite. Universities surely ought to be part of the 'political' rather than a mere branch of institutional politics; a forum for free debate rather than a mouthpiece for the authorities; a permanent source of critique from within the system, with an open-ended brief to keep it under surveillance for the greater good.

Trying to maintain an optimistic note, despite rapidly encroaching commercialism and managerialism, as well as considerable government pressure to embrace the free market as its future, there are still substantial reserves within academic life, particularly within the humanities area, to build on in order to ensure that scepticism remains a significant force in our intellectual life. Suspension still has its advocates, who will see it as a public duty to continue outlining its virtues and putting its methods into practice, as philosophers from Sextus through Hume have been encouraging us to do. The commitment to dissent is not dead yet, although one suspects the ruling authorities would be much happier if it were – such is the nature of all empires, to close down opposition, and to strive to keep it closed down.

It is to be hoped that scepticism could be fostered in the Islamic university system as well, drawing on the tradition of scepticism that we have noted is certainly there within the Islamic philosophical tradition – even if it does tend to be hostage to belief in the main (as, to be fair, it was also in the Christian world until quite recently, as we saw with Descartes at the birth of modern Western philosophy). There really ought to be much more contact between the humanities and social science departments in the two systems than there currently is; much more dialogue about methods of thought and analysis, and about the universty's role in the community. The sense of mutual distrust of each other's culture that marks out Western–Islamic relations at present urgently needs to be dispelled, and communication at the level of ideas seems a particularly good place to start the process. The relationship of the academy to belief could usefully be debated across the cultural divide.

Again, this needs to be approached in a positive way, such that the benefits to each system of dialogue are apparent. Our own ideas about democracy need to be kept fluid if we are to convince the other side that we are not attempting a take-over of their institutional ethos in a new imperialist initiative. But this should not pose a problem: like all ideas, democracy has to be kept under constant scrutiny and open to change. Postmodern scepticism towards institutional authority is a phenomenon we can point to in order to demonstrate that radical questioning of the political system does indeed take place, and much of the impetus for this comes from within academe. The 'wind of teaching' may not be to the liking of the new pope and the current Catholic church hierarchy (or to such neoconservatives as Francis Fukuyama, for whom the end of history is nigh), yet it is precisely what ideology needs constantly to be exposed to if it is to be kept honest. And where better than the university system, for all its flaws and regrettable commercial and managerial trends at present, to foster the process? I would repeat the point made earlier that universities are not there to shore up particular regimes or intellectual paradigms, but to scrutinise and challenge received ideas and systems of belief. They would be failing in their public duty were they to neglect to do this on a permanent basis.

Voices are beginning to be raised within the Muslim world for the kind of contact I am suggesting. The Aga Khan University in the UK, for example, ran a conference in London in 2005 about the future of Muslim universities around the world. The director of the university's Institute for the Study of Muslim Civilisations, Abdou Filali-Ansary, has emphasised the need for a historical rather than religious-based approach to the Institute's work: 'We want to look at Muslims in their diversity, different languages and cultures and historical processes. It's an alternative to some existing programmes in the Muslim world, which look at norms, but not at facts.'[1] Tariq Ramadan has made a similar observation about Muslim life in the West: 'there is a great difference between historical models and universal principles, and today everything is proving that the formalistic imitation of models in an age other than one's own is in fact the betrayal of principles'.[2]

The conference itself debated teaching and research methods within the Muslim system, with a view to encouraging a more critical approach by practitioners. Reform was high on the agenda, with another senior member of the Institute insisting that it was necessary to look closely at 'the cultural forces fostering or hindering the reform activities' in Muslim universities.[3] The laudable objective, as with Ramadan, is to preserve Islam's principles at the expense of an uncritical imitation of its tradition. Perhaps this is a beginning of a reawakening of the sceptical strain within Islamic thought? If so, it is a welcome development.

Scepticism and the Media

The media can be asked to make a greater contribution to the project of creating a sympathetic climate for scepticism and doubt. Commercialism and managerialism are rife within this area too, and in general the profit motive works against the sceptical impulse and dissent. Nevertheless, the latter can still find room for expression, depending on how it is packaged. Satire, as noted in Chapter 6, can be a powerful vehicle for counter-cultural sentiments, and the broadcast media in particular should be encouraged to be sympathetic to such material, even if it involves taking some risks on their part. Essentially, I am speaking here about the relationship between creative artists and the media, and the extent to which the former group are given their head in challenging the establishment and dominant ideology of our culture.

What the broadcast media must never do, however, is to give in to the campaigns of pressure groups, whether religiously or politically motivated, to prevent belief systems from being satirised or in other ways having their integrity or validity called into question. Better that we have several *Jerry Springers* than an absence of debate; better that the notion of blasphemy is constantly challenged than silently accepted as a curb on freedom of speech. When plays suffer the fate of *Behzti*, perhaps that is a reason for seeking wider exposure on national television or radio to take the fight back to the dogmatists? The censorship lobby within the religious community has to be resisted at every turn, and the broadcast media will be in the front line of this struggle. They should be supported vigorously by all campaigners for scepticism. The distinction between believer and belief needs to be tested, and tested regularly, by creative artists (writers, producers, directors), and the media ought to be prepared to follow the gut instincts of those artists. Universities can initiate such debates, and produce sceptically minded individuals to keep pressing away at them; but when it comes to bringing these issues to the attention of the wider public, then the media are in a uniquely powerful position and should be cultivated accordingly.

We could certainly do, too, with more questioning of the scientific and technological enterprises by the broadcast media. In the main, the latter tend to be over-respectful. While some investigative journalism does occur on topical subjects like cloning, the notion of science as a belief system could come in for more searching examination. This is particularly so when it comes to techno-science, where the profit motive drives the science. GM crop experimentation on oilseed rape has led to claims of the emergence of a 'superweed' which is apparently resistant to herbicide.[4] Scientists had considered this to be a remote possibility, and no doubt were acting in good faith in conducting the trials. But we are unlikely to have gone down this road so far and so quickly without pressure from a techno-scientific establishment seeking yet another source of profit. Even though some scientists have criticised the press coverage as sensational, this is still a worrying phenomenon.[5] Once again, until a very advanced stage science has been given the benefit of the doubt and not monitored as closely as it might have been; not subjected to enough doubt and scepticism. We certainly need much more media questioning of the techno-scientific ethic, and a greater sense of scepticism being encouraged about its rationale and objectives. 'Oh brave new world' is no longer a viable response: techno-science cannot always be trusted to know what is best for humankind.

The national newspaper set-up in the UK today can give the appearance of pluralism in action. The spectrum of political positions covered is fairly wide, although it is weighted towards a centre-right outlook and can hardly be described as revolutionary or radical. Support rarely strays ouside the three main political parties, as represented in Parliament, which, as we've noted before, can come to look like a monolithic bloc to radicals and dissenters outside the official channels. Nevertheless, various competing sub-ideologies are offered for inspection, although the scope for 'conversion' of the newspapers themselves to other viewpoints has to be seen as very limited. Whether the press succeed in turning antagonism into agonism is another question. Too often there is a party line in operation in most national newspapers which discourages examination of their own position and a fair assessment of others. We could do with a measure of soft scepticism across the reporting front: arguing from a position, but without dogmatic emphasis. It ought to be possible to have convictions but to be open-minded at the same time; possible not to sound as if one had an easy answer to all political problems. An acknowledgement that certainty is a rare phenomenon in human relations would be a useful start.

Newspapers certainly need to be challenged on their 'special interest' scepticism. Euroscepticism, as we have seen, is too often a cover for prejudice and reactionary politics, which merely increases the 'democratic deficit'. That kind of populism is to be deplored, and merely substitutes one kind of authority for another – precisely what a sceptic wishes above all to avoid. Arguments against religion need to guard against lapsing into prejudice as well. It's all too easy for this to happen these days when discussing Islam. Islamic fundamentalism is a problem, yes, but so is every other kind of religious dogmatism; something which is not always made clear in the popular press in the West. It's not the other we have to fear, but the dogmatist. Cures by argument are what the current situation calls for, not emotional appeals to deep-seated cultural prejudices which merely fuel the growth of dogmatism further.

Scepticism: Generosity, Optimism, and Fighting Back

Overall, scepticism ought to develop a trait of generosity within us. There are more reasons to doubt what we believe than to treat it as gospel; more reasons to be circumspect in acting on our beliefs than to adopt an authoritarian or dogmatic stance over them which precludes opposition. Scepticism ought to prevent the development of prejudice against others, to encourage a sense of doubt about our own judgement and its sources, to be the bedrock of pluralism. Our own position is never any more than provisional, as even the most committed supporter of agonistic pluralism would have to admit – conversion always has to remain a live possibility, even if it is one we shall argue against for as long as we can. It is an argument to be prosecuted with an open mind, however, rather than dogmatically. None of us can assume that our belief system will hold good for ever, or that it is beyond challenge from others, beyond reasonable doubt as to the claims it makes. We need to retain the humility of the true Pyrrhonist, recognising that all of us face the same problem and should therefore keep a sense of proportion about our claims – social, political, theological, metaphysical, or whatever else. Sextus' philanthropic attitude applies across humanity, as do the virtues of suspension. More doubt, more scepticism, more suspension – those are the goals.

That is not, however, by any means the same thing as saying that 'anything goes'. We've considered a wide range of beliefs throughout this book, some of them claiming to be 'scepticisms' in their own right, that patently do not 'go': creationism (both Young and Old Earth varieties), Euroscepticism, global warming scepticism, Holocaust denial, fascism in any of its forms. None of these shows generosity towards opposing views. In fact, they are designed to stamp out all opposing views, to which they do not grant any credibility whatsoever. Debate is an irrelevance to such interest groups, as it is to most religions: suspension only applies to others. Scepticism as it is being defended in these pages, however, is about continuing the debate over belief, ensuring that neither one's opponents nor one's supporters ever take up residence in the intellectual comfort zone; never certain that they, and they alone, are in possession of 'the truth', which can then be imposed unilaterally on everyone else. Incalculable harm can be done when people do believe the latter. Sceptics are duty bound to do all that they can, using all the media at their disposal, to limit the scope for that state of affairs to occur, and to make it clear that there is a whole range of hypotheses we just do not need any more, hypotheses that do far more harm than good, and that can be discredited if we work away at them enthusiastically enough. 'To cure by argument' must always be the goal.

But the sceptic must set about the activity of 'curing' with a sense of generosity, and also of optimism: dogmatism can be challenged, dogmatists can be made to climb down. If the Holy Ghost is indeed not a sceptic, that is all the more reason for us to be (if that is blasphemy, then I'm quite happy to own up to it). We have to believe that it is still all to play for, and scepticism, with its long cultural history of being the irritant to all belief systems, philosophy's very own internal critique, is uniquely qualified to lead the fight-back that the times demand. Scepticism is in humanity's best interests: the representative sceptic rests his case.

Notes

Introduction: Empires of Belief, Campaigns for Scepticism

1 See my *Fundamentalist World: The New Dark Age of Dogma*, Cambridge: Icon Books, 2004, for more on the workings of these various fundamentalisms. Francis Wheen also deals with this issue in *How Mumbo-Jumbo Conquered the World: A Short History of Modern Delusions*, London: Fourth Estate, 2004.

2 Jeremy Seabrook, *Consuming Cultures: Globalization and Local Life*, Oxford: New Internationalist Publications, 2004, p. 4.

3 The Vatican's intervention in the 2005 Italian referendum on the laws surrounding infertility treatment is a case in point. The pope called for Catholics to abstain from voting in order to prevent the referendum from reaching the necessary threshold of participation to be valid – and was successful in his plea.

4 For a detailed analysis of the rise of religious fundamentalism, see Malise Ruthven, *Fundamentalism: The Search for Meaning*, Oxford: Oxford University Press, 2004.

5 Fundamentalism is the term coined to describe the content of *The Fundamentals* (A. C. Dixon, ed. [1910–15], New York and London: Garland, 1988), a series of pamphlets published in America setting out the principles of evangelical Christian belief, principles taken to be so 'fundamental' as to be beyond any possible doubt or need for interpretation by believers. It is worth noting that the Islamic world tends to reject

the notion that it can be fundamentalist, regarding the term as applicable to Christians only. Although that is a fair point, in the West fundamentalism has become a blanket term for all kinds of religious extremism.

6 Stuart Sim, *Contemporary Continental Philosophy: The New Scepticism*, Aldershot and Burlington, VT: Ashgate, 2000, p. 2.

7 Sextus Empiricus, *Outlines of Scepticism*, trans. Julia Annas and Jonathan Barnes, Cambridge: Cambridge University Press, 1994, p. 72.

8 Richard H. Popkin, *The History of Scepticism from Erasmus to Spinoza*, Berkeley, Los Angeles, and London: University of California Press, 1979, p. xiii. This book is an extended version of the author's earlier *The History of Scepticism from Erasmus to Descartes*, New York: Humanities Press, 1964.

9 Richard H. Popkin, *The History of Scepticism from Erasmus to Spinoza*, p. xv.

10 Ibid.

11 Christopher Hookaway, *Scepticism*, London and New York: Routledge, 1990, p. 145.

12 Martin Keeley, quoted in Fred Pearce, 'Climate Change: Menace or Myth?', *New Scientist*, 12 February 2005, pp. 38–43 (p. 40).

13 See Jean-François Lyotard, *The Postmodern Condition: A Report on Knowledge* [1979], trans. Geoff Bennington and Brian Massumi, Manchester: Manchester University Press, 1984.

14 Brian Brivati, 'Invasion Reduced to the Threat of Terror', *Guardian*, 12 July 2005, p. 22.

15 M. F. Burnyeat, 'The Sceptic in his Place and Time', in Richard H. Popkin and Charles B. Schmitt, eds, *Scepticism from the Renaissance to the Enlightenment*, Weisbaden: Harrassowitz, 1987, pp. 13–43 (p. 14).

1 Scepticism: A Brief Philosophical History

1 C. H. Whiteley, 'Epistemological Strategies', *Mind*, 78 (1969), pp. 25–34 (p. 26).

2 Mohsen Sazegara, 'Floodgates of Reform', *New Humanist*, May/June 2005, pp. 12–14 (p. 13).

3 Quoted in Ewen MacAskill, 'UK Fears a Return to the Bad Old Days in Iran', *Guardian*, 27 June 2005, p. 14.

4 Fouad Zakarayyi, *Myth and Reality in the Contemporary Islamist Movement*, trans. Ibrahim M. Abu Rabi, London: Pluto Press, 2005.

5 Jonathan Barnes, *The Toils of Scepticism*, Cambridge: Cambridge University Press, 1990, p. ix.

6 Julia Annas and Jonathan Barnes, *The Modes of Scepticism: Ancient Texts and Modern Interpretations*, Cambridge: Cambridge University Press, 1985, p. 8.

7 See Jonathan Barnes, *The Toils of Scepticism*.

8 For a full discussion of these, see Julia Annas and Jonathan Barnes, *The Modes of Scepticism*.

9 Sextus Empiricus, *Outlines of Scepticism*, p. 4.

10 Ibid., p. 5.

11 Richard H. Popkin, *The History of Scepticism from Erasmus to Spinoza*, Berkeley, Los Angeles, and London: University of California Press, 1979, p. xi. There are interesting parallels to be drawn between Pyrrhonism and deconstruction, which similarly claims not to be a method as such but a tactic for undermining all philosophical positions, including its own: 'deconstruction, as I have often had to insist, is not a discursive or theoretical affair, but a practico-political one, and it is always produced within the structures . . . said to be institutional' (Jacques Derrida, *The Post Card: From Socrates to Freud and Beyond* [1980], trans. Alan Bass, Chicago and London: University of Chicago Press, 1987, p. 508).

12 Sextus Empiricus, *Outlines of Scepticism*, p. 216.

13 Richard H. Popkin, *The History of Scepticism from Erasmus to Spinoza*, p. xi.

14 R. J. Hankinson, *The Sceptics*, London and New York: Routledge, 1995, p. 306.

15 See Michel de Montaigne, *The Complete Essays*, trans. and ed. M. A. Screech, Harmondsworth: Penguin, 2003, pp. 489–683.

16 Richard H. Popkin, *The History of Scepticism from Erasmus to Spinoza*, p. 18.

17 Quoted in ibid., p. 7.

18 François Rabelais, *Gargantua and Pantagruel* [1532, 1534], trans. J. M. Cohen, Harmondsworth: Penguin, 1955, p. 389.

19 René Descartes, *Philosophical Writings*, revised edition, trans. and eds Elizabeth Anscombe and Peter Thomas Geach, London: Thomas Nelson, 1970, p. 76.

20 Christopher Hookaway, *Scepticism*, London and New York: Routledge, 1990, p. 41.

21 Bernard Williams, *Descartes: The Project of Pure Enquiry*, Penguin: Harmondsworth, 1978, p. 162.

22 Christopher Hookaway, 'Scepticism, History of', in Ted Honderich, ed., *The Oxford Companion to Philosophy*, Oxford: Oxford University Press, 1995, pp. 797–9 (p. 798).

23 David Hume, *Dialogues and Natural History of Religion* [1779, 1757], ed. J. C. A. Gaskin, Oxford: Oxford University Press, 1993, p. 161.

24 Ibid., p. 179.

25 David Hume, *A Treatise of Human Nature* [1739], ed. D. G. C. Macnabb, Glasgow: Fontana/Collins, 1962, p. 216.

26 Ibid., pp. 300, 301.

27 Ibid., p. 301.

28 Ibid., pp. 301, 302.

29 David Hume, *Dialogues and Natural History*, p. 36.

30 It was Averroes' commentaries on Aristotle that sparked the revival of interest in Greek philosophy in medieval Europe, where Aristotle soon became the most feted of classical thinkers – 'the philosopher', as he reverentially came to be styled.

31 Arthur Hyman and James J. Walsh, eds, *Philosophy in the Middle Ages: The Christian, Islamic, and Jewish Traditions*, Indianapolis, IN: Hackett Publishing, 1973, p. 263.

32 Al-Ghazali, *Deliverance from Error*, in *The Faith and Practice of Al-Ghazali*, trans. W. Montgomery Watt, Lahore: Sh. Muhammad Ashraf, 1963, pp. 19–85 (p. 25).

33 Ibid., pp. 30, 43.

34 Arthur Hyman and James J. Walsh, *Philosophy in the Middle Ages*, p. 264.

35 Diane Collinson, Robert Wilkinson, and Katherine Plant, *Fifty Key Eastern Thinkers*, London and New York: Routledge, 1999, p. 39.

36 Al-Ghazali, *The Incoherence of the Philosophers* [c. 1100], trans. Michael E. Marmara, Provo, UT: Brigham Young University Press, 1997, p. 2.

37 Ibid.

38 Ibid., p. 3.

39 Introduction to ibid., p. xv.

40 Quoted in Majid Fakhry, *Islamic Philosophy, Theology and Mysticism: A Short Introduction*, Oxford: Oneworld, 1997, p. 35 (insertion of 'Arabic' in quote by Fakhry).

41 Quoted in ibid., p. 36.

42 Ibid., p. 3.

43 Ninian Smart, *Doctrine and Argument in Indian Philosophy*, Atlantic Highlands, NJ: Humanities Press, 1976, p. 16.

44 Ibid., p. 15.

45 Edward Conze, *Buddhist Thought in India: Three Phases of Buddhist Philosophy*, Ann Arbor, MI: University of Michigan Press, 1967, p. 208.

46 For some, Nagarjuna's work prefigures deconstruction. See Robert Magliola, *Derrida on the Mend*, West Lafayette, IN: Purdue University Press, 1984.

47 Frederick J. Streng, *Emptiness: A Study in Religious Meaning*, Nashville, NY: Abingdon Press, 1967, p. 43.

48 Robert Magliola, *Derrida on the Mend*, p. 87.

49 Nagarjuna, *Fundamentals of the Middle Way*, trans. Frederick J. Streng, '1. An Analysis of Conditioning Clauses', paras 2, 7; Appendix A, in Frederick J. Streng, *Emptiness*, pp. 183–220 (p. 183).

50 Frederick J. Streng, *Emptiness*, p. 169.

51 Nagarjuna, *Averting the Arguments*, trans. Frederick J. Streng, para 70; Appendix B, in Frederick J. Streng, *Emptiness*, pp. 222–7 (p. 227).

52 Karl Potter, *Presuppositions of India's Philosophies*, Westport, CT: Greenwood Press, 1972, p. 241.

53 Arthur Hyman and James J. Walsh, *Philosophy in the Middle Ages*, pp. 654, 656.

54 Nicholas of Autrecourt, *Letters to Bernard of Arezzo* [c.1338], in ibid., pp. 656–64 (pp. 658, 659).

55 Ibid., p. 661.

56 Julius R. Weinberg, *Nicolaus of Autrecourt: A Study in Fourteenth Century Thought*, Princeton, NJ: Princeton University Press, 1948, p. 101.

57 George Berkeley, *Three Dialogues Between Hylas and Philonous, In Opposition to Sceptics and Atheists* [1713], in *The Works of George Berkeley*, I–IX, eds A. A. Luce and T. E. Jessop, London: Thomas Nelson, 1949–58, II, pp. 165–263 (p. 172).

58 Ibid., p. 261.

59 Ibid., p. 173.
60 Ibid., p. 212.
61 Ludwig Wittgenstein, *On Certainty*, trans. Denis Paul and G. E. M. Anscombe, eds G. E. M. Anscombe and G. H. von Wright, Oxford: Blackwell, 1974, paras 211, 151.
62 Ibid., para. 105.
63 Barry Stroud, *The Significance of Philosophical Scepticism*, Oxford: Clarendon Press, 1984, p. viii.
64 Hilary Putnam, *Reason, Truth and History*, Cambridge: Cambridge University Press, 1981, p. 7.
65 Ibid., pp. 16–17.
66 Ibid., p. 163.
67 Robert Nozick, *Philosophical Explanations*, Cambridge, MA: Harvard University Press, 1981, p. 167.
68 Ibid., p. 13.
69 Ibid., p. 204.
70 Ibid., p. 287.
71 Barry Stroud, *The Significance of Philosophical Scepticism*, p. viii.
72 Ibid., p. 38.
73 Ibid., p. 66.
74 Ibid., p. 71.
75 Ibid., p. 255.
76 Ibid., p. 273.
77 Christopher Hookaway, *Scepticism*, p. x.
78 Ibid., p. 145.
79 Ibid., p. 132.
80 Ibid., p. 167.
81 See, for example, R. J. White, *The Anti-Philosophers: A Study of the Philosophes in Eighteenth-Century France*, London: Macmillan, 1970. White defends the *philosophes* against attacks from modern academic philosophers as to their derivativeness, on the grounds that their 'historic function . . . was not to originate new ideas but to translate the ideas of the previous century . . . into the language of every day for everyday men, and women' (p. 11).

2 *Enlightenment Scepticism: A Campaign Against Unnecessary Hypotheses*

1 The remark, 'I have no need of that hypothesis', is attributed to Laplace in reply to Napoleon's question as to where God fitted into his cosmology. Apocryphal or not, the remark does capture the iconoclastic character of Enlightenment thought, with theology unceremoniously banished from the intellectual realm.

2 Margaret C. Jacob, *The Radical Enlightenment: Pantheists, Freemasons and Republicans*, London: George Allen and Unwin, 1981, pp. 23, 25, 20.

3 Ibid., p. 23. Jacob notes elsewhere that even Helvétius' wife was 'deeply involved in freemasonry' (*Living the Enlightenment: Freemasonry and Politics in Eighteenth-Century Europe*, New York and Oxford: Oxford University Press, 1991, p. 200).

4 Margaret C. Jacob, *The Radical Enlightenment*, p. 263.

5 Diderot suffered a similar fate at the hands of the same body. Ironically enough, d'Holbach later became a supporter of the *parlements* as an alternative source of power to the monarchy, when they were suppressed by the latter.

6 For more on d'Holbach's intellectual milieu, see Alan Charles Kors, *D'Holbach's Coterie: An Enlightenment in Paris*, Princeton, NJ: Princeton University Press, 1976. Diderot is thought to have contributed some material to *The System of Nature*.

7 Maurice Cranston, *Philosophers and Pamphleteers: Political Theorists of the Enlightenment*, Oxford: Oxford University Press, 1986, p. 121.

8 Baron d'Holbach, *The System of Nature*, I [1770], trans. H. D. Robinson and Alastair Jackson, Manchester: Clinamen Press, 1999, pp. 4–5.

9 Ibid., p. 5.

10 Ibid., p. 11.

11 Ibid., p. 12.

12 Ibid., pp. 114, 78.

13 Ibid., p. 131.

14 Ibid., p. 289.

15 Ibid., p. 5.

16 Maurice Cranston, *Philosophers and Pamphleteers*, p. 139.

17 Baron d'Holbach, *Christianity Unveiled: Being an Examination of the Principles and Effects of the Christian Religion* [1761], trans. William Martin Johnson, in *The Deist, or Moral Philosopher*, vol. II, London: R. Carlile, 1819, pp. 16–125 (p. 17). The work was originally published under the name of Nicolas Boulanger (1722–59), and is so credited in this edition.

18 Ibid., p. 35.

19 Claude-Adrien Helvétius, *De l'Esprit or Essays on the Mind and its Several Faculties* [1758], Whitefish, MT: Kessinger Publishing, 2004, pp. 6–7 (facsimile of 1809 London edition; no translator given).

20 Ibid., p. 173.

21 Ibid., p. 175.

22 Ibid., p. 183.

23 Quoted in Alan Charles Kors, *D'Holbach's Coterie*, p. 60.

24 James W. Cornman, *Skepticism, Justification, and Explanation*, Dordrecht, Boston, and London: D. Reidel, 1980, p. xi.

25 David Hume, *Dialogues and Natural History of Religion* [1779, 1757], ed. J. C. A. Gaskin, Oxford: Oxford University Press, 1993, p. 185.

26 Ibid.

27 Ibid., p. 184.

28 Stephen Eric Bronner, *Reclaiming the Enlightenment: Towards a Politics of Radical Engagement*, New York: Columbia University Press, 2004, p. xii.

29 Daniel Brewer, *The Discourse of Enlightenment in Eighteenth-Century France: Diderot and the Art of Philosophizing*, Cambridge: Cambridge University Press, 1993, p. 252.

30 Ibid.

3 Super-Scepticism: The Postmodern World

1 Jean-François Lyotard, *The Postmodern Condition: A Report on Knowledge* [1979], trans. Geoffrey Bennington and Brian Massumi, Manchester: Manchester University Press, 1984, p. 60.

2 See Jürgen Habermas, 'Modernity: An Unfinished Project' [1981; trans. Nicholas Walker], in Maurizio Passerin D'Entreves and Seyla Benhabib, eds, *Habermas and the Unfinished Project of Modernity*, Cambridge and Oxford: Polity and Blackwell, 1996, pp. 38–55.

3 Friedrich Nietzsche, *On the Genealogy of Morals: A Polemic* [1887], trans. Douglas Smith, Oxford and New York: Oxford University Press, 1996, p. 19.

4 Friedrich Nietzsche, 'On Truth and Lying in a Non-Moral Sense', in *The Birth of Tragedy and Other Writings* [1873], trans. Ronald Spiers, eds Raymond Geuss and Ronald Spiers, Cambridge: Cambridge University Press, 1999, pp. 139–53 (p. 146).

5 Theodor W. Adorno and Max Horkheimer, *Dialectic of Enlightenment* [1944], trans. John Cumming, London and New York: Verso, 1972, p. 3.

6 Jürgen Habermas, *The Philosophical Discourse of Modernity: Twelve Lectures* [1985], trans. Frederick Lawrence, Cambridge: Polity, 1987, p. 129.

7 Theodore W. Adorno and Max Horkheimer, *Dialectic of Enlightenment*, p. 205.

8 Theodor W. Adorno, *Negative Dialectics* [1966], trans. E. B. Ashton, London: Routledge and Kegan Paul, 1973, p. 5.

9 Ibid., p. xx. Commentators have pointed up the close links between Adorno and Derrida in this respect.

10 Roland Barthes, *Mythologies* [1957], trans. Annette Lavers, London: Paladin, 1973, pp. 41–2.

11 'Introduction to the Structural Analysis of Narratives', in Roland Barthes, *Image Music Text*, trans. Stephen Heath, London: Fontana, 1977, p. 79.

12 Roland Barthes, *S/Z* [1970], trans. Richard Miller, New York: Hill and Wang, 1974, pp. 5–6.

13 Ibid., p. 6.

14 Ibid., p. 16. The codes are also referred to as 'voices' in the text: 'the Voice of Empirics (the proairetisms), the Voice of the Person (the semes), the Voice of Science (the cultural codes), the Voice of Truth (the hermeneutisms), the Voice of Symbol' (ibid., p. 21).

15 'The Death of the Author', in Roland Barthes, *Image Music Text*, pp. 142–8.

16 Jacques Derrida, 'Living On • Border Lines', in Harold Bloom, Jacques Derrida, Geoffrey H. Hartmann, Paul de Man, and J. Hillis Miller, *Deconstruction and Criticism*, London and Henley: Routledge and Kegan Paul, 1979, pp. 75–176 (p. 152).

17 Gilles Deleuze and Felix Guattari, *A Thousand Plateaus: Capitalism and Schizophrenia* [1980], trans. Brian Massumi, London: Athlone Press, 1988, p. 3.

18 Gilles Deleuze and Felix Guattari, *Anti-Oedipus: Capitalism and Schizophrenia* [1972], trans. Robert Hurley, Mark Seem, and Helen R. Lane, London: Athlone Press, 1984, p. 26.

19 Ibid., p. 3.

20 Ibid., p. 8.

21 Michel Foucault, preface to ibid., p. xiii.

22 Gilles Deleuze, *Difference and Repetition* [1968], trans. Paul Patton, London: Athlone Press, 1994, p. 50.

23 Michel Foucault, *Madness and Civilization: A History of Insanity in the Age of Reason* [1961], trans. Richard Howard, London: Tavistock, 1967, p. 38.

24 See Michel Foucault, *The History of Sexuality: Volume I, Introduction* [1976], trans. Robert Hurley, Harmondsworth: Penguin, 1981.

25 Jean Baudrillard, *America* [1986], trans. Chris Turner, London and New York: Verso, 1988, p. 10.

26 Ibid., pp. 123, 124.

27 Jean Baudrillard, 'The Structural Law of Value and the Order of Simulacra' [1976], in John Fekete, ed., *The Structural Allegory: Reconstructive Encounters with the New French Thought*, Manchester: Manchester University Press, 1984, pp. 54–73 (p. 59).

28 Jean Baudrillard, *The Perfect Crime* [1995], trans. Chris Turner, London and New York: Verso, 1996, preface (unpaginated).

29 Jean Baudrillard, 'The Year 2000 Will Not Take Place', trans. Paul Foss and Paul Patton, in E. A. Grosz, Terry Threadgold, David Kelly, Alan Cholodenko, and Edward Colless, eds, *Futur-Fall: Excursions into Post-Modernity*, Sydney: Power Institute Publications, 1986, pp. 18–28 (p. 22).

30 Luce Irigaray, *This Sex Which Is Not One* [1977], trans. Catherine Porter, with Carolyn Burke, Ithaca, NY: Cornell University Press, 1985, p. 29.

31 Ibid.

32 Ibid., p. 28.

33 Hélène Cixous and Catherine Clément, *The Newly Born Woman* [1975], trans. Betsy Wing, Manchester: Manchester University Press, 1986, p. 82.

34 Hélène Cixous, 'The Laugh of the Medusa', in Elaine Marks and Isabelle de Courtivron, eds, *New French Feminisms: An Anthology*, Brighton: Harvester, 1981, pp. 245–64 (p. 247).

35 Jean-François Lyotard, *Heidegger and 'the Jews'* [1988], trans. Andreas Michel and Mark Roberts, Minneapolis, MN: University of Minnesota Press, 1990, p. 22.

36 Kinky Friedman, *Elvis, Jesus and Coca-Cola*, London and Boston: Faber and Faber, 1993, p. 44.

37 On a personal note, my father-in-law, the late Professor Sydney Brandon, an eminent psychiatrist, instituted a programme amongst victims of the civil war in Rwanda (widows) to write down their personal narratives as a way of trying to come to terms with their experiences. This was a very practical, and successful, method of ensuring that such horrific experiences were not forgotten at local level, and equates to Lyotard's idea that we must always strive to 'bear witness' to what happens around us (in fact, Lyotard regards that as an obligation each of us owes the rest of the human race). Most of the world has tended to turn a blind eye to the horrors of the Rwandan civil war, although the recent film *Hotel Rwanda* (2004) was a brave attempt to counter this trend and bring knowledge of the event into the international political mainstream.

38 Victor Farías, *Heidegger and Nazism* [1987], trans. Paul Burrell and Gabriel R. Ricci, Philadelphia: Temple University Press, 1989.

39 Jean-François Lyotard, *Heidegger and 'the Jews'*, p. 3; Jean-François Lyotard, *The Differend: Phrases in Dispute* [1983], trans Georges Van Den Abbeele, Manchester: Manchester University Press, 1988, p. xiii.

40 See, for example, Derrida's claims that, 'An interpretive decision does not have to draw a line between two intents or two political contents . . . . There can always be a Hegelianism of the left and a Hegelianism of the right, a Heideggerianism of the left and a Heideggerianism of the right, a Nietzscheanism of the right and a Nietzscheanism of the left, and even, let us not overlook it, a Marxism of the right and a Marxism of the left. The one can always be the other. The double of the other' (Jacques Derrida, *The Ear of the Other: Otobiography, Transference, Translation*, trans. Peggy Kamuf, ed. Christie McDonald, Lincoln, NE, and London: University of Nebraska Press, 1988, p. 32). For Lyotard, however, Heidegger was inextricably of the fascist right and could not be trusted as a philosopher in consequence.

41 From a speech given by Heidegger in 1933 (quoted in Jean-François Lyotard, *Heidegger and 'the Jews'*, p. 69).
42 Lyotard describes his goal as being 'to set up a philosophical politics apart from the politics of "intellectuals" and of "politicians"' (Jean-François Lyotard, *The Differend*, p. xiii).
43 Jean-François Lyotard, *Heidegger and 'the Jews'*, p. 82.
44 See *The Differend*, pp. 3–4.
45 Deborah Lipstadt, 'Witness Statement', High Court of Justice 1996-1-No. 1113, Queen's Bench Division, http://www.holocaustdenialontrial.com/evidence/wsdl.html, paragraph 29.
46 David Irving, *Hitler's War*, London: Hodder and Stoughton, 1977, p. 12.
47 Ibid., p. xv.
48 Deborah Lipstadt, *Denying the Holocaust: The Growing Assault on Truth and Memory*, Harmondsworth: Penguin, 1994, p. 181.
49 David Irving, 'Witness Statement', High Court of Justice 1996, Queen's Bench Division, http://www.fpp.co.uk/Legal/Penguin/witness/Irving/html.
50 Robert Nozick, *Philosophical Explanations*, Cambridge, MA: Harvard University Press, 1981.

4 Science and Technology as Belief Systems

1 Sue Mayer and Robin Grove-White, 'A Bitter Harvest', *Guardian*, 22 February 2005, p. 21.
2 Ibid.
3 Colin Douglas, 'Aristotle, the NHS, and Davie's Henhouse', *British Medical Journal*, 14 May 2005, p. 1157.
4 Ibid.
5 Ibid.
6 Peter Davies, 'A Conduit to Imbecility', *British Medical Journal*, 14 May 2005, p. 1157.
7 Ibid.
8 Ibid.
9 Sharon Sanders, 'Clever Searching for Evidence', *British Medical Journal*, 21 May 2005, pp. 1162–3.
10 Ibid., p. 1162.

11 Quoted in Robin McKie, 'Creationists Take their Fight to the Really Big Screen', *Observer*, 20 March 2005, p. 24. The person in question will no doubt be pleased to hear of the opening of the Museum of Earth History in in a Bible-based theme park in Eureka Springs, Arkansas, which manages to include dinosaurs in a Young Earth creationist perspective by arguing that they were wiped out by the Flood (see Paul Harris, 'Would You Adam 'n' Eve It . . . Dinosaurs in Eden', *Observer*, 22 May 2005, p. 20).

12 Some critics are unhappy about the respectability that even being dubbed an 'ism' grants such ideas. Massimo Pigliucci, for example, prefers the blunter formulation of 'evolution denial' (*Denying Evolution: Creationism, Scientism, and the Nature of Science*, Sunderland, MA: Sinauer Associates, 2002, p. 2).

13 Ralph O. Muncaster, *Creation vs. Evolution*, Eugene, OR: Harvest House Publishers, 2000, p. 13.

14 Ibid.

15 Ibid. pp. 13, 36.

16 Ibid., p. 42. Not every theologian grants the Bible such credibility as a historical record. Eric J. Hildeman, for example, argues in *Creationism: The Bible Says No!* (Bloomington, IN: Author House, 2004), that it contains too many errors and contradictions to count as such.

17 See, for example, Michael Drosnin, *The Bible Code*, London: Weidenfeld and Nicolson, 1997. Some national papers in the UK have seen fit to serialise such works, giving them a further degree of credibility with the general public. Muncaster's own 'scientific' analysis of biblical predictions can be found in *The Bible – Scientific Insights. Volume 5: Investigation of the Evidence*, Newport Beach, CA: Strong Basis to Believe, 1996.

18 Ralph O. Muncaster, *Creation vs. Evolution*, p. 12.

19 Ibid., p. 13.

20 Ibid.

21 Ibid., p. 33. I've consulted a scientist friend on this, Prof. Brett Wilson (Sheffield Hallam University), and it transpires that light would have to slow down to somewhere around twice the speed of sound for 10,000 years to give the appearance of 5 billion light years to contemporary observers. Even assuming a God able to alter the laws of physics at will, or the wilder speculations of M-theorists (for whom the

184

speed of light is now considered to be a limit rather than a constant, thus potentially variable), this severely taxes credibility. One is tempted to ask distinctly metaphysical questions, such as: how slow can light become and still be classifiable as light? Prof. Wilson's calculations are as follows:

Taking the generally accepted age of Earth as 4.55 billion years (4.55 $\times$ 10^9 years) as against the creationist age of 10,000 years (10^4 years) would require a simple (non-relativistic) slowing ratio of 4.55 $\times$ 10^5. This would imply a value for the speed of light of (3 $\times$ 10^8 m/s) / (4.55 $\times$ 10^5), equal to 660 m/s (1,476 mph) – or approximately twice the speed of sound. Matters are a little more complex as the age of the universe is normally taken as 13.7 billion years, so there's additional latitude there for argument over precisely when in the development of the universe the Earth came into existence – but that would only change matters by a factor of 3 at most (13.77/4.55 = 3.01).

As Prof. Wilson goes on to note, however: 'the whole shape, form, structure and nature of physics and our perceived physical environment would have to be outrageously different to support such an enormously slower value' (personal communication to author). Not that this would faze the creationists, one suspects.

22 Ralph Muncaster, *Creation vs. Evolution*, p. 33.
23 Hank Hanegraaff, *Fatal Flaws*, Nashville, TN: W Publishing Group, 2003, p. xiii.
24 Richard Dawkins, *The Selfish Gene*, 2nd edition, Oxford: Oxford University Press, 1989, p. 1.
25 Hank Hanegraaff, *Fatal Flaws*, p. xiv.
26 Richard Dawkins, *The Selfish Gene*, p. 195; Hank Hanegraaff, *Fatal Flaws*, p. 9. Darwin's words are as follows: 'At some future period, not very distant as measured by centuries, the civilised races of man will almost certainly exterminate, and replace, the savage races throughout the world' (*The Descent of Man* [1871], Harmondsworth: Penguin, 2004, p. 183).
27 Hank Hanegraaff, *Fatal Flaws*, p. 11.
28 Ibid., p. 80.
29 David Berlinski; quoted in ibid., p. 80.

30 David Sloan Wilson, *Darwin's Cathedral: Evolution, Religion, and the Nature of Society*, Chicago and London: University of Chicago Press, 2003, p. 1. Pascal Boyer puts a slightly different spin on this, arguing for what he calls 'cultural selection': 'The invisible hand of cultural selection makes it the case that the religious concepts people acquire and transmit are in general the ones most likely to seem convincing to them, given their circumstances' (*Religion Explained: The Human Instincts that Fashion Gods, Spirits and Ancestors*, London: William Heinemann, 2001, p. 379).

31 David Sloan Wilson, *Darwin's Cathedral*, p. 35.

32 Ibid., p. 126.

33 Ibid., p. 38.

34 Ibid.

35 Ibid., p. 44.

36 Nick Brooks (senior research associate, Tyndall Centre for Climate Change Research, University of East Anglia); quoted in Kate Ravilious, 'What a Way to Go', *Guardian*, Life Section, 14 April 2005, pp. 6–7 (p. 6).

37 Fred Pearce, 'Climate Change: Menace or Myth?', *New Scientist*, 12 February 2005, pp. 38–43 (p. 40).

38 Ibid., p. 38.

39 Maria Zambon (Head of the Influenza Laboratory, Health Protection Agency); quoted in Kate Ravilious, 'What a Way to Go', p. 6.

40 Fred Pearce, 'Climate Change: Menace or Myth?', p. 43.

41 Patrick Michaels, quoted in ibid.

42 It is worth noting, however, that David Bellamy has been accused of a cavalier attitude to scientific evidence, with one critic referring scathingly to the 'inaccurate and selective figures' he relies on in his denial of climate change (George Monbiot, 'Junk Science', *Guardian*, 10 May 2005, p. 23).

43 Quoted in Fred Pearce, 'Climate Change: Menace or Myth?', p. 40.

44 Hans Moravec (research professor at the Robotics Institute, Carnegie Mellon University, Pittsburgh); quoted in Kate Ravilious, 'What a Way to Go', p. 7.

45 For a detailed survey of the worlds of AI and AL, see Mark Ward, *Virtual Organisms: The Startling World of Artificial Life*, London: Macmillan, 1999. Ward is fairly phlegmatic about the spread of AI and AL: 'More likely we

will learn to live with ALife creations for a long time before we feel any kind of threat from them. . . . They will become familiar tools and possibly companions long before they are smart enough to think about doing away with us' (p. 280). From a Lyotardean perspective, this is merely delivering ourselves into the hands of the enemy, and giving techno-science *carte blanche* to carry on developing the inhuman at our expense.

46 Justin Mullins, 'Whatever Happened to Machines that Think?', *New Scientist*, 23 April 2005, pp. 32–7 (p. 37).

47 See, for example, the arguments put forward in Donna Haraway, *Simians, Cyborgs, and Women: The Reinvention of Nature*, London: Free Association Books, 1991, where cyborgs are celebrated as a means of breaking down patriarchal power structures, and their further development eagerly anticipated.

48 Jean-François Lyotard, *The Inhuman: Reflections on Time* [1988], trans. Geoffrey Bennington and Rachel Bowlby, Oxford: Blackwell, 1991, p. 2.

49 Ibid., p. 20.

50 Ibid., p. 65.

51 William Paley, *Natural Theology* [1802], Charlottesville, VA: Lincoln-Rembrandt, 1986, pp. 2–3.

52 Ibid., pp. 17–18.

53 Michael J. Behe, *Darwin's Black Box: The Biochemical Challenge to Evolution*, New York: Simon and Schuster, 1996, p. 252.

54 Quoted in Banesh Hoffman, with Helen Dukas, *Albert Einstein: Creator and Rebel*, London: Hart-Davis, MacGibbon, 1973, p. 193.

55 'For Wit's false mirror held up Nature's light; / Shew'd erring Pride, WHATEVER IS, IS RIGHT; / That REASON, PASSION, answer one great aim; / That true SELF-LOVE and SOCIAL are the same; That VIRTUE only makes our Bliss below; / And all our Knowledge is, OURSELVES TO KNOW' (Alexander Pope, *An Essay on Man*, Epistle IV, l. 393–8; in *The Poems of Alexander Pope*, ed. John Butt, London: Methuen, 1968, p. 547).

56 Fazale Rana and Hugh Ross, *Origins of Life: Biblical and Evolutionary Models Face Off*, Colorado Springs, CO: NavPress, 2004, p. 222.

57 'The Proofs for the Existence of God in the Light of Modern Natural Science'; quoted in Simon Singh, *Big Bang: The Most Important Scientific Discovery of All Time and Why You Need to Know About It*, London and New York: Fourth Estate, 2004, p. 360.

58 For more on this debate, see ibid. Interestingly enough from our point of view, the Steady State theorists saw a sinister element in this conjunction of religion and science. In Fred Hoyle's words: 'The passionate frenzy with which the Big Bang cosmology is clutched to the corporate scientific bosom evidently arises from a deep-rooted attachment to the first page of Genesis, religious fundamentalism at its strongest' (quoted in ibid., pp. 438–9). While the Big Bang can be used in the way Hoyle deplores, it does not necessarily lead back to a religious explanation, nor is it as incompatible with scepticism as he is implying. Given that Steady State theory has been more or less discredited by recent advances in physics, this is just as well: religion must not be allowed such an easy victory.

59 Fazale Rana and Hugh Ross, *Origins of Life*, p. 16.

60 Ibid., p. 225.

61 Ibid., p. 43.

62 'Reason to Believe' is described as an interdenominational institute, based in California, which 'researches and communicates how God's revelation in the words of the Bible harmonizes with the facts of nature' ('About the Authors', *Origins of Life*, p. 297). Ross is both founder and president; Rana, vice-president for science apologetics at the institute. Ralph O. Muncaster, whose views were considered earlier in the chapter, feels the need to be even more positive about his own project, also based in California, which is entitled 'Strong Basis to Believe'. Doubt clearly is not being contemplated in either case.

63 Fazal Rana and Hugh Ross, *Origins of Life*, pp. 43–4.

64 Theologians have traditionally been critical of those who want to go back beyond creation. The late Pope John Paul once admonished a group of cosmologists that, '[i]t is not for you to question what happens before the big bang' (quoted in John Cornwell, 'Against Holy Orders', *New Scientist*, 23 April 2005, p. 23).

65 Massimo Pigliucci, *Denying Evolution*, p. 65.

66 Ralph O. Muncaster, *Creation vs. Evolution*, p. 13.

67 Although many theologians still took refuge in the 'God's punishment for the wicked' line. Theodicy dies hard, and is seemingly always available for the unquestioning believer in times of trouble.

68 Fazale Rana and Hugh Ross, *Origins of Life*, p. 216.

69 For a detailed analysis of this historical debate, see Thomas Kuhn, *The Copernican Revolution: Planetary Astronomy in the Development of Western Thought*, Cambridge, MA, and London: Harvard University Press, 1957.

70 Fazale Rana and Hugh Ross, *Origins of Life*, p. 42.

71 Ibid., p. 225.

5 Towards a Sceptical Politics

1 Ernesto Laclau and Chantal Mouffe, *Hegemony and Socialist Strategy: Towards a Radical Democratic Politics*, London: Verso, 1985, p. 1.

2 See, for example, the arguments of Joseph E. Stiglitz, in *Globalization and its Discontents*, London: Penguin, 2002.

3 Chantal Mouffe, *The Democratic Paradox*, London: Verso, 2000, p. 111.

4 Ibid., p. 113.

5 Ibid., p. 101.

6 Ibid., p. 102.

7 William E. Connolly, *Identity/Difference: Democratic Negotiations of Political Paradox*, Ithaca, NY, and London: Cornell University Press, 1991, pp. 178–9.

8 Ibid., pp. 14–15.

9 Ibid., p. x.

10 Chantal Mouffe, *The Democratic Paradox*, p. 102.

11 See Thomas Kuhn, *The Structure of Scientific Revolutions*, 2nd edition, Chicago and London: University of Chicago Press, 1970.

12 Chantal Mouffe, *The Democratic Paradox*, p. 103.

13 Ibid., p. 105.

14 Ibid., p. 96.

15 Ibid., p. 105.

16 See, for example, Roger Lewin, *Complexity: Life at the Edge of Chaos*, London: Phoenix, 1993.

17 Every species has a fitness landscape in which it can attain 'peaks' of fitness, or slide back to lower levels with correspondingly less development taking place. Fitness in this case equates to adaptability to the landscape, which is only one of a host of such interacting with each other. The balance of such interactions dictates whether the system manages to survive at the edge of chaos. (See ibid.)

18 '[T]he Resolutions of a Monarch, are subject to no other Inconstancy, than that of Humane Nature; but in Assemblies, besides that of Nature, there ariseth an Inconstancy from the Number. . . . [A] Monarch cannot disagree with himselfe, out of envy, or interest; but an Assembly may; and that to such a height, as may produce a Civill Warre' (Thomas Hobbes, *Leviathan, or, The Matter, Forme, and Power of a Commonwealth Ecclesiastical and Civill* [1651], ed. C. B. Macpherson, Harmondsworth: Penguin, 1968, pp. 242, 243). Hobbes's prescriptions were specifically designed by him to prevent civil wars of the type that had occurred in England in the 1640s, and he had no time for either agonism or antagonism.

19 See Martin Pugh, *Hurrah for the Blackshirts!: Fascists and Fascism in Britain Between the Wars*, London: Jonathan Cape, 2005.

20 Francis Fukuyama, *The End of History and the Last Man*, London: Hamish Hamilton, 1992.

21 See Ziauddin Sardar and Merryl Wynn Davies, *Why Do People Hate America?*, 2nd edition, Cambridge: Icon Books, 2003, for a discussion of the source of those grievances.

22 Richard H. Popkin, *The History of Scepticism from Erasmus to Spinoza*, Berkeley, Los Angeles, and London: University of California Press, 1979, p. xiv.

23 Chantal Mouffe, *The Democratic Paradox*, p. 140.

24 It is noticeable that commentators are increasingly willing to use the term 'theocracy' when discussing the current American political scene. See, for example, Mark Lawson: 'Travelling around the US in the past few days, I was astonished by the extent to which the country seems to have become a theocracy: even beyond the evidence offered six months ago in the re-election of George Bush by the God-fearing' ('One Miracle Too Many', *Guardian*, 25 June 2005, p. 23). Although there is an element of hyperbole in such assessments, there are still worrying trends to note.

25 The term was coined by the international financier and currency speculator George Soros.

26 Friedrick Nietzsche, 'On Truth and Lying in a Non-Moral Sense', in *The Birth of Tragedy and Other Writings* [1873], trans. Ronald Spiers, eds Raymond Geuss and Ronald Spiers, Cambridge: Cambridge University Press, 1999, pp. 139–53 (p. 146).

Notes

6 Reasonable Doubt?

1 See 'Lectric Law Library Lexicon, http://www.lectlaw.com/def2/q016.htm.
2 See Law.com Law Dictionary, http://dictionary.law.com/affiliate.html.
3 P. B. Carter, *Cases and Statutes on Evidence*, 2nd edition, London: Sweet and Maxwell, 1990, p. 65.
4 Ibid., p. 66 (*Dawson v. The Queen*; Australia, 1961).
5 Ibid. (*The People (Attorney-General) v. Byrne*; Ireland, 1974).
6 Ibid., 59.
7 Law.com Law Dictionary.
8 P. B. Carter, *Cases and Statutes*, p. 66 (*Walters v. Regina*; 1969).
9 John Bunyan, *The Holy War* [1682], eds James F. Forrest and Roger Sharrock, Oxford: Clarendon Press, 1980, p. 226.
10 Ibid., pp. 204–5.
11 For an argument suggesting that Bunyan's religious fundamentalism is the cornerstone of his appeal to radical thinkers – including many Marxists – over the centuries to the present day, see my 'John Bunyan – Fundamentalist?', in W. R. Owens and Stuart Sim, eds, *Reception, Appropriation, Recollection: John Bunyan's Pilgrim's Progress*, Bern and Oxford: Peter Lang (forthcoming).
12 See, for example, his spiritual autobiography, *Grace Abounding to the Chief of Sinners* [1666], ed. Roger Sharrock, Oxford: Clarendon Press, 1962, where the author records contending voices in his head at various points in his life.
13 John Bunyan, *The Pilgrim's Progress*, Parts One and Two [1678, 1684], ed. J. B. Wharey, rev. Roger Sharrock, Oxford: Clarendon Press, 1928, 1960, Part One, p. 135.
14 Ibid., p. 118.
15 Stephen Bates, 'African Bishop Spurns Aids Cash from Pro-Gay Diocese', *Guardian*, 22 March 2005, p. 13.
16 Giles Fraser and William Whyte, 'Don't Hand Religion to the Right', *Guardian*, 18 March 2005, p. 26.
17 Ibid.
18 Quoted in Stephen Bates and John Hooper, 'From Hitler Youth to the Vatican', *Guardian*, 20 April 2005, p. 3.

19 For more on this topic, see Youssef M. Choueiri, *Islamic Fundamentalism*, 2nd edition, London and Washington: Pinter, 1997.

20 Irshad Manji, *The Trouble with Islam Today: A Wake-up Call for Honesty and Change*, Edinburgh and London: Mainstream Books, 2004, p. 13.

21 Ibid., p. 12.

22 Quoted in Stephen Bates, ' "Bin Laden's Nightmare" Seeks Islamic Reformation', *The Guardian*, 9 May 2005, p. 10. For more on the campaign, see Irshad Manji's official website, http://www.muslim-refusenik.com/ijtihad.html.

23 See Christoph Luxenberg, *Die Syro-Aramaische Lesart des Koran* (*The Syro-Aramaic Reading of the Koran*), Berlin: Das Arabische Buch, 2000. Tellingly, despite its obvious topicality, the book has not yet been translated from the German.

24 'Profile: Playwright Gurpreet Kaur Bhatti', http://news.bbc.co.uk/1/hi/uk/4109017.stm.

25 Gurpreet Kaur Bhatti, foreword, *Behzti*, London: Oberon Books, 2004, p. 17.

26 Ibid.

27 Quoted in 'Gurpreet Kaur Bhatti's Play', http://www.artnewsblog.com/2004/12/gurpreet-kaur-bhattis-play.htm.

28 Gurpreet Kaur Bhatti, *Behzti*, p. 136.

29 During the 1980s a Sikh separatist movement waged war against the Indian state, with over 40,000 deaths occurring – including, significantly enough, that of the prime minister, Indira Gandhi, at the hands of her own Sikh bodyguards. The present prime minister of India, Manmohan Singh, is, however, a Sikh, which only goes to point up the complexity of the political situation.

30 'Protests as BBC Screens Springer', http://news.bbc.co.uk/1/hi/entertainment/tv_and_radio/4154071.stm.

31 Editorial, 'Speak up For Humanity', *New Humanist*, March/April, 2005, p. 3.

32 'Springer Opera Draws 1.7m Viewers', http://news.bbc.co.uk/1/hi/entertainment/tv_and_radio/4159217.stm.

33 Fiona MacTaggart, 'It Will Still Be OK to Ridicule Religion', *Guardian*, 14 March 2005, p. 18.

34 While there are organisations such as the Secular Society, their scope is limited, and they do not really act as focal points for non-believers, who are a much more diverse group than believers tend to be.

35 Fiona MacTaggart, 'It Will Still Be OK to Ridicule Religion'.

36 Ibid.

37 Editorial, March/April 2005, p. 3. For a defence of Muslim faith schools, however, see Dilpazier Aslam, 'Islam is the Secret of Our Success', *Guardian*, Education Section, 25 January 2005, p. 9.

38 For a wry account of an encounter with this organisation, see Jon Ronson, *Them: Adventures with Extremists*, London: Picador, 2002.

39 Malise Ruthven, *The Divine Supermarket: Travels in Search of the Soul of America*, London: Chatto and Windus, 1989.

40 David Nokes, *Raillery and Rage: A Study of Eighteenth Century Satire*, Brighton: Harvester, 1987, p. 1.

41 Ibid., pp. 2–3.

42 Alexander Pope, *The First Epistle of the Second Book of Horace Imitated* [1737], in *The Poems of Alexander Pope*, ed. John Butt, London: Methuen, 1968, 1.262, p. 644.

43 Alexander Pope, *The Dunciad*, II [1728], 1.1–12, in *Poems*, pp. 372–3.

44 David Nokes, *Raillery and Rage*, p. 58.

45 P. K. Elkin, *The Augustan Defence of Satire*, Oxford: Clarendon Press, 1973, p. 1.

46 Ibid., p. 12.

47 J. Trusler; quoted in ibid., p. 24.

48 Ibid., p. 201.

49 Ibid.

50 Jonathan Swift, *Gulliver's Travels* [1726], ed. Robert DeMaria, Jr, Harmondsworth: Penguin, 2001, pp. 167, 168.

51 Ibid., p. 48.

52 'The tendency of all satire . . . is to resolve into a vituperative or ironic speaker' (Ronald Paulson, *The Fictions of Satire*, Baltimore: Johns Hopkins University Press, 1967, p. 221).

53 Henry Fielding, *The History of Tom Jones, A Foundling* [1749], eds Thomas Keymer and Alice Wakely, Harmondsworth: Penguin, 2005, p. 595.

54 David Rodgers, 'James Gillray', in Hugh Brigstocke, ed., *The Oxford Companion to Western Art*, Oxford: Oxford University Press, 2001, p. 664.

55 Richard Godfrey, *James Gillray: The Art of Caricature*, London: Tate Gallery Publishing, 2001, p. 13.
56 Ibid., p. 14.
57 Not just for his *If* series in the *Guardian*, but for strips like *Maggie's Farm* in *Time Out* magazine.
58 David Nokes, *Raillery and Rage*, p. x.

Conclusion: The Sceptic Fights Back

1 Quoted in Donald MacLeod, 'Bound by Islam', *Guardian*, Education Section, 22 February 2005, p. 22.
2 Tariq Ramadan, *Western Muslims and the Future of Islam*, Oxford: Oxford University Press, 2004, p. 133.
3 Donald McLeod, 'Bound by Islam', p. 22.
4 See Paul Brown, 'GM Crops Created Superweed, Say Scientists', *Guardian*, 25 July 2005, p. 3.
5 As reported in *New Scientist*, the researchers at the Centre for Ecology and Hydrology in Dorset insist that gene transfer cannot be confirmed as yet, but the Environment Minister, Elliot Morley, still feels 'it is a finding we cannot ignore' ('Reports of Superweed Greatly Exaggerated', 30 July 2005, p. 4).

Bibliography

Adorno, Theodor W., *Negative Dialectics* [1966], trans. E. B. Ashton, London: Routledge and Kegan Paul, 1973.

— and Horkheimer, Max, *Dialectic of Enlightenment* [1944], trans. John Cumming, London and New York: Verso, 1979.

Al-Ghazali, *The Faith and Practice of Al-Ghazali*, trans. W. Montgomery Watt, Lahore: Sh. Muhammad Ashraf, 1963.

— *The Incoherence of the Philosophers* [1091–5], trans. Michael E. Marmara, Provo, UT: Brigham Young University Publishing, 1997.

Annas, Julia, and Barnes, Jonathan, *The Modes of Scepticism: Ancient Texts and Modern Interpretations*, Cambridge: Cambridge University Press, 1985.

Aslam, Dilpazier, 'Islam is the Secret of Our Success', *Guardian*, Education Section, 25 January 2005, p. 9.

Barnes, Jonathan, *The Toils of Scepticism*, Cambridge: Cambridge University Press, 1990.

Barthes, Roland, *Mythologies* [1957], trans. Annette Lavers, London: Paladin, 1973.

— *S/Z* [1970], trans. Richard Miller, New York: Hill and Wang, 1974.

— *Image Music Text*, trans. Stephen Heath, London: Fontana, 1977.

— *The Fashion System* [1967], trans. Matthew Ward and Richard Howard, London: Jonathan Cape, 1985.

Bates, Stephen, 'African Bishop Spurns Aids Cash from Pro-Gay Diocese', *Guardian*, 22 March 2005, p. 13.

Bates, Stephen, ' "Bin Laden's Nightmare" Seeks Islamic Reformation', *Guardian*, 9 May 2005, p. 10.

— and Hooper, John, 'From Hitler Youth to the Vatican', *Guardian*, 20 April 2005, p. 3.

Baudrillard, Jean, 'The Structural Law of Value and the Order of Simulacra' [1976], in John Fekete, ed., *The Structural Allegory: Reconstructive Encounters with the New French Thought*, Manchester: Manchester University Press, 1984, pp. 54–73.

— 'The Year 2000 Will Not Take Place', trans. Paul Foss and Paul Patton, in E. A. Grosz, Terry Threadgold, David Kelly, Alan Cholodenko, and Edward Colless, eds, *Futur-Fall: Excursions into Post-Modernity*, Sydney: Power Institute Publications, 1986, pp. 18–28.

— *America* [1986], trans. Chris Turner, London and New York: Verso, 1988.

— *The Perfect Crime* [1995], trans. Chris Turner, London and New York: Verso, 1996.

Behe, Michael J., *Darwin's Black Box: The Biochemical Challenge to Evolution*, New York: Simon and Schuster, 1996.

Berkeley, Bishop George, *The Works of George Berkeley*, I–IX, eds A. A. Luce and T. E. Jessop, London: Thomas Nelson, 1949–58.

Bhatti, Gurpreet Kaur, *Behzti*, London: Oberon Books, 2004.

Bloom, Harold, Derrida, Jacques, Hartman, Geoffrey H., de Man, Paul, and Miller, J. Hillis, *Deconstruction and Criticism*, London and Henley: Routledge and Kegan Paul, 1979.

Boyer, Pascal, *Religion Explained: The Human Instincts that Fashion Gods, Spirits and Ancestors*, London: William Heinemann, 2001.

Brewer, Daniel, *The Discourse of Enlightenment in Eighteenth-Century France: Diderot and the Art of Philosophizing*, Cambridge: Cambridge University Press, 1993.

Brigstocke, Hugh, ed., *The Oxford Companion to Western Art*, Oxford: Oxford University Press, 2001.

Brivati, Brian, 'Invasion Reduced to the Threat of Terror', *Guardian*, 12 July 2005, p. 22.

Bronner, Stephen Eric, *Reclaiming the Enlightenment: Towards a Politics of Radical Engagement*, New York: Columbia University Press, 2004.

Brown, Paul, 'GM Crops Created Superweed, Say Scientists', *Guardian*, 25 July 2005, p. 6.

Bibliography

Bunyan, John, *The Pilgrim's Progress*, Parts One and Two [1678, 1684], ed. J. B. Wharey, rev. Roger Sharrock, Oxford: Clarendon Press, 1928, 1960.

— *Grace Abounding to the Chief of Sinners* [1666], ed. Roger Sharrock, Oxford: Clarendon Press, 1962.

— *The Holy War* [1682], eds James F. Forrest and Roger Sharrock, Oxford: Clarendon Press, 1980.

Burnyeat, M. F., 'The Sceptic in his Place and Time', in Richard H. Popkin and Charles B. Schmitt, eds, *Scepticism from the Renaissance to the Enlightenment*, Wiesbaden: Harrassowitz, 1987, pp. 13–43.

Carter, P. B., *Cases and Statutes on Evidence*, 2nd edition, London: Sweet and Maxwell, 1990.

Choueiri, Youssef M., *Islamic Fundamentalism*, 2nd edition, London and Washington: Pinter, 1997.

Cixous, Hélène, 'The Laugh of the Medusa', in Elaine Marks and Isabelle de Courtivron, eds, *New French Feminisms: An Anthology*, Brighton: Harvester, 1981, pp. 245–64.

— and Clément, Catherine, *The Newly Born Woman* [1975], trans. Betsy Wing, Manchester: Manchester University Press, 1986.

Collinson, Diane, Wilkinson, Robert, and Plant, Katherine, *Fifty Key Eastern Thinkers*, London and New York: Routledge, 1999.

Connolly, William E., *Identity/Difference: Democratic Negotiations of Political Paradox*, Ithaca, NY, and London: Cornell University Press, 1991.

Conze, Edward, *Buddhist Thought in India: Three Phases of Buddhist Philosophy*, Ann Arbor, MI: University of Michigan Press, 1967.

Cornman, James W., *Skepticism, Justification, and Explanation*, Dordrecht, Boston, and London: D. Reidel, 1980.

Cornwell, John, 'Against Holy Orders', *New Scientist*, 23 April 2005, p. 23.

Cranston, Maurice, *Philosophers and Pamphleteers: Political Theorists of the Enlightenment*, Oxford: Oxford University Press, 1986.

Darwin, Charles, *The Descent of Man* [1871], Harmondsworth: Penguin, 2004.

Davies, Peter, 'A Conduit to Imbecility', *British Medical Journal*, 14 May 2005, p. 1157.

Dawkins, Richard, *The Selfish Gene*, 2nd edition, Oxford: Oxford University Press, 1989.

The Deist, or Moral Philosopher, vol. II, London: R. Carlile, 1819.

Deleuze, Gilles, *Difference and Repetition* [1968], trans. Paul Patton, London: Athlone Press, 1994.

— and Guattari, Felix, *Anti-Oedipus: Capitalism and Schizophrenia* [1972], trans. Robert Hurley, Mark Seem, and Helen R. Lane, London: Athlone Press, 1984.

— *A Thousand Plateaus: Capitalism and Schizophrenia* [1980], trans. Brian Massumi, London: Athlone Press, 1988.

D'Entreves, Maurizio Passerin, and Benhabib, Seyla, eds, *Habermas and the Unfinished Project of Modernity*, Cambridge and Oxford: Polity and Blackwell, 1996.

Derrida, Jacques, 'Living On • Border Lines', in Harold Bloom, Jacques Derrida, Geoffrey H. Hartmann, Paul de Man, and J. Hillis Miller, *Deconstruction and Criticism*, London and Henley: Routledge and Kegan Paul, 1979, pp. 75–176.

— *The Post Card: From Socrates to Freud and Beyond* [1980], trans. Alan Bass, Chicago and London: University of Chicago Press, 1987.

— *The Ear of the Other: Otobiography, Transference, Translation*, trans. Peggy Kamuf, ed. Christie McDonald, Lincoln, NE, and London: University of Nebraska Press, 1988.

Descartes, René, *Philosophical Writings*, revised edition, trans. and eds Elizabeth Anscombe and Peter Thomas Geach, London: Thomas Nelson, 1970.

Dixon, A. C., ed., *The Fundamentals* [1910–15], New York and London: Garland, 1988.

Douglas, Colin, 'Aristotle, the NHS, and Davie's Henhouse', *British Medical Journal*, 14 May 2005, p. 1157.

Drosnin, Michael, *The Bible Code*, London: Weidenfeld and Nicolson, 1997.

Editorial, 'Speak Up For Humanity', *New Humanist*, March/April 2005, p. 3.

Elkin, P. K., *The Augustan Defence of Satire*, Oxford: Clarendon Press, 1973.

Fakhry, Majid, *Islamic Philosophy, Theology and Mysticism: A Short Introduction*, Oxford: Oneworld, 1997.

Farías, Victor, *Heidegger and Nazism* [1987], trans. Paul Burrell and Gabriel R. Ricci, Philadelphia: Temple University Press, 1989.

Fekete, John, ed., *The Structural Allegory: Reconstructive Encounters with the New French Thought*, Manchester: Manchester University Press, 1984.

Bibliography

Fielding, Henry, *The History of Tom Jones, A Foundling* [1749], eds Thomas Keymer and Alice Wakely, Harmondsworth: Penguin, 2005.

Foucault, Michel, *Madness and Civilization: A History of Insanity in the Age of Reason* [1961], trans. Richard Howard, London: Tavistock, 1967.

— *The History of Sexuality: Volume I, Introduction* [1976], trans. Robert Hurley, Harmondsworth: Penguin, 1981.

Fraser, Giles, and Whyte, William, 'Don't Hand Religion to the Right', *Guardian*, 18 March 2005, p. 26.

Friedman, Kinky, *Elvis, Jesus and Coca-Cola*, London and Boston: Faber and Faber, 1993.

Fukuyama, Francis, *The End of History and the Last Man*, London: Hamish Hamilton, 1992.

Godfrey, Richard, *James Gillray: The Art of Caricature*, London: Tate Gallery Publishing, 2001.

Grosz, E. A., Threadgold, Terry, Kelly, David, Cholodenko, Alan, and Colless, Edward, eds, *Futur-Fall: Excursions into Post-Modernity*, Sydney: Power Institute Publications, 1986.

'Gurpreet Kaur Bhatti's Play', http://www.artnewsblog.com/2004/12/gurpreet-kaur-bhattis-play.htm.

Habermas, Jürgen, *The Philosophical Discourse of Modernity: Twelve Lectures* [1985], trans. Frederick Lawrence, Cambridge: Polity, 1987.

— 'Modernity: An Unfinished Project' [1981; trans. Nicholas Walker], in Maurizio Passerin D'Entreves and Seyla Benhabib, eds, *Habermas and the Unfinished Project of Modernity*, Cambridge and Oxford: Polity and Blackwell, 1996, pp. 38–55.

Hanegraaff, Hank, *Fatal Flaws*, Nashville, TN: W Publishing Group, 2003.

Hankinson, R. J., *The Sceptics*, London and New York: Routledge, 1995.

Haraway, Donna, *Simians, Cyborgs, and Women: The Reinvention of Nature*, London: Free Association Books, 1991.

Harris, Paul, 'Would You Adam 'n' Eve It . . . Dinosaurs in Eden', *Observer*, 22 May 2005, p. 20.

Helvétius, Claude-Adrien, *De l'Esprit or Essays on the Mind and its Several Faculties* [1758], Whitefish, MT: Kessinger Publishing, 2004 (facsimile of 1809 edition; no translator given).

Hildeman, Eric, J., *Creationism: The Bible Says No!*, Bloomington, IN: Author House, 2004.

Hobbes, Thomas, *Leviathan, or, The Matter, Forme, and Power of a Commonwealth Ecclesiastical and Civill* [1651], ed. C. B. Macpherson, Harmondsworth: Penguin, 1968.

Hoffman, Banesh, with Dukas, Helen, *Albert Einstein: Creator and Rebel*, London: Hart-Davis, MacGibbon, 1973.

Holbach, Baron d', *Christianity Unveiled: Being an Examination of the Principles and Effects of the Christian Religion* [1761], trans. William Martin Johnson, in *The Deist, or Moral Philosopher*, vol. II, London: R. Carlile, 1819 (published under the name of Nicolas Boulanger in this edition).

— *The System of Nature*, I [1770], trans. H. D. Robinson and Alastair Jackson, Manchester: Clinamen Press, 1999.

Honderich, Ted, ed., *The Oxford Companion to Philosophy*, Oxford: Oxford University Press, 1995.

Hookaway, C. J., *Scepticism*, London and New York: Routledge, 1990.

— 'Scepticism, History of', in Ted Honderich, ed., *The Oxford Companion to Philosophy*, Oxford: Oxford University Press, 1995, pp. 797–9.

Hume, David, *A Treatise of Human Nature* [1739], ed. D. G. C. Macnabb, Glasgow: Fontana/Collins, 1962.

— *Dialogues and Natural History of Religion* [1779, 1757], ed. J. C. A. Gaskin, Oxford: Oxford University Press, 1993.

Hyman, Arthur, and Walsh, James J., eds, *Philosophy in the Middle Ages: The Christian, Islamic, and Jewish Traditions*, Indianapolis, IN: Hackett Publishing, 1973.

Irigaray, Luce, *This Sex Which Is Not One* [1977], trans. Catherine Porter, with Carolyn Burke, Ithaca, NY: Cornell University Press, 1985.

Irving, David, *Hitler's War*, London: Hodder and Stoughton, 1977.

— 'Witness Statement', High Court of Justice 1996, Queen's Bench Division, http://www.fpp.co.uk/Legal/Penguin/witness/Irving/html.

Jacob, Margaret C., *The Radical Enlightenment: Pantheists, Freemasons and Republicans*, London: George Allen and Unwin, 1981.

— *Living the Enlightenment: Freemasonry and Politics in Eighteenth-Century Europe*, New York and Oxford: Oxford University Press, 1991.

Kors, Alan Charles, *D'Holbach's Coterie: An Enlightenment in Paris*, Princeton, NJ: Princeton University Press, 1976.

Kuhn, Thomas, *The Copernican Revolution: Planetary Astronomy in the*

Bibliography

Development of Western Thought, Cambridge, MA, and London: Harvard University Press, 1957.

— *The Structure of Scientific Revolutions*, 2nd edition, Chicago and London: University of Chicago Press, 1970.

Laclau, Ernesto, and Mouffe, Chantal, *Hegemony and Socialist Strategy: Towards a Radical Democratic Politics*, London: Verso, 1985.

Law.com Law Dictionary, http://dictionary.law.com/affiliate/html.

Lawson, Mark, 'One Miracle Too Many', *Guardian*, 25 June 2005, p. 23.

'Lectric Law Library Lexicon, http://www.lectlaw.com/def2/q106.htm.

Lewin, Roger, *Complexity: Life at the Edge of Chaos*, London: Phoenix, 1993.

Lipstadt, Deborah, *Denying the Holocaust: The Growing Assault on Truth and Memory*, Harmondsworth: Penguin, 1994.

— 'Witness Statement', High Court of Justice 1996 – 1 – No. 1113, Queen's Bench Division, http://www.holocaustdenialontrial.com/evidence/wsdl.html.

Luxenberg, Christoph, *Die Syro-Aramaische Lesart des Koran (The Syro-Aramaic Reading of the Koran)*, Berlin: Das Arabische Buch, 2000.

Lyotard, Jean-François, *The Postmodern Condition: A Report on Knowledge* [1979], trans. Geoffrey Bennington and Brian Massumi, Manchester: Manchester University Press, 1984.

— *The Differend: Phrases in Dispute* [1983], trans. George Van Den Abbeele, Manchester: Manchester University Press, 1988.

— *Heidegger and 'the Jews'* [1988], trans. Andreas Michel and Mark Roberts, Minneapolis, MN: University of Minnesota Press, 1990.

— *The Inhuman: Reflections on Time* [1988], trans. Geoffrey Bennington and Rachel Bowlby, Oxford: Blackwell, 1991.

MacAskill, Ewen, 'UK Fears Return to the Bad Old Days in Iran', *Guardian*, 27 June 2005, p. 14.

MacLeod, Donald, 'Bound by Islam', *Guardian*, Education Section, 22 February 2005, p. 22.

MacTaggart, Fiona, 'It Will Still Be OK to Ridicule Religion', *Guardian*, 14 March 2005, p. 18.

Magliola, Robert, *Derrida on the Mend*, West Lafayette, IN: Purdue University Press, 1984.

Manji, Irshad, *The Trouble with Islam Today: A Wake-up Call for Honesty and Change*, Edinburgh and London: Mainstream Books, 2004.

— http://www.muslim-refusenik.com/ijtihad.html.

Marks, Elaine, and Courtivron, Isabelle de, eds, *New French Feminisms: An Anthology*, Brighton: Harvester, 1981.

Mayer, Sue, and Grove-White, Robin, 'A Bitter Harvest', *Guardian*, 22 February 2005, p. 21.

McKie, Robin, 'Creationists Take their Fight to the Really Big Screen', *Observer*, 20 March 2005, p. 24.

Monbiot, George, 'Junk Science', *Guardian*, 10 May 2005, p. 23.

Montaigne, Michel de, *The Complete Essays*, trans. and ed. M. A. Screech, Harmondsworth: Penguin, 2003.

Mouffe, Chantal, *The Democratic Paradox*, London: Verso, 2000.

Mullins, Justin, 'Whatever Happened to Machines that Think?', *New Scientist*, 23 April 2005, pp. 32–7.

Muncaster, Ralph O., *The Bible – Scientific Insights. Volume 5: Investigation of the Evidence*, Newport Beach, CA: Strong Basis to Believe, 1996.

— *Creation vs. Evolution*, Eugene, OR: Harvest House Publishers, 2000.

Nagarjuna, *Averting the Arguments*, trans. Frederick J. Streng; Appendix B, in Frederick J. Streng, *Emptiness: A Study in Religious Meaning*, Nashville, NY: Abingdon Press, 1967.

— *Fundamentals of the Middle Way*, trans. Frederick J. Streng; Appendix A, in Frederick J. Streng, *Emptiness: A Study in Religious Meaning*, Nashville, NY: Abingdon Press, 1967.

Nicholas of Autrecourt, *Letters to Bernard of Arezzo* [c.1338], in Arthur Hyman and James J. Walsh, eds, *Philosophy in the Middle Ages: The Christian, Islamic, and Jewish Traditions*, Indianapolis, IN: Hackett Publishing, 1973, pp. 656–64.

Nietzsche, Friedrich, *On the Genealogy of Morals: A Polemic* [1887], trans. Douglas Smith, Oxford and New York: Oxford University Press, 1996.

— 'On Truth and Lying in a Non-Moral Sense', in *The Birth of Tragedy and Other Writings* [1873], trans. Ronald Spiers, eds Raymond Geuss and Ronald Spiers, Cambridge: Cambridge University Press, 1999, pp. 139–53.

Nokes, David, *Raillery and Rage: A Study of Eighteenth Century Satire*, Brighton: Harvester, 1987.

Nozick, Robert, *Philosophical Explanations*, Cambridge, MA: Harvard University Press, 1981.

Bibliography

Paley, William, *Natural Theology* [1802], Charlottesville, VA: Lincoln-Rembrandt, 1986.

Paulson, Ronald, *The Fictions of Satire*, Baltimore: Johns Hopkins University Press, 1967.

Pearce, Fred, 'Climate Change: Menace or Myth?', *New Scientist*, 12 February 2005, pp. 38–43.

Pigliucci, Massimo, *Denying Evolution: Creationism, Scientism, and the Nature of Science*, Sunderland, MA: Sinauer Associates, 2002.

Pope, Alexander, *The Poems of Alexander Pope*, ed. John Butt, London: Methuen, 1968.

Popkin, Richard H., *The History of Scepticism from Erasmus to Descartes*, New York: Humanities Press, 1964.

— *The History of Scepticism from Erasmus to Spinoza*, Berkeley, Los Angeles, and London: University of California Press, 1979.

— and Schmitt, Charles B., eds, *Scepticism from the Renaissance to the Enlightenment*, Wiesbaden: Harrassowitz, 1987.

Potter, Karl, *Presuppositions of India's Philosophies*, Westport, CT: Greenwood Press, 1972.

'Profile: Playwright Gurpreet Kaur Bhatti', http://news.bbc.co.uk/1/hi/uk/4109017.stm.

'Protests as BBC Screens Springer', http://news.bbc.co.uk/1/hi/entertainment/tv_and_radio/4154071.stm.

Pugh, Martin, *Hurrah for the Blackshirts!: Fascists and Fascism in Britain Between the Wars*, London: Jonathan Cape, 2005.

Putnam, Hilary, *Reason, Truth, and History*, Cambridge: Cambridge University Press, 1981.

Rabelais, François, *Gargantua and Pantagruel* [1532, 1534], trans. J. M. Cohen, Harmondsworth: Penguin, 1955.

Ramadan, Tariq, *Western Muslims and the Future of Islam*, Oxford: Oxford University Press, 2004.

Rana, Fazale, and Ross, Hugh, *Origins of Life: Biblical and Evolutionary Models Face Off*, Colorado Springs, CO: NavPress, 2004.

Ravilious, Kate, 'What a Way to Go', *Guardian*, Life Section, 14 April 2005, pp. 6–7.

'Reports of Superweed Greatly Exaggerated', *New Scientist*, 30 July 2005, p. 4.

Rodgers, David, 'James Gillray', in Hugh Brigstocke, ed., *The Oxford Companion to Western Art*, Oxford: Oxford University Press, 2001.

Ronson, Jon, *Them: Adventures with Extremists*, London: Picador, 2002.

Ruthven, Malise, *The Divine Supermarket: Travels in Search of the Soul of America*, London: Chatto and Windus, 1989.

— *Fundamentalism: The Search for Meaning*, Oxford: Oxford University Press, 2004.

Sanders, Sharon, 'Clever Searching for Evidence', *British Medical Journal*, 21 May 2005, pp. 1162–3.

Sardar, Ziauddin, and Davies, Merryl Wyn, *Why Do People Hate America?*, 2nd edition, Cambridge: Icon Books, 2003.

Sazegara, Mohsen, 'Floodgates of Reform', *New Humanist*, May/June 2005, pp. 12–14.

Seabrook, Jeremy, *Consuming Cultures: Globalization and Local Life*, Oxford: New Internationalist Publications, 2004.

Sextus Empiricus, *Outlines of Scepticism*, trans. Julia Annas and Jonathan Barnes, Cambridge: Cambridge University Press, 1994.

Sim, Stuart, *Contemporary Continental Philosophy: The New Scepticism*, Aldershot and Burlington, VT: Ashgate, 2000.

— *Fundamentalist World: The New Dark Age of Dogma*, Cambridge: Icon Books, 2004.

— 'John Bunyan – Fundamentalist?', in W. R. Owens and Stuart Sim, eds, *Reception, Appropriation, Recollection: John Bunyan's Pilgrim's Progress*, Bern and Oxford: Peter Lang (forthcoming).

Singh, Simon, *Big Bang: The Most Important Scientific Discovery of All Time and Why You Need to Know about It*, London and New York: Fourth Estate, 2004.

Smart, Ninian, *Doctrine and Argument in Indian Philosophy*, Atlantic Highlands, NJ: Humanities Press, 1976.

'Springer Opera Draws 1.7 m Viewers', http://news.bbc.co.uk/1/hi/entertainment/tv_and_radio/4159217.stm.

Stiglitz, Joseph E., *Globalization and its Discontents*, London: Penguin, 2002.

Streng, Frederick J., *Emptiness: A Study in Religious Meaning*, Nashville, NY: Abingdon Press, 1967.

Stroud, Barry, *The Significance of Philosophical Scepticism*, Oxford: Clarendon Press, 1984.

Bibliography

Swift, Jonathan, *Gulliver's Travels* [1726], ed. Robert DeMaria Jr, Harmondsworth: Penguin, 2001.

Ward, Mark, *Virtual Organisms: The Startling World of Artificial Life*, London: Macmillan, 1999.

Waugh, Evelyn, *Decline and Fall* [1928], Harmondsworth: Penguin, 1937.

— *Vile Bodies* [1930], Harmondsworth: Penguin, 1938.

Weinberg, Julius R., *Nicolaus of Autrecourt: A Study in Fourteenth Century Thought*, Princeton, NJ: Princeton University Press, 1948.

Wheen, Francis, *How Mumbo-Jumbo Conquered the World: A Short History of Modern Delusions*, London: Fourth Estate, 2004.

White, R. J., *The Anti-Philosophers: A Study of the Philosophes in Eighteenth-Century France*, London: Macmillan, 1970.

Whiteley, C. H., 'Epistemological Strategies', *Mind*, 78 (1989), pp. 25–34.

Williams, Bernard, *Descartes: The Project of Pure Enquiry*, Penguin: Harmondsworth, 1978.

Wilson, David Sloan, *Darwin's Cathedral: Evolution, Religion, and the Nature of Society*, Chicago and London: University of Chicago Press, 2003.

Wittgenstein, Ludwig, *On Certainty*, trans. Denis Paul and G. E. M. Anscombe, eds G. E. M. Anscombe and G. H. von Wright, Oxford: Blackwell, 1974.

Zakarayyi, Fouad, *Myth and Reality in the Contemporary Islamist Movement*, trans. Ibrahim M. Abu Rabi, London: Pluto Press, 2005.

Index

Index